Ice Fishing Secrets

The In-Fisherman®
Library Series

Ice Fishing Secrets

The In-Fisherman® Library Series

Dave Genz
Al Lindner
Doug Stange

Published by In-Fisherman® Inc.

In-Fisherman Corporate Educational Publications
Book Division

Director *Al Lindner*
Publisher *Ron Lindner*
General Manager *Dan Sura*

Editor In Chief *Doug Stange*
Editor *Steve Quinn*
Editor *Dave Csanda*
Managing Editor *Joann Phipps*
Associate Editor *Eileen Firkus*
Editorial Assistant *Rose Baldwin*
Production Manager *Scott Pederson*

ICE FISHING SECRETS

Compiled by *Mark Strand*
Cover Photograph by *Doug Stange*
Back Cover Photo by *Mark Strand*
Edited by *Doug Stange and Joann Phipps with Steve Quinn*
Layout and Design by *Dan Vickerman, Nelson Graphic Design*
Litho Prep by *Quality Graphics*
Printing by *Bang Printing*

Acknowledgment:

Robert Reznak: ideas shared in in Chapter 2 as a contributor to *In-Fisherman* magazine

ISBN: 0-929384-19-9

The In-Fisherman® Library Series

One of the
(F) Fish + (L) Location + (P) Presentation = (S) Success
Educational Services

Published by In-Fisherman®Inc.
Two In-Fisherman Drive, Brainerd, MN 56401-8097

First Edition, 1991
Second Printing, 1992
Third Printing, 1995

For . . . People of Good Passion, Doing Not For Money But As A Daily Offering Of Selves As Living Sacrifices Feeding the Spirit Lake That Sustains Art In Many Forms From Generation To Generation As It Flows From God As A Token Of His Love.

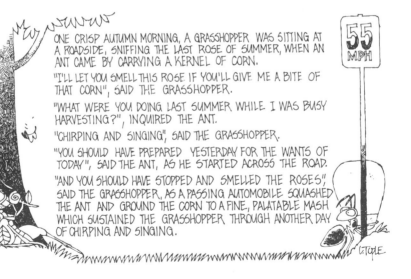

ONE CRISP AUTUMN MORNING, A GRASSHOPPER WAS SITTING AT A ROADSIDE, SNIFFING THE LAST ROSE OF SUMMER, WHEN AN ANT CAME BY CARRYING A KERNEL OF CORN.

"I'LL LET YOU SMELL THIS ROSE IF YOU'LL GIVE ME A BITE OF THAT CORN", SAID THE GRASSHOPPER.

"WHAT WERE YOU DOING LAST SUMMER WHILE I WAS BUSY HARVESTING?", INQUIRED THE ANT.

"CHIRPING AND SINGING", SAID THE GRASSHOPPER.

"YOU SHOULD HAVE PREPARED YESTERDAY FOR THE WANTS OF TODAY", SAID THE ANT, AS HE STARTED ACROSS THE ROAD.

"AND YOU SHOULD HAVE STOPPED AND SMELLED THE ROSES", SAID THE GRASSHOPPER, AS A PASSING AUTOMOBILE SQUASHED THE ANT AND GROUND THE CORN TO A FINE, PALATABLE MASH WHICH SUSTAINED THE GRASSHOPPER THROUGH ANOTHER DAY OF CHIRPING AND SINGING.

5

TABLE OF CONTENTS

CHAPTER 1

Larry Tople

THE ICE AGE

"Ice Fishing Is Alive And Well, But The Times, They Are A Changin'!"
Al Lindner

Time seems to stand still on the frozen surface of a lake, almost as if ways of doing things are preserved in the cold. The history of ice fishing suggests that equipment and tactics live in an ageless vacuum, seldom changing, mostly blind to what's happening in other parts of the world.

We're opening our special session of the fishing revolution—the Ice Fishing Summit, you might call it—a think tank consisting of Al Lindner, Doug Stange, and Dave Genz, fishermen who each in his own way has changed the course of ice fishing.

We're talking history in the making. Equipment and tactics. Thinking. How many people fish through the ice. This will set a background for the rest of the book. We'll get a few "worldly" ice fishermen on the phone, too, for information on what's happening beyond the United States and Canada.

For the moment, the scene is at In-Fisherman where a conference table overflows with old and new ice equipment. Lindner, Stange, and Genz— Al, Doug, and Dave from now on—have settled in with coffee at hand, as if they're ready for a day on the ice. They'll stay until they finish their story.

"Ice fishing is changing, thank goodness," Doug began, "but it would change faster if so many ice fishermen and fishing tackle manufacturers didn't have tunnel vision so serious they're destined to travel by tricycle, toot-tooting their horns as they pedal slowly down a tunnel toward a dim and distant light. With furrowed brows and squinting eyes, they look neither left nor right, but travel the established course—the only course—their course. Advice is unheeded, opinions don't change, and approaches aren't modified. Life's simple. The world's flat.

"To catch more fish and have more fun, fishermen and manufacturers must expand horizons and explore new techniques and tackle.

The summit begins. Dave Genz, Doug Stange, and Al Lindner, respectively. Three among an estimated 15 million ice fishermen in North America.

"This is a historic ice-fishing period. The present-day ice-fishing scene is much like the open-water scene a decade ago when there was no consensus about fishing techniques. Techniques that applied to one region weren't applied to other regions. Each region was a tiny fishing kingdom. Techniques and tackle were a product of how difficult the fishing was and how innovative fishermen were."

"What you're saying," Al offered, "is that techniques and tackle that worked well in New York were often unheard of in Wisconsin. There just was no easy way for fishermen to talk with each other. When they did talk, pride in local techniques and a lack of total country-wide fishing perspective kept them from trying new techniques."

"Absolutely!" Doug responded. "The age of educated fishing was just beginning. Ditto for ice fishing, today, though. It's still easy to find ice fishermen who haven't jigged, haven't used a tip-up, haven't fished with ultralight tackle, haven't used a depthfinder, and haven't moved their shack more than once a season.

"Ice fishing is a frontier," Doug continued. "Increase catches and fishing fun by becoming more versatile and tackling up appropriately. But

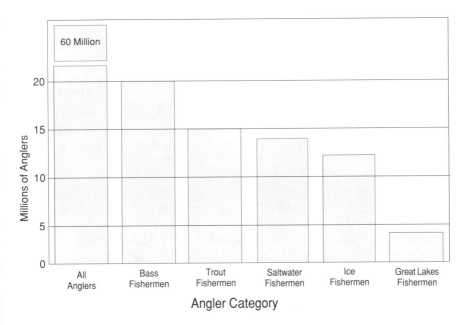

Several surveys indicate that about 60 million Americans fish each year. The bar graph illustrates the approximate number of people who participate in various types of fishing compared to Doug Stange's and Al Lindner's estimate of the number of ice fisherman (about 12.5 million) in America. In combination with Canada, where ice statistics aren't available for their 5.4 million anglers, they estimate a universe of 15 million ice fisherman.

we need help from manufacturers—products!

"To manufacturers I say, there's an ice-fishing market out there. Fishermen need and want a choice of rods, reels, lines, lures, augers, gaffs, snow machines, ice shelters, heaters, and clothing. Not just 'a choice,' but innovative 'choices.' While ice fishermen can benefit by tackling up right, manufacturers can benefit by catering to this solid market.

"But there aren't many ice fishermen, right? And they use only home-made tackle, right? And besides, if you develop a product, you can't reach ice fishermen with it because they're simple folks of modest means who rarely read and thereby won't—can't—respond to advertising. The ice-fishing market doesn't count, right? Wrong!"

"No one knows for sure, but we estimate at least 12 million ice fishermen in the U.S. alone. Forty percent of our 60 million U.S. anglers (25 million) live in the area surrounding the Great Lakes," Doug continued. "Those states also happen to be the main ice fishing area. Of that 25 million universe, we figure at least one person in three ice fishes. That's 8 million ice anglers right there, before we look elsewhere in the U.S., before we include Canada."

"Realize this," Al said, banging his fist on the table. "That makes ice fishing almost bigger than saltwater fishing—bigger than the open-water Great Lakes market.

"Including Canada, I think the ice fishing market may be 15 million anglers. Maybe more. I did a survey—admittedly unscientific—for about two years in the mid 1980s, at every seminar I gave. I asked for a show of hands of who fished through the ice. Tremendous responses. And you know what? A surprisingly high percentage of people only ice fish—don't care about summer fishing. But sheer numbers of people who said they ice fished was impressive. Made me realize what Doug had been telling me for years—the In-Fisherman Network should be doing more for ice fishermen.

"Spend any time on popular lakes during winter. Four thousand fish houses appear on Mille Lacs, a lake near our office in central Minnesota. Droves of cars travel to major winter fisheries throughout North America. I'm saying, ice fishermen have been bypassed by the fishing media and equipment manufacturers. It's almost larger than the saltwater market, for heaven sakes. Doug's right. It's not the simple hook, line, and sinker sport it's been treated as in the past."

The picture is changing, though, the boys agree. Major tackle companies are entering the game. For the first time, ice fishing is being viewed as part of the total fishing picture.

"As recently as the early 80s," Doug said, "ice fishing was a fragmented world, separate from open-water fishing. Ice fishing has always had a steady following; now it's probably one of the few manufacturing markets in fishing that's expanding.

"Demand can mean profit for manufacturers and pleasure for fishermen. Deliver the right product. Help ice fishermen catch fish and enjoy the sport by providing appropriate products for a fair price and there's profit."

Of course, a few versatile ice fishermen use tackle already on the market or fashion their own to make ice fishing the exciting, challenging, enjoyable, and successful sport it can be. And yes, a few manufacturers have seen the lantern burning on the lake and have produced products

Can't believe this guy uses plankton for bait.

that help ice fishermen. Ice fishermen and tackle manufacturers need each other.

Many of the tackle items you need for successful ice fishing are available at your tackle merchandiser. But out of necessity, ice fishing remains partially a do-it-yourself sport.

Nobody knows this better than Dave Genz, who has developed two products that solve two pieces of the puzzle. His portable Fish Trap shelters are easily pulled by hand, snowmobile, or ATV. They set up in seconds—flip a framework over your head. Dave's Ice Box holds a flasher, liquid crystal, or paper graph; a 12-volt motorcycle battery for power; and a swivel arm for leveling the transducer in the hole.

Dave has spent years of trial and error refining his products. As he hawked his wares to distributors, retailers, and individual anglers, he learned firsthand how archaic the winter fishing market was.

"Those early years were frustrating," he said. "'Who needs to change?' was the constant response. But it's tough to sit on the same lake with someone who's outfishing you 5 to 1 because he has the right equipment and not want to change. Ice fishing is growing now, as ice fishermen realize they don't have what they need. They're looking for better fishing than they've had."

Yet Owen Taylor wrote in the September 1988 Fishing Tackle Retailer, a trade magazine: ". . .the average ice angler has a reputation as the Jack Benny of piscatorial pursuits. With a few bucks, he buys rudimentary tackle. For a bit more, he purchases the simple tools needed to hack through the ice. And for bait, he carries minnows in a half-pint whiskey bottle, which he slips into his jacket to keep the morsels from freezing."

Taylor was implying that the same guy who doesn't bat an eye while cutting a deal for an $8,000 to $20,000 boat and motor package recoils at the prospect of spending $500 on ice fishing equipment.

Ice fishing is a sport struggling for respect and advancement. Guys like Dave Genz, Doug Stange, and Al Lindner, along with many of you reading this, are on the front lines, pushing back the envelope of custom, bucking a tradition of crude equipment and marginal catches.

Perhaps part of the problem is timing in relation to promotion. Open-water promoters have time, beginning in early winter, to promote new equipment. By March, anglers are in tackle shops buying whatever's new and hot. Hunting shows and promos start about August, too early to excite consumers about ice fishing. By the time hunting seasons wind

THUS IT BEGAN

Although Al Lindner had been an ice fisherman early in his career, he had quickly tired of the sport because of his inability to fish as efficiently as he could in open water. From 1975, the beginning of In-Fisherman magazine, until 1983, the magazine did without a mention of ice fishing.

Doug Stange, an avid ice fan had joined the staff in early 1981. Doug, used to fishing in the heav-

In-Fisherman *magazine published its first ice article in 1983, the first technical articles in 1984.*

ily pressured "Great Lakes" region of northwest Iowa, found northern Minnesota an untapped paradise by comparison. Using a depthfinder to locate prime structural elements ignored by other fishermen, and using some of the first graphite rod and reel combinations, Doug began making big catches of walleyes—9s, 10s, and 11s—during the winter of 1981.

The itch rekindled, using Doug's tackle advancements, Al was back in the game with passion. In the meantime, Doug continued to suggest ice articles. Wary of "wasting" space in the magazine on something only a "few people" did, the first meager ice article, a trip tip about jumbo perch, didn't appear until In-Fisherman Book #46, 1983.

down, ice fishing has suddenly arrived. No time to hype what's new and hot.

But the fledgling poor sister to open-water angling has an image and a timing problem that's beginning to change. In December 1989, for example, the Madison, Wisconsin, Area Technical College hosted an ice fishing show. Booths and customers filled an auditorium, solely to talk ice fishing, display what's new, and buy what's hot.

By 4 p.m. on the first day, our show scout reported that more than 80 speciality ice fishing rods had been sold by one booth alone—Steve Gerhardt's Sports Center. History being made. The turnout and enthusiasm surprised even the optimists.

"I think it shows," said Wally Banfi of Gerhardt's, "that people are starved for information on ice fishing and a place to gather and talk about it. A lot of people are ready to start spending money to get what they need. Ice fishing is

following October (Book #51). "Trap Attack" discussed mobility on ice via Dave Genz's portable Fish Trap ice shack. And "Walking the Plankton to Winter Panfishing Success," discussed the importance of phyto- and zooplankton in the diets of panfish during winter, and how ice fishermen could use the information to ensure success.

These articles are arguably the first technical articles ever published on ice fishing. Readership for fall and winter magazines quickly increased by almost 20,000, an indication of the number of ice fishermen looking for information. Thus began the revolution among In-Fishermen, the movers and shakers in the fishing world. Thus began the revolution in the ice-fishing world.

Back in the saddle. Al Lindner with big walleyes from Gull Lake in northcentral Minnesota in 1982. The fish were the subject of In-Fisherman's first TV coverge of ice fishing, and an inspiration for Al to get serious about ice fishing.

In-Fisherman magazine coverage of ice fishing began in 1983, and readership for fall and winter magazines quickly increased by over 20,000, an indication of the hunger among fishermen for ice-fishing information.

cheaper than summer fishing. And for anglers who don't own a boat, winter's the only time of year they can go anywhere they choose on the water."

Al: "Remember what I said about those folks at my seminars who said they only ice fish? They're out there, believe me. Because of the success of that first Wisconsin show, the second annual Midwest Ice Fishing Show was booked for Madison, with another set for Minneapolis. Other cities will follow."

"No doubt the market is being created by people like Dave Genz and by *In-Fisherman* magazine," Doug offered. "We're seeing results."

"Absolutely," Dave responded. "The fact that you've been writing seriously about ice fishing for almost a decade has made a lot of this happen. A lot of fishermen out there reading this are as much a part of the revolution in their own areas as we may be on a larger scale."

Pick up a local or regional outdoors magazine in the northern tier of states, and the scope of advertising related to ice fishing and ice products is amazing, compared with just a few years ago. To prove the point, Doug rummaged through a pile of materials and produced a thick orange folder full of clipped ads and articles related to ice fishing.

"Found these in about three issues of tabloids from Minnesota, Wisconsin, and Michigan," he said, offering them to Dave and Al for inspection. "The world's waking up to winter fishing!

"In these same issues 10 years ago, in the off-season you would have seen only articles about how to sharpen your hooks and clean your tackle box. The off season."

"Things are set to happen in ice fishing," Al said. "It's a big, solid, expanding market; you can't say that about many other segments of the

Stampede!

Jan Eggers

Ice fishing is an important sport in Finland and very important in Norway and Sweden, too—big business for companies like Rapala, Kuusamo, and Nils Master, located in Scandinavian countries.

The photograph is of the start of a Rapala-sponsored ice-fishing tournament with more than 5,000 Finns charging out to catch fish.

Portrait Of A Modern Ice Angler

Rigged and ready for panfish by the dozens during late ice. In-Fisherman TV and video director Jim Lindner dressed in lightweight, warm, comfortable clothing fit for temperatures to 20 below. The portable shack's his "bass boat on ice," his ticket to mobility and the ability to easily carry everything he needs.

He can be fishing inside in a moment by simply flipping up the light canvas cover. Freedom from wind, snow, and the eyes of other fishermen. They'll never know he's on fish. And he can concentrate!

He needs the power auger for ice three feet thick, although a sharp hand auger suffices for much of the season—all season for some anglers in milder parts of the country.

The graphite rod makes fishing more fun as well as more successful. And the depthfinder powered by a 12-volt motorcycle battery, perhaps the most important of all the elements in his rigging, lets him see his lure in relation to fish below.

This book asks you to apply this basic system, with appropriate modification, to the ice fishing you do.

sportfishing world. I think soon you'll see manufacturers signing top ice anglers to promotional contracts. More time and money will be spent designing and testing products for the winter fisherman. Fishermen with expertise on the ice are going to become hot commodities, you might say."

Both Canadian and American natural resources agencies are monitoring angling pressure through the ice and the impact it has. More attention than ever is being paid to this segment of the fishing public.

The market exists. Ice anglers are eager to spend money on their sport. They want information on how to catch more fish—how to stay warm and dry.

THE FIRST WORLD ICE FISHING CHAMPIONSHIPS

April 27-28, 1990. The frozen surface of crystal-clear Lake Vastusjarvi in the Finnish Lapland. Assembled were the accumulated experiences of some of the world's best ice anglers.

The first World Ice-Fishing Championship brought teams from eight countries—USA, Canada, USSR (Russia), Norway, Sweden, Luxembourg, Italy, and Finland. At stake were medals and national pride, but the gathering accomplished the more powerful purpose of sharing ideas, knowledge, equipment, and techniques.

Competition is good for the future of fishing, because the lessons learned affect all anglers. Even before the World Championships, American Coach Mick Thill had made several trips to Finland, where he learned many local methods from leading Finnish ice angler Ari Pattier. Thill predicted the fish would be extremely spooky, calling for ultralight rigs and a keen eye for sensitive bites.

He was right. As more than 1,000 anglers and spectators made their way across the Finnish lake, the fish were driven into deep water, where they became difficult to catch.

Thill reported big char, big pike, whitefish, grayling, and perch in the lake, but the people walking on the ice spooked the big fish—no chance of catching them during the event. Even small perch moved from where they'd been in 5 or 6 feet of water into 30 to 50 feet. This called for tiny jigs with tiny hooks and, at the most, 1-pound-test line.

Armed with the Scandinavian equipment and mindset, the Americans did well, nearly upsetting the Russians, which would have been a major accomplishment. Finland, as expected, won the gold medal. Russia second, the United States third.

"Beating the Russians would have been a major coup," Thill said. "Because food is such an important commodity in Russia, catching fish means having food, so fishing is extremely important. The best ice fishermen there are revered, because they can bring home food to their families nearly every day.

"About 20 million Russians ice fish, with about 300,00 participating in organized ice-fishing events. Their team was hand-picked. We, on the other hand, were a collection of people with almost no experience in Scandinavian methods fishing against their best pros."

Through the practice days, the American team learned three basic Russian and Scandinavian styles. "Wind was heavy the day of the team competition," Thill said. "It really hampered the Russians with their 6- to 8-ounce ultralight systems, but we switched to a style that fit the day. The Swedes and Norwegians didn't."

The measure of a complete angler, Thill says, is the ability to go anywhere, adapt to prevailing conditions, and catch fish. Americans and Canadians, blessed with tremendous fishing, often have the luxury of fishing unpressured waters, where fish are relatively aggressive and therefore easier to catch.

That isn't always the case, of course. Many North American waters, especially near major cities, face heavy pressure. And natural forces like weather can also make fishing tough.

"Many of the things we learned," said American team member Steve Pennaz, "will work on panfish in America when fishing gets tough. I can't wait to try some of them."

With increasingly sophisticated fishing pressure, we will experience more finicky fish. The ultimate goal of the American Fishing Association is to bring the World Championships to the United States and to win. But traveling to other areas and bringing home what we learn probably benefits the average fisherman more. Long after the bronze medals won by that historic first American ice-fishing team have tarnished, the lessons they learned will be helping us catch fish under difficult conditions.

"And yet," Dave said, "not everyone who ice fishes has seen the light. Compare ice fishing to open-water fishing. Anglers have to get out of their flat-bottom wooden boats; away from their steel rods, level-wind reels and dacron line; and start using available modern equipment. They wouldn't dream of fishing with yesterday's tackle in open water, but they think nothing of using it all winter. There's no excuse for not doubling or tripling your catch during winter. No excuse!

"We've taken the equipment that made us more successful open-water fishermen and adapted it to ice fishing," Dave added. "More anglers are catching more fish in open water now than they were 10 or 15 years ago. They can do the same with their ice fishing.

"A guy who'd bought a Fish Trap and an Ice Box came to my shop the other day. He said he's catching more fish than ever, even in the summer, and he likes ice fishing better than open-water fishing. We talked rods. He bought an even better graphite rod. He said his buddies would think he was crazy using such sensitive equipment. I assured him they'd shut up when he outfished them.

"Fishermen can be totally set up, down to the right line, lures, livebait and even a heater for about $600. Compare that to summer fishing. I can't believe anyone would call modern ice fishing expensive."

Ice fishing history is happening around the world. Trials were held in the winter of 1989-90 for Ice Team U.S.A. to compete in Finland for the first-ever World Ice Fishing Championships. The preceding spring, the official governing body of international fishing competition (the "Confederation International de la Peche Sportive," or CIPS) voted to hold this historic event. Officials of America's arm of CIPS, the American Fishing Association, hope one day to bring the competition to the United States. In the short term, however, they scrambled along with the rest of the world to assemble a team of ice anglers for the competition in Finland.

The world, it would seem, is beginning to realize the importance of this sport. Organizations, sport shows, and seminars will promote new methods, new products, more enthusiasm, and new ice anglers. The future is, indeed, bright. This book is dedicated to helping you catch more fish and have more fun as we also work together to ensure a future for fishing.

CHAPTER 2

EQUIPMENT

"The revolution in ice fishing is expressed in the quantity and quality of equipment available—making fishing more successful and more fun!"
                                                                    Doug Stange

Historically, fishing equipment was crude and inefficient. Tunneling to China would have been easier than punching a hole in the ice with a poorly designed auger. We froze, because boots and clothing left warmth to the imagination. We fished blindly, sitting outside on five-gallon buckets in a snowstorm without depthfinders. In most cases, we fished without reels. And line—usually 20-pound test or heavier—was old and brittle. And we wondered why we didn't catch fish and why we didn't enjoy ice fishing more.

We fish for many reasons. We enjoy getting away for a day on the water. But many, probably most memorable days are days when we catch fish. Action means fun and fun means memories. Catching fish is exciting. And with the right equipment, we catch more fish.

Sonar Units

"A sonar unit—depthfinder or liquid crystal display unit—more than any other individual product," Al offered, "increases ice-fishing success. Use it right and it doubles or triples your catch."

"Agreed," Dave said. "Know what depth fish are at and where your bait is in relation to them and it's amazing how many more fish you catch. But promise folks five times more fish by using a locater and they won't believe you—until they see it!"

"Of course, nothing in fishing is guaranteed," Doug offered. "People have different ability levels. But the same person in the same situation with a good depthfinder and the ability to use it will catch more fish. Indeed, a depthfinder is more useful in ice fishing than in open-water fishing. In open water, two moving objects (your boat and the fish) and many stationary objects (structure and cover) combine to give a quickly changing picture that's difficult to interpret.

"But when fish move below a stationary ice fisherman, they're right there, give or take a bit, depending on the degree angle of the cone and the depth of the fish. A fish marked at 15 feet on a depthfinder with an 8-degree cone is no more than two feet left or right from directly below your hole. He's there and you know it.

"Are fish coming through at 20 feet when your bait's on the bottom at 30 feet? Probably crappies, or maybe ciscoes, whitefish, or lake trout. Bring

Ice action inside a portable shack. With a properly rigged depthfinder, you know when fish are below, what depth they're at, and a bit about how they're acting. But most importantly, you also know where your bait is in relation to them.

your lure, which you can see on the depthfinder, to the level of those fish. You're on fish you can see. One major problem solved. Now you need to make them strike.

"They won't bite? Try a different presentation—type of jig, live or dead bait, hook size, color, jigging action. But you're on fish. You know it. You can see them! It changes your entire fishing perspective. Learn to use a properly rigged depthfinder on ice and you'll never again be without one."

Power Source

A 12-volt motorcycle battery is critical because it provides the power necessary for a sonar unit to read a tiny ice jig as well as fish. Try at least a 12-amp battery. It's rechargeable, too, and therefore a money saver compared to 6-volt batteries that quickly lose a charge. One charge to a 12-amp battery provides about three 8-hour days of fishing, and a battery lasts one, maybe two seasons.

We've also used the new dry-cell battery from Vexilar that comes with its own charger. It's a good compromise, especially in remote areas. Bush pilots don't like carrying acid batteries.

Flashers

All good flashers are applicable to ice fishing. To be effective, a flasher should show exactly where your lure is in relation to what's directly below. If your unit forces you to turn the gain extremely high to see your bait, a transducer with a narrower cone angle concentrates the signal and improves the unit's performance.

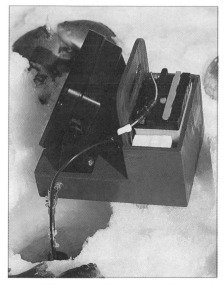

A 12-amp motorcycle battery set snugly inside an "Ice Box."

"A 30-foot scale is best if most of your fishing is for panfish in shallow water," Doug said. "Try a 60-foot scale if you usually fish deeper for perch, lake trout or walleyes. Of course, flasher models like the Hondex FL-8 or FL-7 offer multiple depth scales.

"An 'Ice Box' from Dave Genz's Winter Fishing Systems is the best way to easily combine the motorcycle battery, depthfinder, and transducer. The Ice Box or a homemade version like it lets you easily move to search for fish. When packing up and moving is a problem, you usually don't move, which means fewer fish."

Liquid Crystal Units

Graphs offer limited applications on ice. For most of your fishing, stick with a flasher or a liquid crystal display (LCD) unit.

"A depthfinder is one of the most important aids an ice fisherman can use," Doug said. "I have often said so in print and on radio and TV. But in the beginning, I always shied from discussing LCD units, because the ones I tried didn't work well on ice.

"Many of the first LCDs functioned

A flasher unit rigged on an "Ice Box."

for 10 minutes and then quit. Others read for a bit and then slowly died, probably because the ice units were portable units powered by 6-volt batteries. Even when the units were working, they were tough to read in sunlight. And the little dots (pixels) that define the picture were so coarse that even the tiniest fish looked like battle cruisers in a space video game.

An LCD rigged and ready for action.

"I found it difficult to say these things, however, because so many other writers said their units worked so well. Was I just getting bad units? Or was the difference my sitting in Frostbite Falls, Minnesota, and their sitting in Balmy Bay, Kansas? At times, I also found myself wondering if these writers spent much time on the ice.

"The problem resolved itself, however, because during the past several seasons, I've had success using the units on ice. Whether you call them LCRs (Liquid Crystal Recorders), LCGs (Liquid Crystal Graphs) or LCDs (Liquid Crystal Displays), many of you will like what you see if you correctly rig one of these current models for ice fishing.

"Few things are perfect, though. LCDs don't give an instant readout of the action below. On the other hand, those units give a pleasant picture. We'll discuss this in more detail in Chapter 3.

Shelters

"Former Minnesota Viking football coach Bud Grant used to say, 'Cold is a state of mind,'" Doug offered. "'Toughen up,' he'd tell the Vikings as they stood without gloves in -10°F weather in snow 2 feet deep. I always wondered what the Vikings thought as they looked across the field at the Oakland Raiders roasting weenies on propane heaters between plays.

"The Vikings won some and lost some, and so did other teams, which is my point: Yea, verily, I suppose cold is a state of mind, and being adaptable, we get used to what we have to get used to. But let's play the game comfortably."

"An ice shelter lets you play comfortably," Al said. "If you live in Kansas or Missouri, maybe a shelter isn't necessary. If it's cold enough, a shelter and heater are nice, especially if the wind's blowing. If you plan to fish all day in the true North, you need a shelter.

"Choose a more permanent shelter or a portable shelter? Depends. Permanent shelters are larger, heavier, more stable, and offer homestead status; once parked on a spot, the spot's yours—most of the time. A fisherman once pried my shack loose and placed his over my holes. Homestead sta-

A bevy of portable shacks during a testing session in the mid-1980s. The Fish Trap is in the foreground. From the left in the rear are 4-, 2-, and 1-man Ins-Tents, and a Clam.

tus didn't matter to him.

"Portable shelters are the way to go. An ice-fishing system designed to find fish must be based on the same search-and-find system we use on open water. Mobility's the key. Search with your depthfinder. Then fish. Fish each spot. Move on if the spot doesn't produce or if the action slows.

"But human nature is to stay too long. The more difficult to move, the more tempted you are to stay. And the longer you stay in one spot, the fewer fish you'll catch."

The key to portable shelters is balancing comfort and mobility. The best shelters offer warmth and a measure of the roominess of permanent shacks while not limiting you to a single location.

Frontier Industries, for example,

The trend toward fishermen accepting portable shelters has had an impact on permanent shelters, which have subsequently become lighter and more mobile—more portable. Models like these are available from Brainerd Outdoor Sports, Inc. and Northern Lite Mfg.

offers the comfort of a permanent shack with the mobility of a knock-down unit. Their roomy two-man "Clam" collapses to a 3- by 5-foot compact unit that holds gear and moves easily on poly runners. The "Clam Sleeper" accommodates four anglers, while the "Clam Jr." offers portability for t. single angler.

We've written frequently about the "Fish Traps" from Dave's Winter Fishing Systems. Fish Traps are essentially sleds that hold fishing gear while you tow them to your fishing spot. Remove the gear, flip up the tentlike shelter, and sit on the sled.

Portable shelters fall into three categories: windbreaks, combination sled/pop-ups, and pop-ups. The Fish Trap is so handy because it's a bass boat on ice, carrying all your gear—plus it pops up and over to keep you warm. The Fish Trap can also function as a windbreak, although it's less portable than windbreaks like the H.T. Enterprise model.

ERECTING A POP-UP TYPE TENT

The Ins-Tent in a carrying case.

Slip it out and unravel it (20 seconds).

Extend the braces (20 seconds).

H.T. Enterprises offers a simple two-sided shelter with a built-in seat. Weighing only six pounds, it's ideal when lightness and portability are paramount. HyPark Speciality offers a similar shelter.

F.O.F. Products advertises 10 models of shelters, including the popular "Pop 'N Fish." All are nylon with solid floors. They erect simply with no parts to lose.

Frabill offers a line of three portable shelters. The "Hideout" and "Ice Express" are nylon tents with poly bases. The "Ice Shuttle" is a sledlike box for carrying gear on the ice. Erect a three-sided windbreak around it and sit on a padded seat.

The "Ins-Tent," a black nylon shack for one, two, or four people is another good option. The tents weigh about 12, 16, and 22 pounds, respectively, and set up quickly with an external frame.

Mankato Tent & Awning offers a line of "EZ-Set" portable ice houses. Walls are canvas, the floor wood, and they come in one-, two- or three-person sizes. The "HECO" shelter by Harmony Enterprises has been around since 1962. This two-person shelter features a fire-retardant black fabric, an internal frame,

Comfort in less than a minute.

Lift!

and weighs 30 pounds.

J-Moe Manufacturing Co. sells a one-person nylon shelter that pops open when you release the ties. The "Ice Fort," a 32-square-foot shelter from Fanatics, provides over 6 feet of head room. Cabela's offers their own two-person shelter—woven poly fabric attached to a nylon base.

Tip-Ups

Tip-ups are temptingly set traps for predators like pike, bass, walleyes, trout, salmon, and big panfish. Unlike fishermen, tip-ups are infinitely patient. Set in the right spot with the right bait, they're often the best presentation. Sit back and wait, or take an active jigging approach with a rod and reel while a tip-up also works for you.

To be effective, tip-ups must accomplish three things. First, they must let you present a bait to a waiting predator. Second, the bait presented must cause the predator to bite. And third, the tip-up must alert you to the predator's presence.

Dozens of homemade tip-up designs serve anglers. They may be as simple as placing the bobber on the ice alongside the hole. When a fish hits, the bobber slides from the ice (hopefully) and into the hole.

Two types of modern tip-ups include either line spools that rest above the ice or in the hole below the surface of the water. Wind often moves the bait on tip-ups that rest above the ice, while underwater models depend on a lively bait for action.

Tip-ups we suggest include:

H.T. Enterprises Polar Tip-Up— Perhaps the most reliable and productive tip-up in recent history, perhaps ever. It offers durability and handy options—one of the best ice-fishing bargains available.

"The spool on the Polar revolves smoothly," Al noted, "because the shaft connected to the spool is pressure-packed and sealed with a lubricant. The spool functions under the worst freeze-up conditions.

"The stainless steel trip mechanism on top of the revolving shaft is a key feature because it lets you set the release tension on the spool from light to heavy, depending on the weight of your bait. A notched end provides a heavy setting for big, actively swimming livebaits or big deadbaits.

"The other side of the trip mech-

An H.T. Windlass "wind" tip-up looking frazzled after doing battle with Toad Smith and a big pike.

The H.T. Polar tip-up. Simple design and function. A classic ice tool.

anism is smooth, offering a light setting for fishing with light baits and light line. A set screw on top of the trip mechanism and revolving shaft lets you adjust the tension (drag) on the spool. This further increases or decreases the tension a fish feels when taking the bait. Wish I had a dollar for every big walleye and pike I've caught on a Polar the past seasons. Wouldn't trade those dollars for the memories, though."

H.T. Enterprises Windlass Tip-Up—Another classic. Consists of a plastic base, adjustable double-hinged center arm, and a top rocker arm with an aluminum fan on one end and a line spool and flag on the other end. The tip-up folds for carrying or assembles into an adjustable position to catch the wind. Your line runs from the spool through a hole in the fan and down into the water. The spool rests above the water, and the fan arm moves with the wind, giving movement to the bait suspended below.

The more perpendicular the fan position, the more wind resistance, resulting in more movement to the bait. A spring mechanism controls the position of the fan arm. "Amazingly effective at times!" Doug added. "Try them, whether you fish for walleyes, trout, or bass."

H.T. Enterprises "Fisherman Tip-Up"—Plastic cross sticks with a line spool and flag mechanism. This low-priced tip-up works somewhat like the Polar Tip-up, but not as efficiently. Still, it's a design preferred by many fishermen.

Of course there are many other tip-ups and rods. The "SWish-Rod" from Handishop Industries, available in two sizes, is a rod and reel that props over the hole on a two-legged stand. When the flag indicates a bite, you fight the fish with the rod. Their new "Beeper Pole" with a buzzer and light emitting diode signals a bite.

The "Ice-N-Easy" is another rod set-up similar to a tip-up. It's equipped with a spinning reel and a frame that holds the tip over the hole. Line feeds through a spring bobber that serves as the bite indicator.

Schooley & Sons sells a "Mighty Slick" tip-up that like the "SWish-Rod" is a rod with a flag. After a fish trips the flag, fight him on the rod.

Fishing Specialities sells three tip-up models. Two have below-ice spools, one with a drag mechanism. The other, a "Wind Jigger," uses wind to give action to the bait.

The Worth Company offers the "Pop-Up," a unique design that looks like a little mortar. A tube sits in the

The H.T. Windlass tip-up. Amazingly effective in the right situations.

hole, held in place by tripod legs. The spool is immersed. A flag pops up from the top of the tube when a fish bites.

Heat Pack Midwest offers the simple "Snap Trap," a coated-wire frame that holds line and hangs from a willow branch or auger set over the hole. A bite frees line from the adjustable release, and the frame jiggles as the fish pulls off line. The Snap Trap is so compact you can put five or six in a coat pocket.

U.S. Line makes a range of tip-ups. Some are preloaded with line, and all have freeze-proof immersed spools. The company makes some spools from aluminum, with handles to aid line retrieval.

The popular "Beaver Dam" is made by Arctic Fisherman. These pin tip-ups have an immersed spool and a freeze-proof tube.

Strike Master sells a "Deluxe Tip-Up." It folds open with crossed sticks that sit above the hole with the spool immersed.

Shurkatch sells two tip-up models.

Three tip-up lights are available: "Strike Lite" by H.T. Enterprises, "Fish Alert" by Frabill, and one by Lake Country Products. Lights flash on when a fish trips the flag, a popular feature for fishing crappies and walleyes after dark.

Rods

Traditional ice-fishing rods were only a stubby stick with pegs that held line. The ice-fishing revolution has changed that.

Rod selection is a matter of personal preference, according to Doug. Your decision is influenced by many things including price; how often you fish; and whether you fish in a small shack, a large shack, or outdoors.

"Several years ago," Doug reflected, "the only way to get a great ice fishing rod—a slightly shrunk replica of the best open-water sticks—was to build it yourself or have it custom-made. For several years, Al and I tried convincing companies to introduce a series of good ice-fishing rods. We offered to help design them. It took awhile, but some good ones are now commercially available. When we fish special situations that demand custom rods, we turn to Thorne Brothers owned by Paul and Greg Thorne who helped design many of the ice rod actions that have become standard on commercial rods."

"The industry had to understand," Dave offered, "that we didn't need rods for certain species. We needed rods to handle certain weights of line and lures.

"That's why more rods aren't manufactured for panfishing, for example, because not many commercially made rods can handle 1-pound-test line without breaking when you set the hook. Stiffness equals sensitivity, but a rod can be too stiff. For ultralight lines, you need a rod with a measure of forgiveness.

"The length of a rod is important. Longer is better for setting and fighting fish in deeper water. Longer is particularly important for removing line stretch and driving the hook home in deep water."

"About light rods," Al said. "Sharp, barb-reduced hooks are vital. Use small pliers to flatten barbs. It takes less force to drive in a barb-reduced or barbless hook than it does to bury one with a barb. A sharp barb-reduced hook will sink into a fish's jaw with a quick snap of 1-pound test if your rod lets you do it.

"There's more to ultralight light-action rods than just a soft tip. A short

A good ice rod must be stiff enough to provide sensitivity and set hooks, yet limber enough to maintain a tight line to surging fish. Rod weight, length, power, and action change, however, given the fish species, water depth, and weight of bait.

rod must bend uniformly (parabolic curve) from the handle to the tip, to protect line yet keep it tight. The whole rod has to bend and stay bent while you're fighting a fish. If the rod has a stiff butt and light tip, it's easier for fish to get off. I'd compare this rod style more to a fly-rod blank than a jigging rod blank. The best 'micro' light rods, in fact, are made from fly-rod tips."

About commercial rod options: The most popular Thorne Brothers custom rods are now in production and are marketed by Jig-A-Whopper/UMM Holdings. Selections include three walleye rods, two panfish rods, and a rod for heavy fish like lake trout. These rods feature solid fiberglass blanks, which Thorne Brothers believes are more sensitive and durable than graphite. Fiberglass also allows them to grind custom tapers.

Berkley offers "Northern Lites" rods with oversized guides, 100 percent graphite blanks, and cork handles. Two models, a medium- and a medium-heavy action are coupled with casting reels. The Berkley line also includes six models of spinning rods.

St. Croix offers eight graphite or fiberglass "Arctic Angler" rods in spinning and casting models. Shakespeare offers several models including casting and spinning rods.

Johnson Fishing has 10 Mitchell rods, plus rod and reel combos with Mitchell reels. Their top-of-the-line "PureBred 100" spinning rods are graphite models with cork handles and oversize guides. Of note are the "Fast Action" with an extremely fast tip and the "Ice-Tote," a 30-inch telescopic rod.

Several of Wisconsin Tackle's rods have tips so soft they serve as spring bobbers. The actions are suitable for

One of the earliest custom graphite rods made for walleyes and lake trout. The rod measured 42 inches and was made from a Sage blank. Note plenty of single-foot rod guides. The reel is a Shakespeare 030. The rod later became known as the "In-Fisherman Special," from Thorne Brothers Custom Rods.

panfish, but other options work for walleyes or pike.

Cabela's line of ice rods includes two graphite gamefish models and a light panfish rod. Tape your reel to the cork handles.

Lake Country Products line includes 31 jigsticks in different sizes and strengths.

Fishing Specialities makes eight ice rods, including three graphite-glass composites and several fiberglass models.

Finally, H.T. Enterprises sells the most complete line of rods and poles— 105 at last count. Their high-quality "Polar Lites" graphite line is new. Models range from panfish actions to laker sticks. Many of their panfish rods include H.T. reels.

Reels

According to Doug, choose a reel to match a rod. Then match that combination with the proper line type and weight for the species you intend to catch. "I use spinning tackle or spincasting tackle whether I'm fishing for

There will always be a place for the basic pegged jigstick, still a handy way to hold line for many ice fishing situations well served by hand-over-handing fish.

bluegills or lake trout," Doug offered. "But the reels are necessary only for holding line, so they don't need to be large.

"I'd couple a comparatively small reel like the Garcia Cardinal 3, the Daiwa 1300, the Shimano 2300, or the Shakespeare 030 with a rod for walleyes, pike, or lakers, switching only the line weight as I changed species. I suggest 10-pound test for walleyes; and 12, 14, or 17 for pike or lake trout. OK, so I might also switch rods depending on the weight of the baits I'm using for pike or lakers.

"Same basic deal for panfish. The reel is an overlooked factor in sensitivity. Light's better. Smaller's better. A reel like the Shakespeare 025 is a fine choice for most situations for perch and other larger panfish in deeper water. In shallow water, well, a plastic reel like the Slater makes sense—can't go lighter than that. But note, the plastic line guide on the Slater can fray light line. Hand-over-hand a fish in or don't run your line through that guide on the reel.

"Dave's also turned lots of fishermen on to using spincasting reels like the Zebco UL4 for panfish."

Dave: "I've found a trick when I'm using the Zebco UL4. Sometimes, no matter how much I clean and adjust the drag, it gets sticky, especially on cold days. And a lot of times, when I set the drag light enough to protect 1-pound or lighter line, it's so light I can't wind in a nice fish.

"When I set the hook, line slips out of the drag. I don't get a good hookset. When I try to fight the fish, my drag slips line out like I have a tuna on. I've learned to leave the drag set a little heavier than usual, heavy enough

For panfish in shallow water, simple reels suffice. The Slater (top) and the Zebco 144, a forerunner of today's Zebco UL4.

to break the line. No problem setting the hook now. Then, when the fish makes a run, squeeze up on the trigger ('FeatherTouch' control) and hold it up. Now line goes out smoothly, like a light drag setting. When the fish stops running, re-engage the reel and pump it toward the hole with the rod. You can land big fish this way, without having to set the drag too light to handle them."

"About drag control on spinning reels for bigger fish," Al added. "All the reels Doug mentioned a moment ago generally have smooth drag systems. Set your drag so it gives when you set into a fish. I set my drag like this by pulling on the line right in front of the reel so it barely gives. After you set into a big fish, either disengage the anti-reverse or loosen the drag.

"But when relying on a drag, always be ready—especially when a big fish is right by the hole—to unstick the drag by pulling line from the drag with your free hand. One hand's on the rod holding the fish; the other hand's on the line just in front of the reel. The fish surges and you pull line from the reel. Give's lots of control. I've never broken off a fish at the hole by being ready like that."

Line

"Talking tip-ups first," Doug said, "the standard has been a small-diameter black dacron casting line like Gudebrod 27- or 36-pound test. It's easy to see and handle. More recently, the standard has been either Gudebrod's teflon-coated tip-up line or black plastic-coated tip-up lines made by 3-M for companies like H.T. Enterprises and Berkley. Both lines are easy to handle. You won't go wrong with either."

As for the hook end of your tip-up lines, according to Al, use monofilament or wire leaders. "I recommend about 36 inches of mono line of your choice," he offered, "or 24 inches of 12-, 18-, or 27-pound-test uncoated stranded wire like Sevenstrand's. Cabela's carries Sevenstrand wire. "Quick-strike" wire is also available from H.T. Enterprises or Bait Rigs.

"As for monofilament, many of the same qualities open-water line offers also make good ice-fishing line. I like limp, small-diameter line. I've read that such lines fray on ice, but I've never had it happen."

At least one major company—Berkley—has a specialty ice-fishing monofilament with characteristics tailored specifically to cold-water fishing. "Their clear or green Trilene XL is great for ice fishing," said Doug, "and so is DuPont MagnaThin. Bagley's Silver Thread's good line, too. What about light line for panfishing, Dave? What do you like?"

"For 2-pound test or less, I like Class Tackle's mono imported from

Panfish in deeper water require a classic "open-water" reel. The reel stores line, but also allows for getting fish up and the lure back down quickly and efficiently. "Walleye-size" open-water reels often make good reels for ice fishing. Bass reels are generally too large.

Germany. But there are others, too, like the H.T. Enterprises Panfish line."

Doug: "Line is the focal point for ultralight fishing. As lines get lighter, the type of line you choose and the knots you tie become critical. Choose soft, supple lines. Compare, for example, Berkley's Trilene XL (a small-diameter, soft, supple line) to Trilene XT (a stiffer, coarser, larger-diameter line). Use XL for winter panfishing. Realize, however, that checking for line abrasion and retying knots is an important part of fishing with limp small-diameter line.

"Even though a lot of the best standard lines are available in 1- and 2-pound break strengths, many tackle shops don't carry those sizes. If you can't find them, order them from Thorne Brothers.

"Three choices exist for line lighter than 1-pound test: (1) nylon sewing thread which unofficially tests at 12 ounces to one pound; (2) fly tippet material rated at 7X (about 1 pound) and 8X (about 12 ounces); or (3) European fishing lines often sold in break strengths of approximately 6, 8, 12, and 14 ounces, as well as 1 pound and over.

"Nylon sewing thread is available from sewing shops," Doug continued.

Classic ice lines include limp, small-diameter lines like Berkley Trilene XL, Berkley Cold Weather Line, DuPont MagnaThin, Bagley Silver Thread, and Class Tackle Line.

"It's stiff and somewhat unforgiving, although it fishes OK with shock tippets—a section of rubber or plastic cord added in-line to absorb the shock from a fish run. Shock tippets are most useful on lines testing less than 1 pound and for anglers who have difficulty adjusting to ultralight line. We'll talk about them in the panfish chapter.

"Fly-fishing tippet (leader) line is available from fly fishing shops or from L.L. Bean.

"One source for European lines is Hengelsporthuis of Holland. Do your business airmail or you'll get your line in July. Call and order via credit card. They speak English, and even though their nylon lines are listed by diameter instead of break strength, they'll know what you want. Super Racine Dichroique is a good line to ask for (spell it for them). Also ask for a Hengelsport catalog. You probably won't be able to read it, but the photos tell the story."

Tackle Boxes—Fill 'Em Up

A tackle box for ice fishing shouldn't be too large; it's a problem to drag around. Yet you want to carry all the lures, hooks, and floats you'll need. Dave, Al, and Doug all have at least one Plano Mini-Magnum for carrying floats; swivels; snaps; stranded wire; wire snips; forceps; fingernail clipper; line spools; hook file; various sizes and styles of teardrop ice flies and lead-head jigs; various split shot; single and treble hooks; flash jigs like Acme Kastmasters, Jig-A-Whopper Rocker Minnows, or Rapala Pilkies; and swimming jigs like the Northland Air-Plane Jig, Jigging Rapala, and Swimmin'

Ratt. And more.

"Actually, I have 3 Mini-Mags at present," Doug said. "One's rigged only for walleyes and bass, another holds wire rigging for pike, and another is a general box I can grab anytime and fish almost anywhere."

Plano makes the smaller Micro-Magnum and a new speciality ice-fishing box. And Flambeau's LiteForce is a nice size.

Also, metal fly boxes—a favorite for carrying an assortment of tiny panfish ice flies. Try a fly-fishing shop or tackle catalog like Cabela's.

Punch Or Drill—But Get Through

Doug: "Nothing's so nice as a sharp chisel for making neat holes early in the season or poking out old holes later on. But once the ice gets thick, it's auger time.

"Hand augers are quiet and light (4-, 5-, 6-, 7-, or 8-inch models) for mobile fishing. Power augers are heavier and noisier, but glorious when you need lots of bigger holes in ice more than a foot thick."

"My choice for a hand auger," Dave continued, "is a drill like the Strike Master Mora or the Jiffy Hand Drill. Keep the blade guards on when you're not using the auger so the blade's sharp to continue cutting well. If the blades dull even slightly, cutting even one hole is difficult.

"Power augers? I love 'em," Al said. "I want a lake to look like Swiss cheese when I'm done. The Jiffy from Feldmann Engineering is a proven bet. So's the Strike Master's Magnum III. Both are reliable and quickly cut a clean hole."

Dave: "Power augers are a lot noisier. At times, they may spook fish, although they may also attract fish. But I look at 'em as equivalent to my big outboard motor. I don't generally run over the top of fish with my outboard and expect to catch them. Likewise, I don't expect to drill a hole with a power auger and immediately catch big fish. But it sure happens a lot with

A fly-box for panfish jigs (left) and a Plano Mini-Magnum for almost any combination of tackle from panfish to large predators.

lakers and perch. Apparently, at times the noise attracts fish."

"Assault areas," Al suggested. "Make Swiss cheese. Cut a bunch of holes along different depths and over different bottom types. Then go back to the first hole you drilled and fish it. Fish each one in turn. The fish should have had enough time to calm down and think about biting.

"For a quieter compromise, Strike Master's 'Electra' electric auger cuts a 7-inch hole. It's comparatively lighter than other power augers. Power the drill off the motorcycle battery that runs your depthfinder. It will cut at least 25 holes through 30 inches of ice in a day without affecting performance of the sonar unit."

Dave: "Right. But don't expect to drill all 25 or 30 holes in a row on a day with below zero temperatures. I like the quietness of the electric auger, but I don't think of it as something I use to drill all my holes and the holes of a bunch of other people.

"Mark Strand, who fishes with me a lot, bolted a little wastebasket about the size of a motorcycle battery to the inside of the tub on his Fish Trap (fish shack). He charges a spare battery, puts it in the basket so it doesn't tip over and spill acid on his tackle, and connects his electric auger to it when he gets on the lake. He lays the auger across the top of the Trap when he moves from spot to spot, grabs it and drills a hole when he wants to fish, and leaves the auger lying alongside the house. He unhooks it only to move to another lake. It's fast, efficient, and drills more than 30 holes on a single charge. The extra battery adds about 9 pounds to his cargo."

You'll need a charger for the motorcycle battery. Standard 10-amp chargers for deep-cycle batteries pump too much juice for those little batteries. Get a 1-amp trickle charger or a 2/6-amp selective charger. A portable battery energy gauge from Altus Technology Corporation will help you track the battery charge.

After fishing, attach the terminal clips of the energy gauge to your motorcycle battery to determine the amount of charge remaining. From there, figure exactly how much charge you need and for how long.

Say you have a 12-amp battery. With 50 percent charge left, you've lost 50 percent—or 6 amps. Replace 6 amps by attaching to a 2-amp charg-

Classic power drills past and present: The Kluge (center), the forerunner of today's two finest options, the Strike Master Magnum (left) and the Jiffy.

The Strike Master "Electra," powered by the motorcycle battery that runs a sonar.

er for 3 hours or a 1-amp charger for 6 hours.

Miscellaneous Equipment

Gaff—You might want a gaff for large predators, not for fish you want to release though. Make your own or choose one from H.T. Enterprises.

Ice Creepers—Without snow, walking across the ice can be treacherous and using a power auger downright dangerous without ice creepers.

Scooper—You'll need a "scooper" to strain slush from the hole you drill and keep it ice free while fishing. Many traditional types are available, but try the "Flipper Dipper" from Tackle Tamer Products. A hinged affair slices down through the slush, then opens like a parachute as you pull it up through the hole. One pull and you can start fishing. Two pulls and the hole is spotless. It's plastic and freezes up a bit in extremely cold weather, but a few controlled knocks on something hard and it's ready to work again.

Waterproof matches—Available at almost any sporting goods or hardware store are invaluable for lighting lanterns and heaters after you drop everything in a snowbank.

Flashlight—Handy for times when you wait too long to light the lantern.

Safety picks—See the safety discussion for details. Picks are a good precaution especially during early- and late-ice periods or anytime you're on unfamiliar waters with a reputation for swallowing winter fishermen.

Take everything you need, but no more. Lightness means more mobility. If it's easy to move, you're more likely to do so. And you must move!

Snow Machines

Do you need a snow machine—snowmobile or four-wheeler—to fish well? Probably not. "But a machine can increase your range (mobility) and thus your efficiency," says Doug. In essence, they serve the same purpose as a boat.

Picture this: The North Country, home of real men and women too poor to move south. Object: Walleyes, also appropriately called "walrus" in some parts of the North.

You're totally rigged and ready, a virtual ice-fishing machine on fast tracks. Indeed, no relationship is more sacred than that personified by the North Country fisherman and his highly personalized snow machine.

Walleyes. You drive your snowmobile pulling a sled loaded with equipment to a distant reef. At the reef, you cut holes with your power auger and check depths and bottom contours with your depthfinder. It's cold and you plan to stay for several hours, so you set a shelter over holes you hope will produce.

Making Your Own Gaff

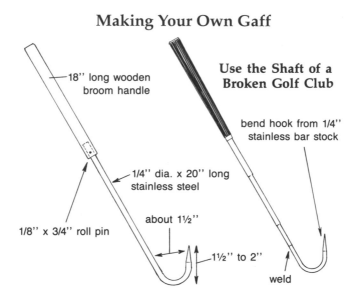

1. Taper a 1/4-inch stainless-steel rod to a sharp point.

2. Drill an 1/8-inch hole for a roll (rod) pin in the 1/4-inch rod.

3. Bend the pointed end of the rod around a 3/4-inch pipe, leaving 1 1/2 to 2 inches from the point to the beginning of the radius. The point to shaft gap should also be about 1 1/2 to 2 inches.

4. Drill a 1/4-inch by 3 1/2-inch deep hole in an 18-inch-long wooden broom handle. Insert the rod and drill and install the roll pin.

5. Drill a hole in the handle for a piece of rope.

You can also make a good gaff by bending 1/4-inch stainless steel bar stock and welding it onto the end of a broken golf club.

Before beginning to jig in the shelter, you set out a tip-up over a nearby spot. You cut extra holes so if fish move into the tip-up area you can quickly move the shelter and jig there. In the tent, you light your lantern. Some days and for some people, the lantern doesn't provide enough heat; if that's the case, try Coleman's Focus 5 propane heater. Heat is sweet!

Adjust the depthfinder to see if walleyes are coming through, but aren't interested in your presentation. Grab your graphite jigging rod because it's light and sensitive and fun to use.

Too much technology? Depends. For north-country fishermen faced with 4 or 5 months of ice cover, it makes as much sense to have an efficient ice-fishing rig as it does a boat. Snow machine, portable shelter, depthfinder, and other assorted gear are in the future of ice fishing for many anglers.

But technology used in pursuit of pleasure is a matter of personal choice. Forget the snow machine if you're willing to walk and fish smaller lakes. The depthfinder or the graphite jigging rods? We wouldn't be without a depthfinder. But the graphite rods? Maybe they could go, although they certainly make fishing more fun.

If you keep cutting the list, you'll be using a stone hatchet to get through the ice and jigging a bone on a grapevine to trigger fish. Come to think of it, even those early ages must have had "tunnel tooters," as Doug calls them, as well as progressive souls willing to try new approaches—thinner diameter vine perhaps—to solve the same old fishing problems. The right tackle is a major step to solving problems.

Ice fishing can be fun—inspiring even! Do it right and you'll catch more fish through ice than in open water.

Yee-haa!

CHAPTER 3

THE SYSTEM

"Understand a bit about location and presentation, and mobility becomes the key to catching more fish than you ever dreamed possible through ice."
                                                                    Dave Genz

Think about the way the best fishermen fish during summer. They head to a lake based on past experience and reports of fine fishing. If the fish aren't biting, they move to a backup lake. Still not biting? They move to yet another lake.

They ask questions before leaving and when they arrive. They study a lake map and move from likely spot to likely spot. Drawing on past experience, they try a variety of baits and presentations, but remain open to constant experimenting. They turn on their depthfinder when they push away from shore and don't turn it off until they return to the dock. The same system works for ice fishing, with modifications for the sheet of ice and accompanying cold weather.

"Think about the way most people ice fish," Dave began. "They drill a hole, usually wherever a bunch of other people are fishing, and sit there whether or not they catch anything.

"That's how I once approached the sport. A big shack sitting in the middle of a bay was more an excuse for a winter picnic than to catch fish. I'd put lines out, have lunch, check lines, have lunch again, and hope fish came to me. I rarely fished outside except during the morning and evening. The locals only went then because that's when the fish were moving so that's when they caught fish.

"I stayed for a few hours and then left because I got cold, or it got dark, or lines got tangled or broken. I got frustrated when things froze.

"That's changed, if you will use ice fishing products available today. Use a depthfinder, and you'll see that even during the middle of the day, if fish are under your hole, you can often make them bite. Don't be content to sit and wait for fish to come under your hole; search for them. Mobility becomes a key.

"And sometimes even when fish are under your hole, mobility is still important, because only so many biters exist. Some days, most fish are what we call sniffers—fish that just look at your bait. Sometimes you catch a few fish right away and your hole goes dead, even though fish are still there. This is the only time I see people handicapped by electronics. They're so fascinated trying to make fish bite that they forget that moving to fresh fish is a better option."

Al: "Doug has been talking for almost a decade about a simple, yet guaranteed system for improving ice-fishing success. Lots of people have listened. Thousands are making consistent catches because of articles featured in *In-Fisherman*. But Doug's right; most ice fishermen still haven't heard.

"It's no surprise to me. For 5 years I spent 300 days a year barnstorming the country selling tackle systems absolutely guaranteed to help fishermen catch more fish. The basis of that tackle system was a slip-sinker rig called the Lindy Rig.

"More than 30 million Lindy Rigs have sold over the years and accounted for millions and millions of fish. Yet, no matter where I went, no matter what I did, no matter how many fish I caught on that foolproof rig, no matter how many times I told people, showed people, and showed them and told them again, some folks wouldn't listen. It's the nature of things, I guess.

"On the other hand, though, a few folks always caught on and became the best fishermen in their area."

"You're right, Al," Dave said. "After you understand a bit about fish location and presentation, mobility is the key to catching more fish through the ice than you ever dreamed possible.

"But mobility is more than moving; it's moving with a purpose and moving efficiently. Components that let you move and fish efficiently are key parts of the system. The system is similar to mobile systems we use on open water."

A Systematic Approach

"As I said," Al continued, "the problem with most ice-fishing approaches is lack of mobility. Most ice fishermen won't move when they're not catching fish. Not moving is a tradition—set out the shack and don't move it until the end of the season.

"But not many good open-water anglers would stay in a few spots on one or two lake points during a day of fishing. Good open-water anglers go to the fish. Too many ice fishermen let the fish come to them. Be willing to search for fish each time you're out and each time the fishing slows. Camp on a spot only when you find fish and they continue to bite.

"Consider components for efficient open-water fishing as a basis for comparison," Al instructed. "Most successful open-water fishermen wouldn't think of venturing out without a properly rigged boat or a proper assortment of tackle. A fisherman with a boat wants a finely tuned gas engine to

A Mobile Panfish System

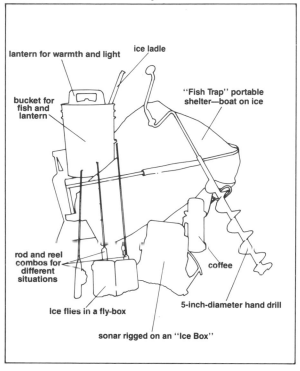

lantern for warmth and light

ice ladle

bucket for fish and lantern

"Fish Trap" portable shelter—boat on ice

rod and reel combos for different situations

coffee

Ice flies in a fly-box

5-inch-diameter hand drill

sonar rigged on an "Ice Box"

get to a spot, an electric trolling motor to position the boat once he's there, and a depthfinder to locate fish-holding structure. The boat carries an assortment of tackle to meet a variety of fishing conditions, plus rain gear, a thermos and a sandwich, extra clothes, bug repellant, a flashlight, and so on.

"Successful open-water fishermen choose from many options to catch fish. Whether casting, trolling, or vertical jigging, sonar plays an integral part. Components and steps taken to catch fish become an efficient fish-catching system. When well-equipped anglers hit the water, they're efficient fishing machines, ready to search for and catch fish.

"Most ice fishermen usually don't move because they can't move—easily! Sitting in a big shack, who's going to spend half a day moving to another spot? They don't have a depthfinder, so they don't know what they're fishing over in the first place, much less where they should move to.

"A trip to the Bass Islands area of Lake Erie in 1988 illustrates advantages and disadvantages of moving," Al said. "It also illustrates the source of some of Doug's frustration. Doug assumed that after years of writing about the advantages of mobility in ice fishing and the success of In-Fisherman's video *Ice Fishing Secrets Part I*, folks at Lake Erie would be moving to catch walleyes.

"We were fishing with Pat Chrysler, one of the best of a good group of Bass Island guides. Chrysler runs a topnotch operation—good bait, and clean, warm shacks in the vicinity of schools of walleyes. But even Chrysler can't guarantee that his shacks will be over the main part of a big school of walleyes every hour of every day.

"We were catching fish. But when the bite just hinted to be slowing about 10:15 a.m., Doug assumed the pack of fishermen sitting in our group of 20 shacks would head this way and that to catch 'his' walleyes. Instantly out of the shack, he was ready to move to find more walleyes

Radio Results

Dave Genz goes wacko, to borrow one of his favorite words, when people complain that his deluxe Fish Trap holds only one person. "We want to fish together," ice anglers say. "Don't you have a two-man Trap?"

He does, mainly because of demand. But he insists and we agree that eventually we'll all be fishing alone, but in constant contact.

"You're not fishing alone, you're fishing independently," Dave says. "What do you do in a big fish house when the other guy is catching fish and you're not? You want to move and he wants to stay. In a one-man house, you move until you're satisfied. That doesn't mean you're fishing alone."

Members of the Winter Fishing Systems team often wear portable walkie-talkie headsets to keep track of each other as they move, searching for fish. Punch holes, read the depthfinder, fish hard. Keep moving. Mayday! Mayday! Panfish in the vicinity! Big ones! Help!

They always know who's catching fish, at what depth, and on what, even a half mile away.

and stay ahead of the crowd.

"As we moved, studying the depthfinder, cutting holes, and catching walleyes, Doug nervously looked back over his shoulder, checking for competition. Reminds me of a kid I knew when I was growing up. He had 8 brothers to compete with at mealtime. So he learned early to guard his plate or leave the table hungry.

In-Fisherman Ice Secrets I and II, *comprehensive instructional videos covering location, presentation, and fishing trends.*

"Doug learned his sport in northwest Iowa where the competition for fish and fishing spots is intense. Publish or perish they say in literary circles. In Iowa, you compete well or catch nothing.

"No one moved from the shacks. Doug assumed they were killing the fish back there in the shacks! A new school must have moved in.

"Eventually when he couldn't take it any longer, he walked back to the shacks to find out what was going on. 'You're not catching fish? Then why are you sitting in there?' I can still hear him asking one group. 'Fish'll be back,' they answered. 'Aren't you guys cold out there?'

"The walleyes did come back in, as they almost always do on Lake Erie. At about 3:30 everyone started banging fish again. Everyone was happy, as they should have been. Fishing is wonderful—comparatively easy—on Lake Erie. You often don't have to move to catch a limit of walleyes on Erie.

"But good guides aren't always available. And walleye fishing through the ice is more difficult almost everywhere compared to Lake Erie. I'm talking about a simple system that makes you so tough, so good, that with a bit of practice you can go almost anywhere, almost any time, fish for almost anything, and almost always catch fish.

"That first day on Erie," Al concluded, "almost everyone caught walleyes early and late. But we caught fish all day. The next day was tough all day. By moving we were the only ones to scratch a limit of fish, including a 10."

Rigged And Ready

"To be consistently successful," Doug emphasized, "you must be rigged, ready, and willing to move when conditions call for it, no matter what you're fishing for—pike, walleyes, lake trout, other large predators, or panfish. Don't tell me it's different if you fish for brookies in Maine, pike in Manitoba, or walleyes in Wyoming. It's not. You must be willing to move and move efficiently.

"Rigged and ready means a depthfinder or LCD, auger, rods and reels, and other tidbits. Nothing special. Nothing very high priced. In colder climates like Minnesota, add a portable shanty to the list. A portable shack allows mobility and acts as a storage unit for fishing gear. It becomes your boat on ice."

"That's what I've been saying about the Fish Trap for years," Dave

THE ART OF DRILLING HOLES

M obile ice fishing means drilling holes—lots of holes. Serious ice anglers often punch 100 to 150 holes in a day.

In your rush to get through the ice, however, don't lose sight of the art of drilling a great hole. "Drilling holes is an art few people understand, including Al Lindner who's always in too much of a hurry," Doug revealed. "Try for a smooth top and a clean hole, not a hole surrounded by a big mound of ice chips and snow."

So drill hard. Then, when you go through:

1. *Punch the auger down sharply.*
2. *Lift it halfway up out of the hole, which removes about half the ice and slush.*
3. *Punch the auger down a little way again.*
4. *Lift the auger all the way out of the hole.*
5. *Kick mounds of ice away from the sides of the hole.*
6. *Insert the auger back in the hole. Run it just a second or two to get it down the hole.*
7. *Lift the auger back out, taking with it a flow of water and the rest of the ice.*
8. *Kick away the mounds one last time and you're ready to start fishing, except for maybe a little straining with something like a Flipper Dipper.*

If you're fishing with tip-ups, clean an even larger area around the hole so it's as smooth as possible. If you do that, line won't get caught in ice chips, snow, and water while you're fishing and especially when you're fighting fish. Shovel a circle about 4 feet across with a lightweight shovel. Now that's a hole in the ice!

said. "I call it my winter bass boat.

"Each time an open-water angler pulls up to a spot, the depthfinder gives instant information about conditions below—a structural element's shape and depth, as well as if fish are present. Then he must choose a presentation that makes fish strike."

More Examples

"Dave and his friends developed a system primarily for panfish—simple, yet deadly," Doug said. "The guys usually target panfish, but the system adapts well to other fish species. I'm willing to bet they could go anywhere in North America—the world for that matter—and outfish local fishermen using traditional methods, with buckets of fish to spare."

"Indeed," Dave answered. "The system works for walleyes, trout, bass, jumbo perch, and pike, as well as panfish. We drill lots of holes, look for fish on the locator, and when we find them, we work on getting them to bite. We've added more rods, baits, and heavier line; but other than that, our equipment's the same. Believe me, the system works on any species of fish."

"For obvious reasons," Doug said, "the Fish Trap is your favorite house (Dave developed it from a plan his family used for about 30 years). It lets you move easily with all your gear and provides welcome relief from an ice fisherman's chief adversary—cold. You can be fishing inside in seconds.

"We've already mentioned the 'Ice Box.' It's vital to the system because it allows for mounting and carrying a gimbal-mount depthfinder wherever you go. Forget problems associated with opening and closing a portable depthfinder. The box lets you power the depthfinder with a 12-volt motorcycle battery—the only way to have enough power to run sonar so you can see tiny lures in relation to fish below, all day, all weekend, no matter how cold it gets.

"When fish come through at 10 feet, you know it. Move your lure to that depth. Watch how the fish react to your presentation. Make adjustments. You fish blindly without a depthfinder."

"Absolutely," Al emphasized. "You're tuned in with a locator. Presentation options exist in ice fishing that can't be accomplished on open water. You're sitting on ice—no boat control problems. You can see the fish, your lure, and the reaction of the fish to lure action."

"Right," Dave replied. "I call my flasher a 'mood indicator' of the fish. I can follow patterns of action, whether fish bite when the bait's moving or sitting still; whether they move off in reaction to what I'm doing. Without that mood indicator, ice fishing wouldn't be nearly as efficient or as much fun."

Doug addressed technical aspects of sonar: "The box has an adjustable arm for the transducer. Glue the 'level' that comes with each Ice Box on top of the transducer, which is mounted on the end of the swivel arm."

"Now wait," Dave interrupted. "If you just willy-nilly glue the level to the transducer, you won't get the best performance from your electronics. Set up the unit and turn it on while it's sitting on a table or workbench. Shoot the signal onto a hard floor, adjusting the swivel arm until the bottom signal is as wide and bright as possible. A good double echo tells you the signal is shooting straight down. Now, without moving it, put silicone on top of the transducer and squish the leveling bubble so it seats firmly and shows the unit as level. Let it dry overnight in that position."

"Good point," Doug continued. "Properly rigged, you can position the transducer level in the hole and get a reading instantly. Pick up and move to a new hole without the frustration of opening and closing a portable box or struggling to get the transducer to hang properly in the hole. The box has a big handle; it's a balanced package. No problem to move. Moving's fun; it's intriguing to see what's over the next hill—below the next hole."

Doug continued. "With due respect, Dave, I'd never be without a Fish Trap, but I'm not saying the Fish Trap is the best shack in each situation.

Mobility In Many Forms

Mobility on ice takes many forms. We've already featured the handy Fish Trap ice shack, which can be pulled by hand or moved by more mobile means. Or with minimal snow cover and thick ice, drive right out and fish (Photo 1).

All terrain vehicles (Photo 2) remain options, although the snowmobile (Photo 3) is undoubtedly the choice of most north-country fishermen.

On bays of the Great Lakes, anglers often pull a boat (Photo 4) behind, in case a portion of ice breaks loose from shore when they're on it.

Fishermen heading into the Canadian wilds need a trailer or sled ((Photo 5) to pack everything they need for a day on ice. Of course, you can always travel "bowzer power"!

Right now, the Ice Box is the best sonar box. But other equipment may be as applicable to a given situation. Your shack, however, is a perfect example of the type of shack that fits the system and flat-out guarantees success.

"Modifications? Again, I have a Fish Trap and use it a lot. I also like the H.T. Wind Break and the Frabill 'Ice Shuttle.' And when I go for lake trout, I take along a bigger shack and pitch it in an area near where I'm searching. I use the shack to stow gear, eat lunch, and to warm up in from time to time. It's still a portable shack, however, like an Ins-Tent or Clam, one that I can pack in a minute when I want to move. I still use a depthfinder every moment I'm out there. The basic system's the same. But the components change to fit the situation."

"How often you move," Al offered, "depends on the species you're after and the fishing situation. Times call for staying put within a given area, say a spot on a reef when you're fishing for walleyes in the evening. Eventually, the fish turn on or come to you.

"Say you're out on the reef by 3 p.m. By 3:30 you know where the

Photo 3

Photo 4

Photo 5

Photo 6

Rigging The Ice Box

To read correctly on ice, depthfinders and LCDs must be adequately powered. That means a 12-volt motorcycle battery, not a pair of 6-volt batteries that poop out quickly.

A 12-volt battery will cost about $20. It's rechargeable, so it saves you money. One charge provides a weekend of fishing—two or three 8-hour days.

A battery should be at least 5 amps, but 10 or 12 is better. Lower amperage means smaller battery size and more portability. But higher amperage means more sustained power.

Most manufacturers seem determined to sell ice fishermen a portable depthfinder. They do indeed work fine powered by a motorcycle battery. Yet it's unhandy to rig portable units with anything but 6-volts. And there's the added problem of how to deal with the transducer.

To get a consistent reading, a transducer must rest parallel to the bottom. It's tough to hang a transducer on a cord and have it parallel to the bottom. The answer is a moveable arm with the transducer anchored in place at the end of the arm. The answer for portability and quick and easy adjustment each time you move is a gimbal-mount depthfinder mounted on a box that holds the motorcycle battery, the depthfinder, and the transducer arm.

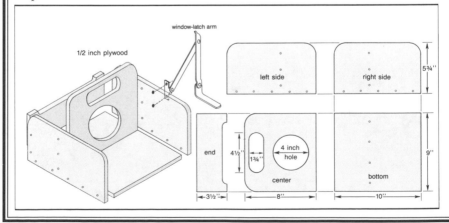

The Ice Box

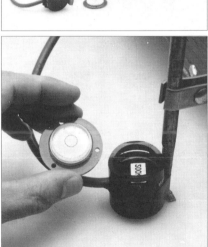

The "Ice Box" is manufactured by Dave Genz. The components necessary to rig a depthfinder or LCD on an Ice Box include the depthfinder or LCD; transducer; 12-volt motorcycle battery; and a carpenter's level.

The present-day Ice Box is made from durable, light plastic, not wood as shown here.

Attach the depthfinder or LCD to the base of the Ice Box. There's room below for extra transducer and electrical cord. Slip the motorcycle battery neatly into the back of the box. Tape or bracket the transducer to the adjustable transducer arm on the side of the box.

Tape or glue the type of level used in refridgerators in mobile homes to the top of your transducer. Puck-type transducers are handiest to use.

points on the breakline are, and you have 20 holes cut with your power auger. You can work the shallow, flat portion of a reef; the edge (drop-off); as well as the deep flat at the base of the drop-off.

"Let things quiet down now, because it's fish time—twilight. Usually

DRESSING FOR SUCCESS

"'Smaah snauw suit,' said one feller when I asked him about the paper-thin garment he was stuffing into dry storage," Doug recalled. "Ever see southern bass pros on their first trip north fish a bass tourney during fall and happen to run into 'coal wather'? They're the ones with the 'tainsy-lil-thaan' suits that pass for snowsuits (called 'birrr suits') down south.

"You gonna wear those cowboy boots?" Doug asked, his toes hunkered nice and cozy-warm in Sorel boots.

"Ah nehver gaw ainywhere withaught mah boots. Nehver!" he answered without considering why Doug had asked. He lived—barely! And learned—lots!

You need to dress right to put up with the cold, and that's usually learned by experience. Experience teaches layering appropriate clothing and always being overdressed.

Get polypropylene or Thermax long underwear. Polypro lifts perspiration from your body and transfers it to the next layer of clothing. That layer should be a heavier pair of cotton-wool blend long underwear (perhaps quilted, or Polarfleece).

Ready for a pair of pants and a shirt. Blue jeans are fine, although wool pants are better. Gore-Tex/Thinsulate pants are maybe the ultimate. A cotton-wool blend shirt is nice, although a lot of folks wear a lighter shirt and then add a wool sweater.

Vest time. Thermopile is wonderful, but most people prefer down. You can fish inside a reasonably warm shelter dressed like this, but if you're going to be outside, you need a snowsuit. The boys recommend a one-piece hooded suit like a Refridgeware. Refridgeware also makes two-piece suits that includes bib pants and a hooded jacket. One-piece suits are nice because it's easy to add one more layer.

this isn't the time to suddenly move to a new reef or point. But move from hole to hole to see where the fish are moving on the reef. The only time I'd sit on one spot for a long time without seeing and catching fish is if I'd fished a reef dozens of times and knew the best spots exactly.

Another layer? Yup, a hooded down parka or hooded Gore-Tex waterfowling parka. Doug, for example, is a 150-pounder who's spent many a 12-hour day fishing outside in -20°F weather. He stays warm. No need to suffer.

If it's reasonably warm and the wind isn't blowing, you can go without the coat. And if it's almost balmy, say 20°F, you can probably forget the snowsuit and go only with the coat covering. But it's no fun to be cold. You'll catch fewer fish.

Boots—Heavily lined Sorel-type boots are the standard footwear because they work. Stick with boots with rubber soles and leather uppers until you can get one of your friends to try the new Gore-Tex Sorels. We haven't had experience with them yet. Dave and Doug have long since gone to LaCrosse Iceman boots and they've found nothing like them.

Socks—Try tissue-thin polypropylene or silk socks under wool-blend socks. That should do it unless your feet get cold easily. A pair of Gore-Tex outer socks help keep your feet warm and dry. *(continued)*

"Camp on spots when you're after one big fish. Even then, though, it might be better to move a bit more.

"Give you another example. Fishing for pike with tip-ups generally isn't thought to be a moving-type affair. Search for a good spot, set your

In extremely cold weather Doug wears polypro socks under electric socks powered with two D-cell batteries. He likes the socks with long electrical cords, not the socks with hook-ups right at the top of the socks. Put the socks on, he says, and tuck the battery pack in the top of your long johns. Put your pants on with one cord running down each pants leg. Hang the cord and the battery pack out of the top of your zippered-up zipper. The battery pack goes in your pants pocket. When your feet get cold, snap the batteries on for a half-hour or so. Toasty Toezzies!

Cold? Shoot an In-Fisherman TV Special in sustained -20°F cold and 20 mph winds. Layer and live.

Hand Wear—Wear loose fitting mittens that cover your wrists.   Cotton gloves are handy when it isn't bitterly cold; or try wool-blend fingerless gloves.

Another option is to combine a pair of fingerless fishing gloves inside the loose-fitting mittens. If you can pop for them, consider gloves like Glacier Gloves. They're neoprene, available in slit-finger models where the thumb and index finger peel back and velcro out of the way so you can tie knots and really fish. Hands get cold? Slip the mittens back on. Berkley also makes neoprene fishing gloves.

Head Wear—Wool-blend balaclavas are great, but you may prefer a stocking cap or a Thinsulate waterfowling hat. Include a mask for bitterly cold and windy days.

A soft hand towel is a good addition, too. Roll it up and tuck it behind your collar to break the wind. And finally, use it to dry wet hands.

tip-ups, and wait. More movement, however, more searching can mean more fish. In the pike chapter, we'll tell you that jigging—moving from hole to hole in a systematic search with the right baits—can outproduce stationary tip-ups.

"The best approach usually is a combination system of jigging and tip-up sets. In other words, cut plenty of holes over a good bar and set tip-ups in a few of them. Then while your tip-ups are working, move quickly from hole to hole, looking for pike that will take a jigged bait. I think you'll be impressed and make it part of your pike system. But again, the point is, moving—efficiently searching—with the right tools means success.

"This isn't meant to be a technical discussion so much as a pep talk. We want you to catch more fish, and you can—more than you've ever dreamed possible. Honestly, catching fish through the ice can be as pleasant and in many ways more exciting and efficient than catching them in open water. The simple steps we've just discussed virtually guarantee consistent catches."

Sonar And The System

The conversation turned to sonar again. Doug began talking experiences with sonar on ice.

"Crappies—For most of my life I believed that crappies fed up, that they positioned below forage because their eyes were set up and forward in their heads, and that a bait had to be placed above them.

"Wrong. Crappies feed down as well as up, and often the best way to get them to bite is to present a bait slightly below them. I've watched it on a depthfinder countless times while ice fishing.

"Lake trout—My jig was 6 inches off bottom in 70 feet of water when the fish moved onto the screen. I jigged the bait and the trout rushed it, but wouldn't take. I cranked the bait up 5 feet, often an effective triggering move. The trout followed, but still wouldn't take. I had to do something!

"I reeled the bait quickly toward the surface. The trout paused momentarily and then shot from 65 feet to 5 feet, took a swipe at the bait, and returned to the bottom. My heart was pounding. Later, again jigging near bottom, a fish appeared on the screen at 60 feet. I raised my jig 10 feet, jigged once, and immediately caught the trout.

"Walleyes—Sunset, and only perch had been hitting the minnow head hanging below my Jigging Rapala. The perch bite slowed. As I jigged, more distinct marks moved onto the screen, paused, and then moved on. Do something!

"I removed the Jigging Rapala, a lure that should be fished fairly aggressively and therefore often works well on aggressive fish. I replaced it with a Jig-A-Whopper Rocker Minnow, a flash lure that doesn't have to be fished so aggressively. The next mark that moved in paused and then

LIVEWELL ON ICE

Make a livewell on ice by drilling a series of holes not quite through the ice. Remove the ice shavings from the hole and chisel a small hole in the bottom to let water in.

Another option is to drill a hole about three inches away from the livewell and ladle water.

Livewells keep fish alive until you're ready to go home. Most importantly, though, they keep fish from freezing. Freezing ruins the fine quality of the flesh, especially when they're thawed to be cleaned and then refrozen for storage.

Too big!

Fish that are to be released should, of course, be released immediately without being held in a livewell. But if you aren't sure if a deeply hooked fish or a tired fish will live, a stay in the livewell lets you hold the fish upright until it's ready to go.

When you leave the ice, mark the livewell with a branch so no one steps or drives into it.

Panfish size!

Just right!

inhaled the minnow head hanging on the treble hook below my lure. The walleyes weren't aggressive. When you're on fish, adjust your presentation to fit the fish's mood.

"Perch—Everyone around us was fishing near bottom, and few perch were being caught. They bit here yesterday, and they bit here this morning, we heard. The depthfinder showed hordes of freshwater shrimp suspended just below the ice. Occasionally we saw large marks suspended high with the shrimp. We moved our baits and caught perch 2 feet below the ice.

"Later, more distinct marks moved through. The perch fishing slowed. I hooked a pike. Five minutes later, marks moved through along the bottom. We caught them—perch—along the bottom until slowly they began to suspend below the shrimp again.

"Bluegills—Fourteen-ouncers were suspended above a rock pile in 20 feet of water. We'd caught several fish on teardrops and Eurolarvae before they quit biting. I replaced the maggot with a tiny minnow and placed a shot 6 inches above it. The bait settled near bottom.

"I could distinctly see the shot and minnow on the screen. A fish hit the minnow and I set and missed. I looked at the screen. The shot was apparent but the teardrop signal was less distinct. My minnow was gone.

"You fish blindly without a depthfinder," Doug emphasized. "Seeing what's happening below enhances the fishing experience. Dave says the fishing experience begins when you see the fish on your screen, not when you get the bite. Seeing makes you think—react. You'll catch more fish and have more fun.

"Ice fishing is moving toward sophistication that makes it more fun, more successful, and more comfortable. But the most important step to better catches is a depthfinder. We'll repeat that until we get everyone's attention."

As we highlighted in the preceding chapter, Dave, Al, and Doug contend that a depthfinder is more useful in ice fishing than in open-water fishing. It bears repeating that in open water, two moving objects—your boat and the fish—and many stationary objects—structure—combine to give a changing picture that's often difficult to interpret.

"When fish move below a stationary ice fisherman, they're right there," Al said, "give or take a bit—depending on the degree angle of the cone and the depth of the fish. A fish marked at 15 feet on a depthfinder with a 10-degree cone is little more than 2 feet left or right from directly below your hole. A fish marked on a 20-degree cone is no more than 6 feet left or right from directly below you."

"This is where that Hondex FL-8 really shines," Dave offered, because the fish show up in different colors depending on whether they're off to the side of the cone or more directly beneath you. It also becomes easy after some experience to tell where a fish is and about how big it is. If it's a thin green signal, it's either a tiny fish or off to the side. When it gets

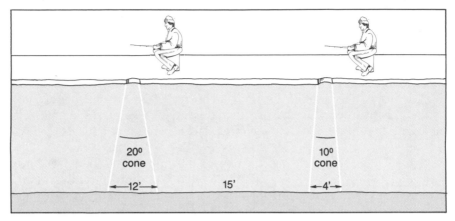

A larger cone angle gives wider coverage of what's below, but less assurance of where objects are within the cone. A small cone angle gives more definitive readings, but less coverage.

wider and turns to yellow and finally red, get ready! We call that a 'Red Alert,' when a fish is right there, ready to bite."

"That's helpful information," Doug continued. "Wide-degree and narrow-degree cones each offer advantages. At 15 feet, a 20-degree cone provides about 800 percent more coverage than a 10-degree cone. You see more fish, more weeds, more bottom. You get the big picture. But it's also a bit more difficult to say exactly what's happening below in relation to your lure.

"For example, when you jig your lure and see a fish at the same level, the fish may not be at that exact level. Fish on the outside edge of the cone appear deeper on a screen because they're farther from the cone. The sonar signal travels farther to hit them than it does to hit something at that same depth in the center of the cone. A fish 15 feet down and several feet from the center of the cone appears deeper than a fish centered 15 feet down. This problem is magnified with a wider cone. The deeper you fish, the more intense the problem becomes.

"With a narrower-degree cone you see less, but more. You're more aware of what you're seeing and

We struggle with details. But where there's will . . .

therefore what's happening in relation to your lure. If a bluegill moves onto your screen at the level of your bait (15 feet), he's there to look at the bait.

"Cones with narrower degrees also give more distinct readings, because power is concentrated within a smaller area. There may be power differences among depthfinder makes and models, though, and also among depthfinders of the same make and model.

"With a Hondex FL-8 unit and a 10-degree cone," Al continued, "in 40 feet of water, I can read a hook and minnow, shot spaced at 6 and 12 inches, and the swivel connecting my monofilament leader to my dacron line 24 inches above the hook. I can tell if the minnow tears off or if a shot slips 6 inches. If I chum maggots, I can watch them drop individually until they reach bottom or are eaten.

"In shallower water, I can tell when a fish steals maggots from an ice fly. That's cracking power that can't be duplicated quite as well with a wider-degree cone. Yet many anglers prefer a wider-degree cone, especially for panfish in shallow water.

"The problem with suggesting a narrow-degree cone is that none are presently available in puck-style transducers. Locator companies consider narrow cones mainly a tool for high-speed use; therefore the bulky designs are shaped hydrodynamically (boat style) for attaching to boats.

"Lowrance offers an 8-degree cone in a boat style and an 18-degree cone in a puck style. Hondex offers a 10-degree cone in a boat style and a 20-degree cone in a puck style.

"The boat-style transducers are so bulky that the puck style with a wider cone angle is probably the best bet for most fishermen, given that most fishing takes place in shallow water where cone angle doesn't play a key role.

"I suggest a depthfinder with a 30-foot scale if more of your fishing is for panfish in shallow water and a 60-foot scale if you usually fish deeper for perch, lake trout, or walleyes. Many depthfinder models offer choices of multiple depth-level readings—versatile choices."

Selecting Sonar Types

About flashers for ice fishing. A new generation of anglers exists. Many of these anglers don't know or care to learn how to use flashers. Al, Doug, and Dave contend that this generation has been swept away by the lure of bells and whistles and the easy-to-interpret pictures of liquid crystal and video sonars. They would also say, though, that liquid crystals are getting better all the time. And they're useful on ice.

"A depthfinder is one of the ice fisherman's most important aids," Doug noted. "Al and Dave agree. Until recently, we shied from discussing LCD (Liquid Crystal Display) units, because the ones we used didn't work well on ice. The problem resolved itself, however, and we're ready to say nice things about the units on ice. Get a top-of-the-line unit made after 1988 and rig it right for ice fishing and I think you'll like what you see.

"Still, LCDs don't give the instantaneous readout of action below as a sonar does. Jiggle your bait and the liquid crystal displays your moves a little later. You don't instantly see how fish react to what you do. But these units provide pleasant pictures—fun to watch.

"Instant read-out is a touchy subject among some folks who manufacture LCDs," Doug continued. "They insist that signal send-out and return are instantaneous. But even on the best machines, the screen displays symbols after a short delay.

"When you jig, the signal appears instantly on a flasher. When you jig, the display appears a moment later on an LCD, even when it's running at the fastest speed. In the units I used last season, the delay was 1/2 second. That's not much, but it's enough to make a difference when you want picky jig movements for panfish nuzzling your bait. Instant feedback lets you make split-second decisions about how to trigger fish.

"In most instances on ice, though, instantaneous decisions aren't critical. When you're jigging for pike, lake trout, or walleyes, for example, or when you're fishing with live minnows for crappies, often it's the big picture that counts. It's knowing fish are there; it's knowing where your lure is in relation to the bottom and the fish. You get that with momentary delay on an LCD."

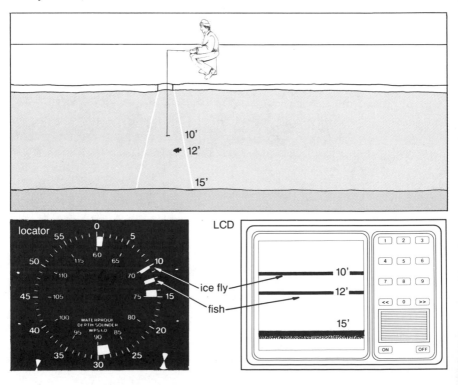

"Say you're fishing for crappies beyond the edge of a drop-off," Al offered. "The crappies are roaming over the lake basin. A depthfinder will mark the bottom. And any fish that come through appear on your screen (dial) as marks between the top and bottom. You know the approximate depth of the fish. Bring your bait, which can also be seen on the screen, to the level of the fish.

"You have to draw an imaginary picture of what's happening below. The quality of the picture depends on how well you know your depthfinder and how much experience you've had reading it. Almost everyone can learn to draw, but some folks can naturally do things with a pencil that other folks never learn. After watching hundreds of fishermen reading depthfinders, I strongly suspect the same's true for interpreting signals from one. The signal may be the same for everyone, but the interpretation isn't."

Doug: "LCDs can be a great equalizer for fishermen because they draw the picture. Interpretation is easy, once you get used to reading lines. The bottom is a straight line across the screen. Your bait appears as a thin suspended horizontal line (row of continuous dots) running across the screen.

"A crappie also appears as a thin line running across the screen. No 'edged' marks and certainly no 'arched' marks will appear as you might have on the screen of an LCD moving over fish in open water. Your transducer is stationary; the fish move. If a fish moves up, the line that represents it moves up. If a fish stops, the line continues across the screen. Again, bring your bait to the level of the fish."

"The flasher remains more of a precision tool," Dave added. "I can tell when I lose a maggot off an ice fly in 35 feet of water. I can read the tiny wiggle of a bait and the instantaneous response of a fish to that minute wiggle. I can read relative fish distance to within inches from a bait."

If you want to buy a new flasher, well, times couldn't be better. New models are competitively priced. Some of the finest flashers ever made were produced during the past 5 years.

"Presently," Doug continued, "few precision actions we've described can be done with an LCD. The point is, though, that the ability to interpret sonar readings precisely require's practice. I've spent 20 years at it. Many casual fishermen don't have the time for this.

"But often such precision reading isn't necessary. Fishermen confused by a flasher may quickly learn to use an LCD picture and profit from it.

"My son Nate, for example, has never shown more than passing interest in my flashers. Yet the instant he saw my new LCD, he was transfixed. At 8, he had more video experience than I did. He had my Lowrance X-40 running in 5 minutes.

"LCDs can't do exactly what flashers can, but perhaps that's good. I do know that anything that helps fishermen see what's going on underwater, anything that helps fishermen get a bait at the same level as the fish will double or triple their catch on the ice. LCDs can do that right now! Times change. Sometimes people."

"As I see it," Al responded, "people have two choices. They can continue to fish like they always have—sit and wait for the fish to come to them. Or, they can move into modern ice fishing. They can make it an

---

AMAZING!

I imagine that people start to figure out how to live just when it's too late. —Bobbie Ann Mason from "With Jazz"

We were ice fishing on a northern Minnesota lake. Taking advantage of the latest in ice fishing technology, we'd had a wonderful afternoon catching panfish, mostly bluegills.

The fish were riding a little less than a foot off the bottom, and they were finicky. We had to tease them into biting, and then only a few from each hole. It was necessary to "run and gun," cutting a lot of holes, to catch fish.

About the time we were quiting, we met a gentleman standing, catching nothing. Two small pieces of plywood, held together with huge, rusting hinges, formed a pseudo windbreak. He'd been at it all afternoon, and had only a few tiny fish.

He'd put one hole through the ice when he started and was still standing over it, watching a bobber destined to lie still for the rest of the afternoon. After looking at our bucket of nice sunnies, he asked how we'd caught 'em.

"We can see on the depthfinder whether fish are down there and how deep," we said. "Then when we work the bait, we can see how the fish react. If we don't catch anything or see anything after a while, we keep moving, keep drilling holes until we find fish that will bite."

"Amazing!" the man said as we walked away.

fish and entice finicky fish to bite. And they'll almost always catch fish and have fun."

CHAPTER 4

JIGGING

"Jigging is the single most effective approach for catching most fish through the ice.
Al Lindner

"**W**hen I fish with Al Lindner, I often think back to Psychology 101 and the age-old debate over the degree to which heredity and environment influence who we become," Doug began the discussion about jigging. "In other words, are we born to be who we become or are we molded by living?

"But fishermen are made, not born. At least that's what I keep telling myself. But Al makes me wonder. Sure, he's a fisherman like you or me. He has bad days and good days. He gets backlashes. He spills his coffee. His depthfinder won't work. His bilge pump quits. And the plugs on his motor foul.

"But when it comes to catching fish, Al can. He'll go down a weedline after other good fishermen have fished it without a strike and take a limit. Perhaps Al is a bit more 'born to fishing' than the rest of us?

"Then logic slaps me back to reality. Presentation is the reason Al catches so many fish. Al understands basic presentation, plus the small, often seemingly insignificant presentation details that make a difference.

Presentation is learned.

"Fishermen are made, not born. Anyone can become a good ice fisherman. Understanding where to fish is important, but the final act of catching fish is a matter of presentation; and jigging is perhaps the most important presentation factor for catching fish big time."

System Basics—Rod Selection

"As we discussed in Chapter 2," Al said, "rod selection, which is critical to jigging well, is a matter of personal preference influenced by things like price; how often you fish; and whether you fish in a small shack, a large shack, or outside. As I've already said, I fish outside and in small portable shacks. I fish a lot and money's no object because fishing's my

By the late 1970s, small companies in sections of America where ice fishing was very popular were offering fiberglass ice fishing rods. None of the companies did well, however, probably because there wasn't any way to reach the mass ice-fishing market via advertising.

business.

"I own several custom-made graphite jigging rods, plus maybe 25 commercial options. Thank goodness a number of manufacturers have begun to market decent sticks. But again, 'good' depends on your point of view.

"Lake Superior jiggers fish for lake trout in 150 feet of water with nothing more than dacron line wrapped around a small, light 'bobbing' stick. You can easily carry the stick, then sit and jig in the type of confined one-

By the mid 1980s, Al Lindner and Doug Stange in conjunction with rod makers Greg and Paul Thorne were beginning to popularize fine graphite rods for walleyes, lake trout, pike, and bass. Meanwhile, Dave Genz and Al and Doug were also promoting smaller versions of the same rods for panfish. Many commercial options were available by 1988.

man tents Lake Superior winds make so necessary."

"I look for a rod that's comfortable, fun to fish with, and lets me do what I want to do efficiently," Doug replied in response to Al's observations. "To me, that means a longer rod than the typical ice-fishing rod. Not a full-size open-water rod, because they're inconvenient to carry. And not a cheap rod because they always have too few line guides, bend in all the wrong spots, or don't bend at all. They also fall apart in one season.

"Back in the early 1980s, I asked Greg Thorne (Thorne Brothers) to make me two perfect jigging sticks: 42- and 45-inch rods made from Fenwick 634 graphite blanks. At that time, the rods cost about $55 apiece. Greg placed the line guides (4 of them) so each blank loaded quickly to get to the power in the butt section. I used both rods outside, which is how I continue to fish most often, although I occasionally used the shorter model inside a small ice shack.

"I still have those two original rods; they still work great. But now more options are available.

"Besides being sensitive, comfortable, and fun to fish with, a high-quality longer rod overcomes jigging mistakes. Stick a fish directly below you, and it often comes straight up so quickly that it rolls over. That can mean slack line. Short stiff rods often give slack line each time you pump. You want fast tip action and sensitivity coupled with butt power packed into a rod that bends. You need a tight line at the initial hookset and during the battle and final surges at the hole.

"If your jigging rods are one of the highest priced parts of your ice-fishing tackle, fine."

Reels

Doug and Al prefer to fish with spinning tackle. They tape a spinning reel on the handle of a jigging rod a bit farther forward than usual, because they often jig with one hand while they search for a lure or hold a cup of coffee with the other hand. A little extra room at the end of the handle makes the rod easy to hold.

Casting equipment offers advantages, though. It's the obvious choice if you choose to fish deep for lake trout with dacron or wire line. Casting reels provide wrenching power. But in ice fishing, that's seldom necessary. The key to landing fish is to keep your line tight, take your time, and let a good rod do the work. Spinning tackle works great in most situations.

Obviously, the reel you choose needs a reliable drag. Always set the drag so it grudgingly gives line on the hookset to prevent rolling fish over and creating slack line.

Triggering Power—Line Weight

Getting fish to bite depends on a subtle blend of elements. A compre-

Whether reels are large or small, the most popular way to attach them to a rod is with electrical tape.

hensive jigging approach includes such things as choosing a jig style based on the mood of the fish, and as we'll discuss later, balancing the "attraction phase" of a jigging motion with the "triggering phase." Other considerations include line weight, lure size and shape, and the addition of scent.

Speed control (of the lure) depends on lure size and line diameter and how aggressively you jig. Say you're fishing with a #9 Jigging Rapala. On 8-pound-test line it scoots to the side and falls back below the hole more rapidly than it does on 12-pound test. Twelve-pound line, being thicker, offers more water resistance and slows the jig as it swims out and falls back. The slower speed is more appropriate for fish in cold water. Never mind the thicker line that most fishermen think fish can see.

The deeper you fish—the more line you have out—the more water resistance. Twelve-pound test line is Doug's choice for fishing a #9 Jigging Rap to about 40 feet for most large predators. "If I'm fishing deeper than 40 feet, say for walleyes or splake," Doug offered, "I drop to 10-pound test. Ten-pound test delivers about the same performance in 60 feet of water that 12-pound test does at 30 feet.

"If lake trout want a 1/2-ounce airplane jig, start with 14-pound test line—drop to 12-pound test in deeper water. Smaller lures for smaller fish? Start with 10-pound test and drop to 8-pound in deeper water."

Line weight is critical to speed control and lure performance. Yet when you're dealing with touchy fish and using a nonaggressive jigging approach, such as a leadhead jig with a lively minnow, a good choice is 8- or even 6-pound test. Eight pound is about as light as you should go for larger predators, although 4 or 6 pound is appropriate in clear water for smaller stocked rainbow or brown trout.

A Slice Of Life

A jigging lure represents a slice of life. How realistic your slice of life must be in order to get a response from fish depends on the fish species, the body of water, and the fishing situation, including how aggressive the fish are.

Lures like Rocker Minnows, Swedish Pimples, Jigging Rapalas, Kastmasters, or Pilkies are often assumed to represent minnows to fish. The reason so many fishermen remain only float and minnow fishermen is because this approach makes sense; if you want to duplicate a minnow, use one.

"But a less realistic slice of life often better represents real life," Al remarked. "Total triggering power

The real thing or a slice of life? There's a time and place for both. But a slice of life often works much better than the real thing.

Margin for Error—Portrait of a Good Jigging Rod

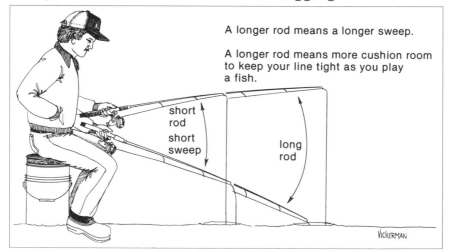

A longer rod means a longer sweep.

A longer rod means more cushion room to keep your line tight as you play a fish.

short rod

short sweep

long rod

VICKERMAN

You're looking for a rod that's comfortable, fun to fish with, and lets you do what you want to do efficiently. That means a rod that's longer than the typical ice-fishing rod, but not as long as a typical open-water rod. Fast tip action and sensitivity coupled with butt power packed into a rod that bends lets you keep a tight line on the initial hook set and during the battle and final surges at the hole.

depends on more than offering a perfectly realistic representation of what a fish eats.

"Say you're fishing for largemouth bass in open water. A crankbait is less real than a live minnow. But you're more apt to trigger bass by moving around and casting the crankbait to likely areas than by soaking a minnow below a bobber. At times, however, adding a minnow to a leadhead jig to cover water will outproduce the crankbait."

So it is in ice fishing. A lively minnow attracts, but often doesn't offer as much attracting power as a moving jig. A minnow may also trigger, but won't trigger unless it first attracts.

"A jigging presentation is a percentage package," Doug responded. "A minnow struggling on a jig may provide the right amount of attraction and triggering on a given day. The added attracting power of a moving and flashing jig, however, often outfishes a live minnow. Jigging is more effective than a bobber and minnow in the same way and for the same reasons a crankbait often outfishes a bobber and minnow in open water.

"Fish react to jigging as well or better than plain live bait for subtle reasons. Cold water seems to dull judgement responses in fish. Apparently, their reduced metabolism makes them respond differently to baits during cold-water periods than during warm-water periods. In warmer water, for example, fish may be so 'keyed up' that they respond quickly and make a mistake. A crankbait speeds by. They respond. Their keyed-up response causes the mistake.

"During winter," Doug continued, "a bait may also make the right series of movements that cause fish to make an aggressive mistake. But more often, mistakes occur during winter because fish are 'keyed down.' They usually don't respond as well to Jigging Rapalas or Kastmasters in warm water. But as the water cools in fall, they respond to them better. And after ice-up, lures that didn't produce well during summer produce best."

Al added, "We've observed that walleyes respond better to lures like the realistic-looking Jigging Rapala in clear water and to flash lures in dirty water. Jigging Rapalas and flash lures bring better responses than minnows. Walleyes in dirty water can't see far and perhaps are programmed to respond to what a flash lure does best, flash. A flash is what they usually see and react to.

"Walleyes in dirty water rarely sense the exact outline of what they eat. So walleyes in dirty water more often respond to larger lures and odd-shaped lures, so long as they flash."

"And don't forget the wobble," Doug interjected. "The feeling's important, too. Along with the flash, vibration is an important attractor; so unless you're using a lively minnow and playing a lift-drop-hold game with it, your lure doesn't have the same attracting ability. A lively minnow can attract as well as a flash lure can, but it doesn't offer the same triggering effect after the attraction.

Tips for Fishing Deep Water

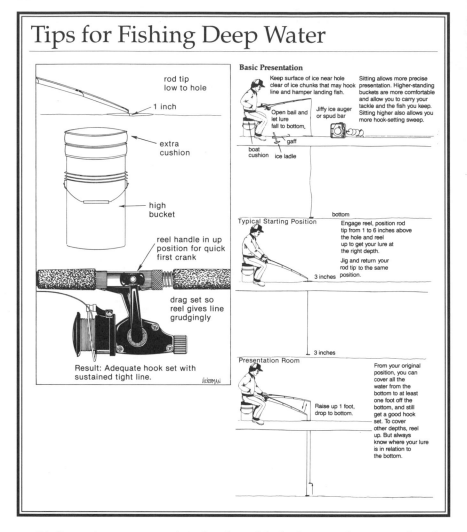

Basic Presentation

rod tip low to hole

1 inch

extra cushion

high bucket

reel handle in up position for quick first crank

drag set so reel gives line grudgingly

Result: Adequate hook set with sustained tight line.

Keep surface of ice near hole clear of ice chunks that may hook line and hamper landing fish.

Open bail and let lure fall to bottom.

Jiffy ice auger or spud bar

Sitting allows more precise presentation. Higher-standing buckets are more comfortable and allow you to carry your tackle and the fish you keep. Sitting higher also allows you more hook-setting sweep.

boat cushion   ice ladle   gaff

bottom

Typical Starting Position

Engage reel, position rod tip from 1 to 6 inches above the hole and reel up to get your lure at the right depth.

Jig and return your rod tip to the same position.

3 inches

3 inches

Presentation Room

Raise up 1 foot, drop to bottom.

From your original position, you can cover all the water from the bottom to at least one foot off the bottom, and still get a good hook set. To cover other depths, reel up. But always know where your lure is in relation to the bottom.

"A live minnow on a plain hook and light line is often considered a great trigger. Not always. A lively minnow is a great attractor, but may be a poor trigger in many cold-water situations. A lively free-swimming minnow on light line may actually intimidate a walleye sedated by cold water. It's too much of a good thing. In essence, the lively minnow keeps attracting, but no triggering pause is built into the presentation. A flash lure, on the other hand, flashes to attract and then pauses to trigger. That's often the right measure, the right blend in cold water."

Then you might ask, Why do walleyes in clear water prefer jigs with a more realistic profile like the Jigging Rapala?

"Probably because in clear water they clearly see what they eat," Al offered. "They see the school of minnows they attack, as well as smell them and feel them through their lateral lines. They usually respond to

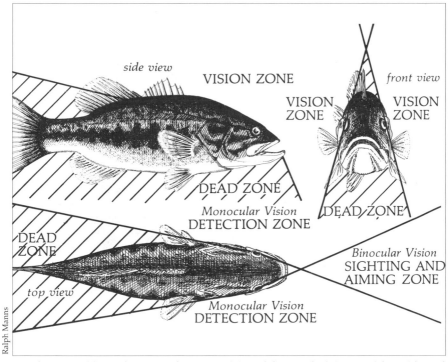

Ralph Manns

The eyes of bass, for example, are positioned for good vision to either side and binocular vision in a forward and slightly upward direction. Blind zones exist to the rear and underneath. Prey or lures in the binocular (sighting and aiming) zone are the most easily and accurately attacked. Prey and lures in other detection zones, however, may also be successfully attacked if the bass has time to turn and focus in the binocular zone. Items in dead zones may go undetected.

distinct profiles and distinctly moving prey. A flash is only part of what they usually see and respond to. Fish in clear water need a bit more than flash."

But walleyes sometimes respond to flash lures in clear water.

"We're offering considerations, not hard rules," Doug responded. "Think and then experiment; don't fish by the book—any book.

"Fish have binocular vision complete with depth perception when they look straight ahead. But their eyes are located on the sides of their head, so they lose their binocular vision right smack in front of their snout. Bigger fish may even have a blind spot directly in front of them because of the increased space between their eyes.

"Most fish in cold water, especially less aggressive species like walleyes, strike only when they get close to a lure. Movement attracts them, but when they get close they don't see so well. If the object that attracted them smells right and feels right (based on lateral line stimulation as they move up to the lure), they often make 'the big mistake.' "

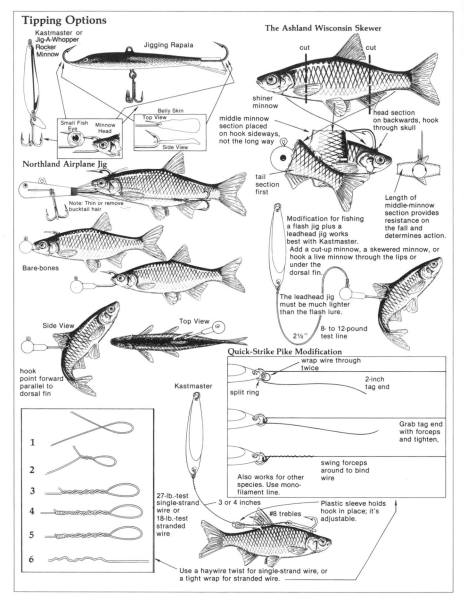

Tipping Options

Kastmaster or Jig-A-Whopper Rocker Minnow

Jigging Rapala

The Ashland Wisconsin Skewer

cut   cut

shiner minnow

head section on backwards, hook through skull

Belly Skin

Top View

Small Fish Eye   Minnow Head

Side View

middle minnow section placed on hook sideways, not the long way

Northland Airplane Jig

Note: Thin or remove bucktail hair

tail section first

Length of middle-minnow section provides resistance on the fall and determines action.

Modification for fishing a flash jig plus a leadhead jig works best with Kastmaster. Add a cut-up minnow, a skewered minnow, or hook a live minnow through the lips or under the dorsal fin.

Bare-bones

The leadhead jig must be much lighter than the flash lure.

2½"   8- to 12-pound test line

Side View   Top View

Quick-Strike Pike Modification

wrap wire through twice

2-inch tag end

split ring

Grab tag end with forceps and tighten.

swing forceps around to bind wire

Also works for other species. Use mono-filament line.

hook point forward parallel to dorsal fin

Kastmaster

1

2

3

4

5

6

27-lb.-test single-strand wire or 18-lb.-test stranded wire

3 or 4 inches

#8 trebles

Plastic sleeve holds hook in place; it's adjustable.

Use a haywire twist for single-strand wire, or a tight wrap for stranded wire.

Doug continued, "Small fish see better up close than large fish. Small fish swim up to a Jigging Rapala and attempt to eat a specific part of the lure, often the fish eye hanging on the hook. Apparently it looks like forage to unwary small fish."

"Big fish, however, don't usually eat a specific part of a lure," Al interjected. "In the case of the Jigging Rap, often as not they engulf it. Perhaps their diminished close-up vision doesn't allow for a distinct judgement about what the lure is. It moved a moment ago, didn't it? I'm too close to see it now, but I can feel it and it smells right. Mistake! Fish on! Man, I love it!"

The right measure of triggering power? The perfect slice of life? The right percentage package? No one knows exactly why fish respond to jigging presentations through the ice. But they do, from predators like lake trout, browns, brookies, rainbows, walleyes, pike, muskies, hybrids, and bass, to panfish like crappies, white bass, perch, and bluegills. If you

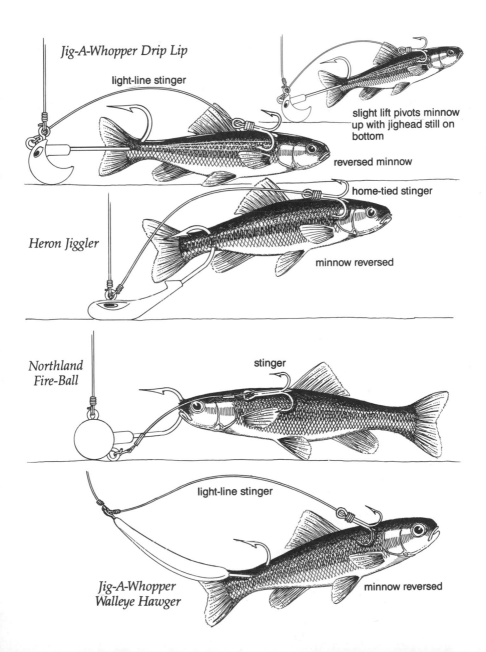

Jig-A-Whopper Drip Lip

light-line stinger

slight lift pivots minnow up with jighead still on bottom

reversed minnow

home-tied stinger

Heron Jiggler

minnow reversed

Northland Fire-Ball

stinger

light-line stinger

Jig-A-Whopper Walleye Hawger

minnow reversed

don't adapt jigging strategies to the species you pursue, you won't catch fish like you could.

Scent

Scent is necessary to consistently trigger some fish species. And when adding scent is so easy, it's foolish not to use it. But should it be a natural scent, a commercial scent, or both?

We often hear that fish rely more on their sense of smell in cold water. Perhaps. Instead of debating this, we'll just remark on what works most of the time. We don't know everything about every situation, though, so experiment.

"Using natural scents works," Al offered. "A fish eye, a piece of fish belly, a minnow head or tail, or a whole minnow. Maggots, wax worms, mousies, grass shrimp, or mayfly larvae. Depends on the fish species and the lure you choose, as well as how you fish the lure.

"Commercial scent products? I've often argued that a commercial scent product can't hurt your fishing. Doug doesn't agree, though. Experiment with commercial products. I've been particularly impressed with the new impregnated baits like Berkley Power Grubs. They'll often outfish maggots. These baits, by the way, are a blend of 'real' stuff, so perhaps they qualify as a natural bait."

"But don't rely on exaggerated claims," Doug cautioned. "Miracle products don't exist, although natural baits coupled with the right jigging lures come close."

General Jigging Principles

If you aren't catching the fish you could because you practice the same old bobber and minnow, tip-up and chub, or deadbait tactics each time you ice fish, it's time to jig. Understanding both jigging and stationary ice-fishing techniques and applying the right approach at the right time is the measure of a fisherman who consistently catches fish.

Questions: Choose a large or small jig; add a natural or a commercial scent; fish deep or shallow; jig aggressively or not so aggressively; use a long rod, short rod, or no rod; use spinning or casting tackle with monofilament or dacron line? Do certain jig types trigger certain species and not others? Does time of day or season affect jig choice, size, and presentation?

General principles help build a foundation toward jigging proficiency for any fish species. The first step is to categorize jigging lures.

Jigging Lures

Jigging lures for larger predators fall into three categories: (1) *flash lures* like the Acme Kastmaster, Jig-A-Whopper Rocker Minnow, or Custom Jigs and Spins' Stinger; (2) *swimming lures* like the Jigging Rapala, Northland Air-Plane Jig, or Wisconsin Tackle Swimmin' Ratt; and (3) *lead-*

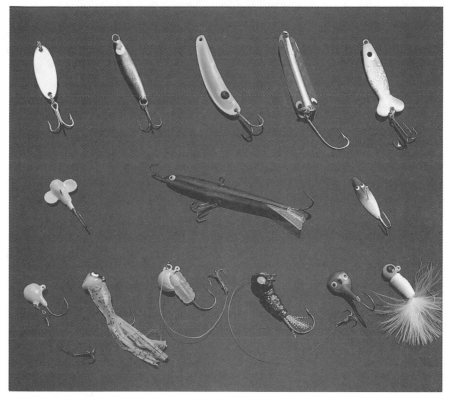

Flash lures—*(left to right)   Acme "Kastmaster"; Jig-A-Whopper "Rocker Minnow"; Jig-A-Whopper "Knocker Minnow"; Jig-A-Whopper "Hawger Spoon"; Northland "Fire-Eye Spoon."*

Swimming lures—*Northland "Air-Plane Jig"; Normark "Jigging Rapala"; Wisconsin Tackle "Swimmin' Ratt."*

Standard leadhead jigs—*Northland "Fire-Ball"; Northland "Lip-Stick"; Jig-A-Whopper "Drip Lip"; Jig-A-Whopper "Competition Head"; Heron "Jiggler"; Lindy-Little Joe "Fuzz-E-Grub."*

head jigs like a Northland Fire-Ball, Jig-A-Whopper Drip Lip, or Heron Jiggler with little or no hair or dressing of any kind, but often with fluorescent or phosphorescent heads.

Flash Lures—Using your wrist and lower arm, jig flash lures up with a sharp 1- to 2-foot lift of your rod tip. Immediately return your rod tip to its original position. The jig flutters and flashes its way down (vertically) to its original position. The flash and movement attract fish.

Jigs weighing from about 1/4 to 3/4 ounce work fine in depths down to about 60 feet or more. It may take at least a 1/2-ounce lure to fish effectively for lake trout in 100 feet of water. Ultradeep fishing is unusual, however; most fish including lakers are caught in water less than 60 feet deep.

Although many lures fall into this general category, many styles of flash lures exist. The Acme Kastmaster is a straight, slim, shiny piece of metal. The Jig-A-Whopper Rocker Minnow or Northland Fire-Eye Spoon, by comparison, are bent lead. The Jig-A-Whopper Hawger Spoon, on the other hand, is distinctly bent metal with a big crease running down the back. Each of these baits offers its own unique flash, fall, and feel. In certain conditions, certain flash baits will outperform others.

Swimming Lures—Swimming lures are jigged much like flash lures, but the resulting action is different. The Swimmin' Ratt swims up and out and then glides back to its original position. Lures like the Jigging Rapala swim up and out and return in a quarter- or half-circle swim. Air-Plane jigs are a bit more erratic and may swim in almost a complete circle. Each of these lures will swim complete circles, however, if you constantly pump your rod up and down. The size of the circles depends on depth (how much line you have out), how hard and high you pump your rod, and the size of the lure.

Jigging Rapalas come in four sizes—#3, #5, #7, and #9, with lengths of about 1½, 2, 2½ and 3½ inches, respectively. A #9 fishes fine in 60 feet of water on 12-pound-test monofilament line. The other sizes can be fished that deep, using progressively lighter line.

Northland Air-Plane Jigs, which could be considered leadhead jigs with wings, come in 1/4-, 3/8-, 3/4- and 1½-ounce sizes. And the Swimmin' Ratt ranges from 1/16 ounce to 1/4 ounce.

Leadhead Jigs—Bare-bones leadhead jigs are tipped with cut-up minnow portions, a live minnow, a dead minnow, or packed with maggots. A jig tipped with a deadbait can be jigged aggressively with 1- to 2-foot rod lifts. A jig tipped with a live minnow hooked through the lips or the back near the dorsal fin should be lifted, not jigged aggressively. Ease it up a foot or two and let it flash and fall back to its original position.

Bare-bones jigs for presenting deadbait should range from about 1/16 to 3/4 ounce depending on the depth and the fish species. Use heavy jigs in deep water or to anchor the baits.

To present a live minnow, match jig weight with minnow size. Use the lightest jig you can effectively fish to keep your minnow alive longer and more active.

But remain in control. A 4- or 5-inch shiner minnow will actively swim on a 1/16-ounce jighead, but you lose control. The bait takes too long to get down and may swim out of the productive zone you want to fish. A better choice is at least a 1/8-ounce jig in water down to about 15 feet; 1/4 ounce down to 30 feet; and 3/8 ounce and heavier in deeper water.

Choosing A Jigging Lure

Different fish species prefer different types of jigging lures at different times. Doug suggests categorizing jigging lures and applying them to different situations based on how "aggressive" the lure category fishes.

Fish Species	General Level of Winter Aggressiveness	Basic Jig Type
lake trout, splake, burbot, pike	Aggressive	Swimming Jig (Jigging Rapala, Airplane Jig, or Swimming Rat)
walleyes, brown trout, rainbow trout, brook trout, coho salmon	Moderately Aggressive	Flash Lure (Kastmaster, Rocker Minnow, or Fire-Eye Spoon)
largemouth and smallmouth bass	Not-So-Aggressive	Bare-bones leadhead jig with minnow

"It's a good general guideline," Al said. "Swimming lures are the most aggressive lure category. They flash and also move vertically and horizontally. Flash lures are the next most aggressive category. They flash, but move mostly vertically. Bare-bones leadhead jigs fall into the same category as flash lures if you skewer a dead minnow on the jig and use a lift-drop-pause routine. When they're fished with a live minnow, though, they fall into a 'least-aggressive' category."

"Now by categorizing general winter activity levels of fish species," Doug offered, "we have a system for choosing baits for certain situations and species. Lake trout, burbot, pike, and splake generally are aggressive; walleyes, browns, rainbows, brook trout, and coho salmon are moderately aggressive; largemouth and smallmouth bass are least aggressive.

"These are general characterizations. Lake trout usually are the most aggressive of all winter biters, but at times they're moderately aggressive or less aggressive. On the other hand, walleyes and even generally lethargic largemouth and smallmouth bass at times may feed aggressively."

"The basic rule," Al added," is to apply aggressive jigging lures to aggressive species or species in an aggressive mood, and vice versa. An Air-Plane Jig works for lake trout, splake, burbot, and pike. A Jigging Rap works for those species, too, and is even more appropriate for aggressive walleyes or even aggressive smallmouth or largemouth bass."

"Likewise, flash lures often are more applicable to aggressive species in a less aggressive mood," Doug suggested. "Walleyes when they're moderately aggressive. Largemouth and smallmouth bass when they're slightly more aggressive than usual.

"A light bare-bones leadhead jig tipped with a live minnow or chub and fished in a slow-and-easy lift-drop-pause manner is the most logical choice for triggering other species when they're less aggressive. Again though," Doug noted, "we're talking general principles, not hard rules. The principles are guidelines to help you move in the right direction."

Phases Of A Jigging Motion

Each jigging motion has two basic phases: (1) an attraction phase, and (2) a triggering phase. When you lift a Jigging Rapala it darts to the side, turns, slides back below the hole, and stops. The purpose of the swim-out and swim-back phase is attraction, although it may also trigger aggressive fish. The pause phase triggers.

Only the most aggressive fish of a generally aggressive species like lake trout hit a Jigging Rapala during its swim-out (attraction) phase.

"Watch out, though," Al observed, "because aggressive species often attack as the lure glides back below the hole. But most of the time, the strike comes as the lure settles, after it settles, or when it momentarily remains motionless. For aggressive species, the attraction phase of a jigging motion may attract and trigger, so minimize the pauses—the portion

Jigging Sequence—Lake Trout (Northland Air-Plane Jig Tipped with a Shiner)

Lake trout may be at any depth. Start by jigging 1 foot off the bottom. "Lake trout water" is usually clear, but it's slightly more difficult for lakers to see at 50 feet than up higher where light penetration is better. High-riding lake trout often are aggressive and may be able to see for 30 or 40 feet. No need to spend much time jigging for them. Spend slightly more time jigging close to the bottom. Concentrate your fishing at the depth you contact fish.

3-foot lift, tight-line return

3' return — 7 seconds / 7 seconds

lift   hold lift   hold

Sequence 6, 1 minute	— 40'	return to Sequence 1
Sequence 5, 1 minute	— 30'	
Sequence 4, 1 minute	— 20'	
Sequence 3, 2 minutes	— 10'	
Sequence 2, 2 minutes	— 5'	
Sequence 1, 2 minutes	— 1' start	50' bottom

Keep your line reasonably tight on the fall because lake trout are often aggressive enough to hit the jig then. A tight-line return means the jig falls at a normal speed, but follow the jig with your rod tip as it falls.

Walleyes (#9 Jigging Rapala, Treble Hook Tipped with Perch Eye)

Most walleyes are within a foot of the bottom. Divide that "key foot" of water into two sections. Make at least three jigs at 6 inches and then three jigs at 1 foot. Repeat. On some days, your jigs should be at 3 and 9 inches.
At the 3-inch level, you'll usually catch small fish. Big walleyes usually take their prey up a bit.

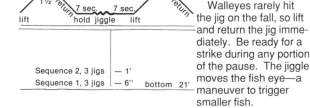

1½-foot lift, immediate return

1½' return — 7 sec. 7 sec.

lift   hold jiggle   lift   return

| Sequence 2, 3 jigs | — 1' | |
| Sequence 1, 3 jigs | — 6" | bottom 21' |

Walleyes rarely hit the jig on the fall, so lift and return the jig immediately. Be ready for a strike during any portion of the pause. The jiggle moves the fish eye—a maneuver to trigger smaller fish.

Largemouth and Smallmouth Bass (1/8-ounce Jig, 3½-inch Shiner Minnow Hooked Parallel to the Dorsal Fin, Hook Point Forward)

Largemouth bass may be found at almost any depth, but you can usually trigger them by using two jigging sequences—one near bottom and the second about halfway up. Largemouths are rarely concentrated at any depth, so continue the two-sequence jigging approach even though you catch a bass at a given depth.

Smallmouth bass are almost always found near the bottom in deep water. Use the same approach as for largemouths in shallow water.

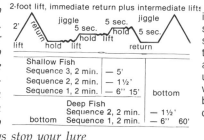

Lift the jig slowly so you don't rip the minnow off, but return the rod tip immediately so the minnow flashes and flutters its way back to the bottom. Pause to let the minnow do its thing. Fish hit during the pause.

Brown Trout and Splake (1/4-ounce Leadhead Jig, Plastic Body Removed, Tipped with Cut Minnow Per the Ashland Skewer)

Brown trout and splake tend to relate to the bottom in both deep and shallow water. Fish in shallow water more likely stray up from the bottom. Lake trout, rainbows, brookies, splake, brown trout, and coho salmon tend to follow lures up to the surface. Always stop your lure about 5 feet below the ice when you retrieve it to the surface..

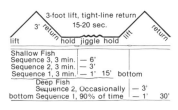

The basic sequence is a 2-foot lift-return with several pauses and slight jiggles to tip the tail end of the bait up and down. Slight upward and then downward changes in the bait often help trigger curious fish.

Pike (Quick-Strike Rig and 6-inch Dead Sucker or Shiner)

In deep water, baits should be fished near the bottom. An exception would be suspending baits over deep water (at the same level as the drop-off) just off a major shallow bar. In shallower water, pike often suspend just below the ice, but still tend to use the lower half of the water column.

The lift-return is an attracting maneuver. The tight-line return keeps the rig from fouling. Pike hit the bait when you pause to let the sucker or shiner set. The jiggle activates the bait.

of the jigging motion that usually triggers less aggressive fish.

"Aggressive fish don't need much time to decide to strike after they see what to strike. Aggressive lures offer the most attraction, and the attraction leads to immediate triggering."

"Of course," Doug suggested, "lures from one of the two less-aggressive lure categories can also be fished more aggressively. Say you're fishing for lake trout. Flash lures might work well fished with 3-foot rod lifts and only a minimal pause in your jigging motion. That rarely works for walleyes. If it doesn't trigger trout, shorten your lifts and slow down.

"For less aggressive species," he continued, "or during times when aggressive species are less aggressive, switch to a lure that naturally provides less attraction. Also minimize the attraction phase of the jig movement and add longer pauses. Switch to a flash lure, which naturally doesn't advertise so much as a lure that swims way out to the side."

"Or choose an aggressive lure like a Jigging Rapala, but jig less aggressively," Al said, smiling at the thought of how this advice must seem contradictory to someone hearing it for the first time. "Lengthen the pause and perhaps add an enticing, but slight jiggle or two during the pause."

Obviously, applications for the three basic lure categories overlap. Calling certain species aggressive and others less aggressive isn't completely accurate when so many variables affect aggression. Likewise, terming lures aggressive or less aggressive is somewhat undependable, too. But it's a start. Consider more exceptions.

Apply aggressive lures to aggressive species, and the walleye is a less aggressive species, the rules say. Fine, but Doug and Al have caught more walleyes, big and small, on Jigging Rapalas—an aggressive lure— than on any other. Flash lures like the Rocker Minnow, however, run a close second. If they had to choose only one jigging lure for big walleyes, though, it would be a #9 Jigging Rapala. But instead of working it aggressively, they confine their moves to a lift-drop-pause; and the pause often lasts as long as 15 seconds.

Again, their experience has shown that a Jigging Rapala produces best in deeper, usually clearer bodies of water; flash jigs produce best in shallower, murkier bodies of water; and bare-bones leadhead jigs tipped with a live minnow produce best in current—rivers.

Exceptions exist for each species. Pike, for example, are an aggressive species, so use an aggressive jigging lure, the rules say. Indeed, experience suggests that a specific aggressive jigging lure, the Northland Air-Plane Jig, tipped with a live or dead minnow or chub is one of the best choices and far outproduces the Jigging Rapala, another aggressive choice.

But a bait choice from the other end of the aggression spectrum has far outfished even the Air-Plane Jig the past few years. In the chapter on pike, we'll talk more about quick-strike rigging 8- to 10-inch dead suckers for pike. The rigged sucker becomes the lure to be lifted and then allowed to fall on a semitight line. The lift-fall attracts pike. The fall sometimes triggers them to strike. The hold after the fall definitely is a triggering maneuver.

Yet pike are an aggressive species, and aggressive techniques should apply, the rule says. But then we told you that only the "right" aggressive techniques apply. And now we're going to tell you that pike often are best fished with a stationary technique such as deadbait suspended below a tip-up.

Jigging generalizations can help form a strong foundation to build on for ice fishing for any fish species. Learning about fishing is like using road maps. A map of the U.S. is fine for getting from Cut Bank, Montana, to Buffalo, New York. But once you get to Buffalo, trade the general map for a city map.

Once you understand jigging basics, experiment with variations for each fish species. Once you have experience on specific lake types during specific winter periods, trade your general map (general jigging guidelines) for a more specific course. But don't throw away your general map; you'll need it when you begin fishing for a different species.

Building On Basics

Traditional Jigging—Countless variations sprout from a basic approach. Start with a standard leadhead jig, a flash lure, or a swimming jig positioned about 6 inches off bottom. A lift-fall attraction phase and drift-back-settle triggering phase works best when fish are feeding up just a bit. That's most of the time. So start with this traditional approach, but experiment with bottom moves.

Bottom Skipping—Begin in traditional fashion with your rod tip positioned about a foot above the water and your jig about 6 inches above the bottom. Then do a bottom-snap instead of a lift-fall. Drop the jig to the bottom with a sharp drop of your rod tip, and immediately snap-lift (skip) the lure off the bottom and back to its original position. Hold, and then repeat.

On semisoft bottom, a snap puffs a cloud of silt when the jig skips bottom. The drop-lift is the attracting maneuver, while the hold triggers fish.

This technique is often effective when used with a traditional jigging approach—lift-fall-hold; then drop-snap-hold. Repeat.

Bottom Upping—Drop your jig to the bottom. Have a tight line to your jig resting on bottom with your rod tip 3 inches above the water. Lift sharply a foot or so and immediately return your rod tip to its original position. Then immediately lift your rod tip 3 more inches (6 inches above the hole) and hold. The jig is 3 inches off the bottom. Before lifting again, drop the jig back to the bottom. Repeat the procedure.

If the fish are seriously bottom oriented, however, you may have to return the jig to the bottom and keep it there before they'll pick it up. This means fishing with a tight line to the bottom.

Traditional Jigging

Bottom Skipping

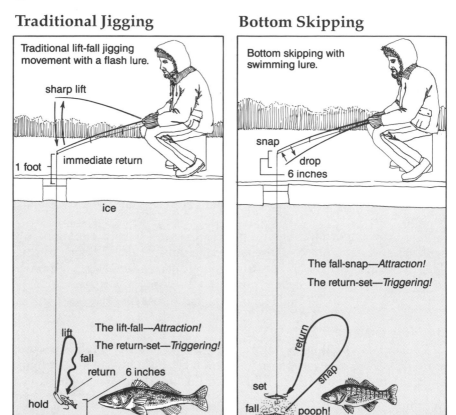

Traditional lift-fall jigging movement with a flash lure.

sharp lift

1 foot — immediate return

ice

The lift-fall—*Attraction!*

The return-set—*Triggering!*

lift

fall

return 6 inches

hold

Bottom skipping with swimming lure.

snap

drop 6 inches

The fall-snap—*Attraction!*

The return-set—*Triggering!*

return

snap

set

fall pooph!

Tight-Line Bottom Techniques

Tight-Line Twitching—Drop your jig to the bottom. Position your rod tip about 3 inches above the water and reel in slack line. Become familiar with the weight of the jig so you know just what it's doing when you barely raise your rod tip or barely jiggle it.

Leadhead jigs and flash lures work well with this technique. Say you're using a 1/16-ounce leadhead jig with the plastic body removed and replaced with either several fish eyes or about 8 maggots.

Be sure your knot is tight and tied directly to the top of the hook eye. With the jig on the bottom, slightly lift your rod tip so you barely feel the head of the jig lift. Now jiggle your rod tip—slight, but quick 1/16-inch up-and-down movements—for about 1 second. The jig will quiver and twitch and move in a semicircle on the bottom.

Stop and hold. An aggressive pickup will be as obvious as a good thump when you're using a traditional jigging technique with the jig resting above bottom. More likely, however, a pickup will be a subtle lift that reduces the weight of the bait as a fish barely sucks in the bait.

Bottom Upping

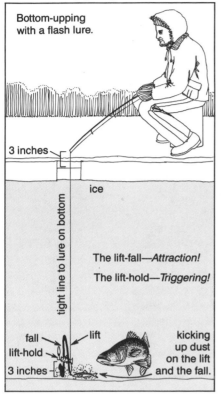

Bottom-upping with a flash lure.

3 inches

ice

tight line to lure on bottom

The lift-fall—*Attraction!*

The lift-hold—*Triggering!*

fall

lift

lift-hold

3 inches

kicking up dust on the lift and the fall.

When fish are reluctant to bite, switch to a 1/32- or 1/64-ounce jig. Use one- or two-pound-test line coupled with tiny jigs on a light-action rod.

Although we've always used traditional leadhead jigs for bottom fishing, in recent years we've switched almost exclusively to Heron Manufacturing's "Mini Jiggler" (1/64 ounce) for perch. Try a 1/8-ounce Jiggler for combination perch and walleye fishing. The Jiggler has a shoe-type head and a hook that projects up. The Jig-A-Whopper Drip Lip also works well in this application.

Pack the hook with maggots to trigger perch, or hook a small minnow just under the dorsal fin, with the point of the hook positioned forward, not to the side. Use a bigger minnow for walleyes.

Say you're using a Jig-A-Whopper #4 "Hawger Spoon" (a flash lure) tipped with a fish eye, another fine option for both perch and walleyes. By lifting your rod tip a half inch, you lift the top of the body of the bait off the bottom, while the triggering portion of the bait—the hook with the fish eye—remains on the bottom.

Jiggle your rod tip—make slight, but quick 1/8-inch up-and-down movements for about 1 second. The body of the bait will swim in a semi-circle while the hook and fish eye puff up and down off the bottom.

Stop and hold. Again, a take will likely be a subtle lift, a barely notice-able reduction in the weight of the lure.

Tight-Line Floating—To become an accomplished tight-line fisher-man, first learn traditional jigging techniques. Even then, however, it may be difficult to lift a jig body 1/8 inch off the bottom while distin-guishing when a fish picks up the bait. A float can help.

Although many floats will work, try the small Carlyles by Wazp Brand Products or Thill Tackle. Slide a Wazp Float Stop on your line, then the slip float, and tie a jig on the end of your line. Inside a shack, the rig func-tions like a slip float. Reel fish up, take them off, and immediately return the rig to the right depth. Outside, the float usually freezes to the stop, but still allows easy bait positioning on the bottom.

Tight-Line Twitching

Drop your bait to the bottom. Move your float up or down to create a tight-line connection between the jig on the bottom and the float on the surface. Jiggling your rod tip jiggles the float and the bait. When a fish picks up the bait, the float tips up, not down. Set the hook and reel or hand-over-hand

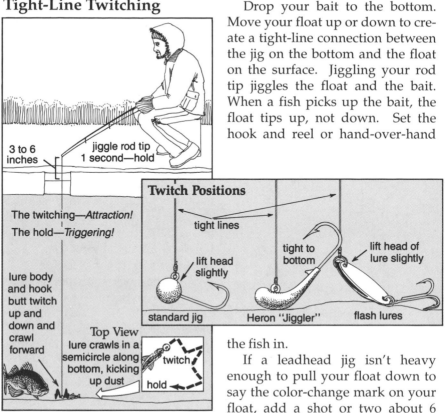

3 to 6 inches

jiggle rod tip 1 second—hold

The twitching—*Attraction!*
The hold—*Triggering!*

lure body and hook butt twitch up and down and crawl forward

Twitch Positions

tight lines

lift head slightly

tight to bottom

lift head of lure slightly

standard jig

Heron "Jiggler"

flash lures

Top View
lure crawls in a semicircle along bottom, kicking up dust

twitch

hold

the fish in.

If a leadhead jig isn't heavy enough to pull your float down to say the color-change mark on your float, add a shot or two about 6 inches below the float. If you want the rig to function as a slip float, add the shot 6 inches above the bait. The addition of shot pulls your float down a bit more, so adjust your float to be sure you still have a tight-line connection to the bottom.

The higher the float rides in the water, the more action you give the jig when you dabble the float. The lower the float rides in the water, the more sensitive the rig is to pick-ups.

Dozens of variations exist to these basic bottom-focused tight-line themes. Basic approaches lead to other options, including "suspender floating," a system we'll cover in the chapter on float fishing.

Jigging For Panfish

Professionals in any sport rely sparingly on mechanical help. Golf pros don't use toe-weighted clubs, because their swings are finely tuned. Professional photographers don't use programmed cameras, because they prefer to make technical and creative decisions themselves. And the best fishermen want nothing between them and their lure but line and a top-quality rod. They rely on educated hands and the touch that comes with talent and experience.

Tight-Line Floating

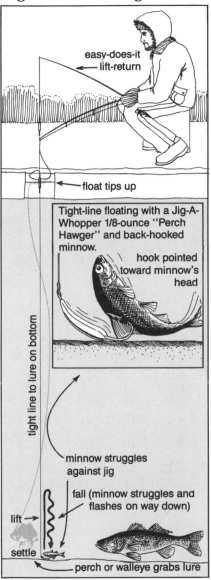

easy-does-it
← lift-return

← float tips up

Tight-line floating with a Jig-A-Whopper 1/8-ounce "Perch Hawger" and back-hooked minnow.

hook pointed toward minnow's head

tight line to lure on bottom

minnow struggles against jig

fall (minnow struggles and flashes on way down)

lift →

settle

perch or walleye grabs lure

But many recreational golfers rely on counterbalanced clubs to forgive their sins; snapshot artists like the ease of automatic cameras; and weekend anglers gladly accept help detecting light-biting fish.

Often the bite of smaller fish—panfish—is hard to detect, especially when you're ice fishing. Winter water is still and as clear as it gets. Fish have time—take time—to inspect things. Under these conditions, you often have to tackle down to get bit.

How light? Certainly no more than 2-pound test. Most of the best panfishermen, however, use 1-pound-test line or less, coupled with tiny ice flies and #10 to #16 hooks. Dangle the right thing—usually the subtle thing—in the face of a big bluegill or crappie, and get ready for a tussle. Often it's difficult to notice when panfish take a tiny lure, unless you know what to look for and how to react.

"A fish can't take a bait without moving it," Doug insisted. "That movement isn't easily measurable, but there's usually something to detect. But it takes an experienced angler to know when to set the hook; so ice fishermen, perhaps more than open-water anglers, have gadgets to help detect subtle takers."

Light Line—A Subtle Connection

Light line helps get more bites and can help you notice them. One- or 2-pound test hangs straight even with the minimal weight of a teeny ice fly. Still, even light line has a drawback for telegraphing strikes. Stretch is the culprit.

"I don't know of any light line that's low stretch and still supple," Dave offered. "Stretch can be a factor even in crappie fishing. In 40 feet of

Bluegills, crappies, perch, white bass, and other panfish are the group of fish most pursued during winter. Jigging far outproduces any other method for putting them on the ice and in the pan.

water, it can feel like you have the fish on a long rubber band."

Hook sharpness, too, as we mentioned earlier, is critical. Laugh at the prospect of sharpening a hook you can barely see, but Dave and Doug carry small diamond sharpeners and touch up every hook before it goes down the hole.

Line

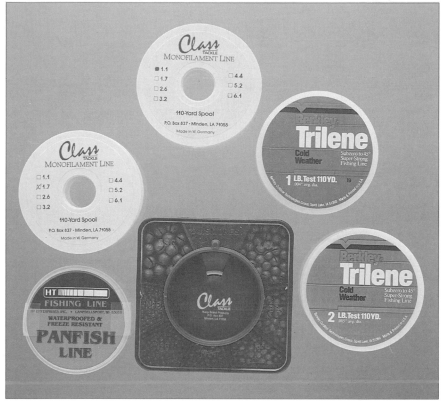

Most monofilament line manufacturers offer lines testing 2 pounds. Often, however, lines of lesser tests can vastly increase your catch.

- Berkley offers "Trilene Cold Weather Line" in 1-pound test, as well as 2-, 4-, 6-, 10-, 12-, 14-, and 17-pound test. The line is blue.
- H.T. Enterprises offers a "Panfish Line" testing 3/4 pound. The line is light grey.
- Class Tackle offers "Class Monofilament" testing 1.1 and 1.7 pounds, as well as 2.6, 3.2, 4.4, 5.2, and 6.1 pounds. The line is clear grey.
- The micro shot is from Class Tackle.

Sharp hooks on your ice flies are vital, according to Dave, because you can't stick the fish hard with light line and a short rod. He pinches the barb down with a needle-nose or files it off. Then the hook sinks in instantly. It also makes unhooking easier.

Spring Tip—Bobber On The Rod

Spring tips, often called spring bobbers, help even experienced anglers detect light bites. They come in many styles, from light wire suspended above the rod tip to springs you thread line through. At the slightest

A spring-tip bite indicator can turn a clumsy ice rod into a functional light-bite system. H.T. Enterprises is one company offering spring tips.

movement, the spring moves downward or settles upward, depending on whether the fish took "down" or "up."

"They can be helpful," Dave observed, "for jigging with light tackle. But they work well with only one presentation—a constant, fairly slow jigging motion. I know guys who pound on the reel or the rod with a closed fist to get a fast-twitching motion. If that works, great."

Doug added, "We've been talking for years about the importance of imitating various zooplankton prey such as copepods and *Daphnia*. To imitate *Daphnia* that panfish feed on especially during low-light periods, make a series of soft bounces followed by a pause and maybe a larger hop or two to catch the fish's attention. You won't get anything except a slow, soft, cushioned hop with a spring tip.

"That's one reason I've never thought of spring bobbers as a weapon, although they do transform a poor rod into a functional light-bite indicator. The spring bobber also offers the advantage of changing depths faster. When you want to fish deeper with a float, you have to adjust the stop."

"Don't bend the spring bobber in a big angle with a wide gap between the rod and the spring so you have to remove slop when you set the hook," Dave cautioned. "Fish don't have to feel resistance to spit the hook. If something doesn't feel right, they'll let go. Instead, bend the spring bobber down close to the rod for a quicker set."

"Sometimes only a lengthy pause, a completely still presentation, will draw a strike," Doug advised. "Even without a spring bobber, you have to place the rod on your leg to get it still enough. Especially in wind, it's impossible to stop a spring from moving the bait. On some days, that costs more bites than the spring helps you see. Always trade-offs."

The Button Indicater

Sitting on the ice too long leads to invention. Someone in the inner circle of Dave's Winter Fishing Systems team thought of threading a shirt button onto the line as a bite indicator.

The button goes on the line between the tip and the first guide, or between the first two guides. Wrap enough fine lead wire (the kind fly-fishermen use to weight sinking flies) to balance the button to the weight of your bait. Drop the bait into the fish zone, and keep your eye on the bouncing button. If a fish takes down, the button goes up. If the fish takes up, the button goes down.

"If the fish are really snapping, it's fun because the button bangs off the rod blank. You can hear the bite," Dave observed.

"To be effective, precisely balance the button with the bait. If the button's too light, it won't pull down line. If it's too heavy, the line falls too far, creating slop and hooksetting problems. Usually, though, some slack occurs in the line even with a properly weighted button.

"When I see fish on the locator screen that won't bite," Dave continued, "I raise, raise, raise. A lot of times, fish will follow, but won't bite. As long as they keep coming, I keep raising; but if the fish suddenly stops following, I drop the lure.

"Instead of the jig falling quickly to the fish, the button falls and creates slack between the first two rod guides. Then the jig sinks slowly to the fish as the button rises, giving an extremely slow and natural drop. The jig doesn't quiver much, even if the rod tip shakes. Sometimes this triggers fish into striking."

The strike is indicated when the button stops rising or actually "jumps" slightly. The "slop factor" still exists when you try to set the hook, but without the button you might not have had the bite. Life's tough.

Eventually some form of "the button" may be available in bait shops.

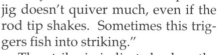

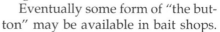

The button!

There's nothing special about the shape, size, or style of a button—just a counterbalance for the bait.

The button system isn't without fault. As you lower your line down the hole, the button may spin around the rod. On a fast drop the line can wrap countless times, leaving a tangle. Also, like spring tips, buttons limit presentation options by cushioning and deadening jigging movements.

"I've played with other gadgets," Dave added, "like the snap-on-and-off slip-sinker from a Northland Tackle Roach Rig. I use a side cutter to trim off lead until the weight's right. Then I snap them on or take them off without having to re-tie."

The Power Of A Good Rod

It shouldn't be surprising that Doug, Dave, and Al choose a good graphite rod and light line as the connection of choice between themselves and finicky panfish. Subtle strikes can be detected without add-on bite-indicators by relying on experience, heightened senses, and the magic of a topnotch rod.

Floats, spring tips, and coiled line sidestep finely tuned senses, the best strike indicators. Floats serve purposes, but we're focusing on ultimate sensitivity under a variety of situations.

"You have at least two senses and possibly a mysterious third on your side," Doug speculated. "Feel is the most important. With a sensitive graphite rod, you'll feel most strikes. Sight—visual clues like line movement—is the second sense. The third clue is an intangible we might call 'anticipation' or 'telepathy.' Concentrate hard enough and you'll set the hook seemingly by instinct; you can't explain how you knew a fish was there. Who knows what controls that?"

H.T. Enterprises, St. Croix, Mitchell, Thorne Brothers, Cabela's, and Berkley (top to bottom) offer graphite panfish rods for ice fishing. Recently, Jig-A-Whopper (marketing rods made by Thorne Brothers) and Wisconsin Tackle have been added to the list. Contact each company for information on their complete line of rods.

"With a straight rod-and-line setup, you can fish the entire column of water under your hole without making big adjustments," Dave added.

Panfish rods, like rods for larger predators, must offer sensitivity, yet provide the type of "measured give" that eliminates mistakes (slack line) and allows fishermen of all ages to use very light line. Beyond that, the rods must be a pleasure to fish with.

"Even if I'm in 35 feet of water, I assume the fish could be at any depth. I constantly raise and lower my bait from on the bottom to just under the ice."

At times, bites can be harder to detect without help from a strike indicator, but sonar readies your senses for the impending bite, making you more capable.

"It's amazing how sensitive you can become," Doug noted, "especially inside a small portable shack away from distractions and wind. Most people just don't—can't—concentrate when they fish. Most fishermen haven't even once coordinated the senses they have for detecting bites. When they do, most 'crutches' aren't necessary.

"In some areas, anglers bend their line to form a sharp angle where it enters the water. They watch for movement. Others coil their line and watch the coils. Trouble is, you have to re-bend the line every time you change depths.

"The best way to detect bites is to watch the line," Doug continued. "Hold your rod at an angle to the ice, with the reel outside your body and the rod coming across it.

"If you're using a light bait, the line at the rod tip hangs outward just a tad before it curves and goes down the hole. That line tightens when a fish bites. Even when the line hangs tight to the rod, there's line movement. As I said before, a fish can't take a bait without moving it."

"My depthfinder is the best strike indicator I have," Dave added. "Some bites are almost impossible to detect. If you know a fish is there, if you can see it on your locator, you're ready, looking for an excuse to set the hook.

"With the locator, ice fishing is a new game. The action doesn't start when you get the bite, but when a fish appears on the screen.

"I've worked a fish for half an hour in what seemed like a minute. Sometimes, you know the fish is right at your hook because the sonar lines are touching. To test for bites, lower your rod tip. If the line doesn't sink, the fish has the bait and it's time to set the hook.

"I don't depend on seeing every fish on the locator; I fish from top to bottom even on a clean screen because fish can be just outside the locator cone. But seeing fish on the screen helps me anticipate bites. I'm concentrating and ready to see or feel the slightest take."

Use the level of strike indication that fits your fishing style. Use "help," but a one-on-one experience—you and the fish and a graphite rod—is there for you when you choose to tackle it.

CHAPTER 5

TIP-UPS AND FLOATS

"Tip-ups? Floats? They mean wild and crazy but consistent action on ice. They're fishing's well-planned attack, especially in conjunction with jigging. The combo approach is one of the best ways to consistently ice fish."
                                                                    Al Lindner

Doug relates a story about a trip to Manitoba in search of monster pike: "For almost three months a year, Ted Jowett of Winnipeg runs a trapline. On this trip in 1984, Ted felt right at home as we set out tip-ups over a quarter-mile section of ice; tip-ups, after all, are temptingly set traps. During winter, when predators like pike, walleyes, burbot, lake trout, salmon, bass, and even big panfish range widely and only feed actively for short periods, a tip-up set in the right spot with the right bait is often the best possible presentation.

"Unlike anglers, tip-ups have infinite patience. Set right and with a minimum of maintenance, they keep working day and night. Granted, jigging often is the most efficient way to catch fish through the ice. It's a matter of percentages, a matter of covering more water searching for fish rather than sitting all day soaking a bait, waiting for fish to come to you. An approach combining jigging with stationary sets, however, often is the best possible compromise.

The brilliantly marked 26-pounder. Note the 10-inch ice hole—room enough for the biggest pike—the big deadbait, quick-strike rig, wire leader, dacron line, forceps (for hook removal), and the Polar Tip-Up.

"In this case, though, we began only with tip-ups, a singular approach we rarely use. The Manitoba limit of two lines per angler allowed our party to set out 12 lines over and around a deep, sunken hump with a saddle area connecting a small shoreline bar. We stood around a cozy fire in the middle of our trapline. In four directions lay traps baited with various sized dead and live baits. Flags were ready to spring as we scanned the maze of tip-ups, waiting for popping flags.

"We'd been out early, drilling at least 50 holes in appropriate spots around the hump—checking depth, checking bottom contour. Now we had 'em covered. One tip-up graced a drop-off along a small shoreline bar, while 2 others were set over the 10- to 25-foot-deep saddle area between the shore and the hump. Several other traps were set over the 12-foot-deep flat topping the hump. The rest were scattered over various depths along the drop-off around the hump. The shallowest tip-ups set at the drop-off held baits suspended near the bottom in 15 feet of water; the deepest baits hung near bottom at almost 40 feet.

"The first pike of the day was a brilliantly marked, well proportioned 26-pounder. About 15 minutes later, a 15-pounder joined our crowd. We returned both fish after taking photos.

"By noon, the pattern was obvious. Pike were moving through the saddle and along the 15- to 25-foot drop-off on the saddle side of the hump. We concentrated our tip-ups in those areas and at those depths. Our two days of fishing were everything an angler could hope for: six pike from 18 to 26 pounds, plus numerous smaller fish. Magnificent!"

Tip-up action can be wild and crazy fun because it can be so effective.

Types of Tip-Ups

Tip-ups must do three things: (1) help present a bait to a waiting predator; (2) trigger the predator; and (3) alert you to the predator's presence.

"Tip-ups aren't new," Al said. "Perhaps for hundreds of years, anglers cut willow sticks and propped them in a snow bank so the limber tip extended over an ice hole. They attached their line to the end of the stick and attached a piece of colored cloth to the line at the point it attached to the stick. The stick waved in the wind, keeping the bait moving, which attracted and triggered fish. The cloth slipped off the stick when a fish took the bait."

Dozens of other homemade tip-ups have been used. Some as simple as laying a bobber and line on the ice alongside the hole. When a fish hits, the bobber slides off the ice and into the hole. Actually, a bobber in a hole is a type of tip-up.

Tip-ups with spools generally fall into two basic categories: (1) Those with a spool that rests below the water surface, and (2) those with a spool that rests above the surface. Many varieties of each type are available, as mentioned in Chapter 2, but we're most familiar with two specific tip-ups.

The Polar Tip-Up

"The Polar Tip-up (H.T. Enterprises) is the most reliable tip-up we've ever used," Doug offered, with Al nodding in agreement. "The spool functions under absolutely the worst freeze-up conditions, always revolving smoothly because the shaft is pressure-packed and sealed with lubricant. The Polar's high-impact plastic is virtually indestructible, and yet it's light and portable.

"Two spool sizes are available. The extra line capacity of the 500-foot spool gives you the option to go light on terminal tackle. Although pike, walleyes, bass or panfish aren't likely to run out much line, a big lake trout, king salmon or steelhead may. Fish confidently with a big spool.

"A stainless-steel trip mechanism on top of the revolving shaft lets you set release tension on the spool from light to heavy, depending on the bait you fish," Doug continued. "A notched end on the trip mechanism provides a heavy setting for baits that swim actively or for big dead baits. We use the heavy setting most often for lake trout and pike, but it applies to other species in specific instances."

"The other end of the trip mecha-

Laker and a Polar. Note the three 8-inch holes drilled side by side and chiseled ice free with a spud bar.

Polar Tip-Up

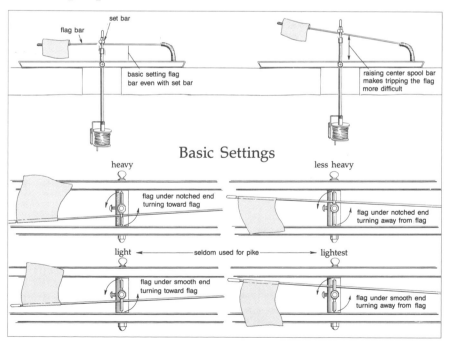

Minnow Size?

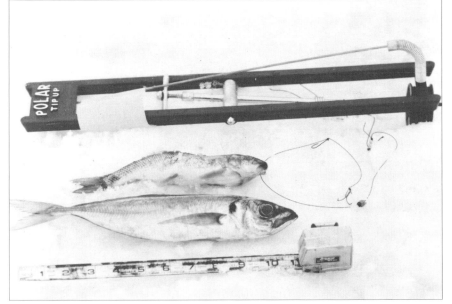

Bait size depends on the size and species of fish you're after. We used the dead-baits pictured here (top bait's a sucker and bottom bait's a mackerel) on a pike fishing trip to Manitoba. We don't prefer mackerel; but it's oily, and smelt weren't available. They worked. The baits ranged from about 8 to 11 inches in length, certainly not too large for pike from 10 to over 20 pounds.

For lake trout, we usually use baits from 5 to 8 inches; and for walleyes, baits from 4 to 5 inches. Crappies and perch usually need minnows ranging from very small to about 3 ½ inches. Larger minnows usually work better after dark, or in deep water.

Whether it's chinook salmon, lake trout, pike, splake, or burbot, you can usually use bigger minnow baits than you'd suspect, especially coupled with quick-strike rigs.

nism is smooth to allow a light setting for light baits on light line," Al offered. "We use this setting most often for crappies, walleyes, and smaller trout.

"Slightly more spool tension is required for fish like lake trout that may make quick runs. If spool tension is too light, backlash could result. Crappies, on the other hand, need the lightest setting or they reject the bait."

Stationary tip-ups like the Polar sometimes offer a distinct advantage over wind tip-ups. Typically, a live bait hung below a stationary tip-up moves only when a predator swims nearby. That movement presents a natural triggering effect.

Live baits also live longer hanging below a stationary tip-up. A wind

Windlass Tip-Up Tips

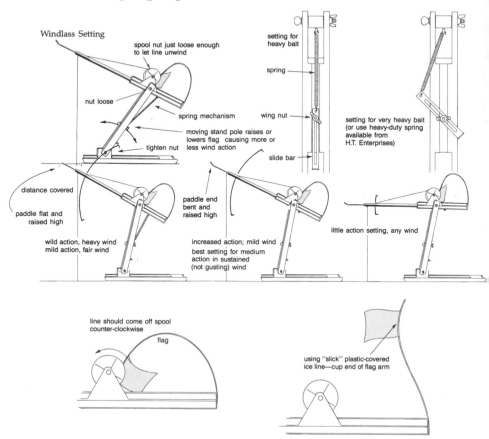

Windlass Setting

spool nut just loose enough
to let line unwind

nut loose

spring mechanism

moving stand pole raises or
lowers flag causing more or
tighten nut less wind action

distance covered

paddle flat and
raised high

wild action, heavy wind
mild action, fair wind

setting for
heavy bait

spring

wing nut

slide bar

setting for very heavy bait
(or use heavy-duty spring
available from
H.T. Enterprises)

paddle end
bent and
raised high

increased action; mild wind
best setting for medium
action in sustained
(not gusting) wind

little action setting, any wind

line should come off spool
counter-clockwise

flag

using "slick" plastic-covered
ice line—cup end of flag arm

tip-up keeps a bait struggling continually. You usually need to change live baits more often with wind tip-ups than with stationary tip-ups.

The Windlass Tip-Up

The H.T. Windlass Tip-up uses wind to keep baits moving. A 200- or 500-foot spool of line is connected to a hinged arm with a tin fan on the end. Line goes from the spool through a hole in the fan and into the water. The spool rests above the water. Wind moves the fan, imparting movement to bait suspended below.

"Although wind tip-ups require more attention because the main parts of the tip-up are above the ice, they can be deadly," Doug said. "They keep a live bait struggling to draw the attention of nearby predators, but they also add movement to dead bait. Although no movement can be a trigger at times, often some movement is important.

"Remember, though, that baits can move too much. No problem. You can get almost any amount of movement by varying tip-up settings.

The Windlass and a walleye.

Basically, the higher or more perpendicular a fan arm rests—as determined by a spring setting—the more fan is exposed to the wind, and the more movement is imparted to the bait. A fan arm resting parallel to the ice catches little wind and imparts little movement.

"With a moderate wind, we usually raise the fan to present dead baits and lower the fan almost parallel to the ice to present live baits. The arm settings depend on what you want your bait to do, based on the mood of the fish."

"Back to the drawbacks of wind tip-ups given that the spool rests above the water," Al interjected. "Line may freeze to the spool or ice up

SWish-Rod

The SWish-Rod is an ice-fishing rod that can function as a tip-up for walleyes, pike, lake trout and other large gamefish, but can function as a panfish rod, too. The SWish-Rod is a stationary tip-up.

A two-legged stand props the rod and holds the rod tip above the hole. The line spool's (two sizes) reliable drag allows you to set tension for releasing line. A tip-up flag clips to the rod, hooks under the spool, and releases when a fish takes the bait. The spool revolves smoothly as the fish takes out line.

in the hole in the fan. But it's worth coping with these problems.

"When line freezes, wind it back onto the spool. As you wind, pinch off ice with your thumb and forefinger. A little Vaseline keeps the fan hole free of ice. For ice in the ice hole you might mount a small PVC tube inside a block of wood or styrofoam. Run your line through it, and then put a few drops of vegetable oil in the tube once it's in the water. This usually keeps line from freezing. Or try a hole cover like the Iceguard from Talon.

"Another option that works in the most adverse conditions is a hot can. Fill a coffee can with burning charcoal briquettes. Drill a shallow hole next to your fishing hole and chisel a passage between the two. Place the can in the shallow hole. Warm water surrounding the hot can filters into the fishing hole, keeping it open and the wind tip-up functioning.

"Be sure to pack the base of your wind tip-up with ice chunks, snow, and slush to prevent it from toppling over when a fish strikes. One of the biggest pike I ever caught jerked the tip-up free and almost pulled it down the hole."

Rigging

Rigging tip-ups depends on the type of tip-up and the fish species you're after. Dacron, specially coated dacron, or special tip-up line is an advantage for handling line. Black or white dacron in about 36-pound test is easy to see and handle compared to monofilament that is hard to see and often becomes stiff and kinky when it gets cold. Tip-up anglers who traditionally have preferred fly-line to dacron will appreciate the smaller diameter and less expensive price of plastic-coated tip-up lines marketed by Tackle Marketing Inc., H.T. Enterprises, Gudebrod, and Berkley.

Rig Polar and Windlass tip-ups with dacron or plastic line. Gudebrod's teflon-coated ice dacron is a good choice, based on ease of handling, not because heavy line is needed to land fish. To avoid spooking fish, tie a swivel on the end of your dacron and add a leader. Again, the type of leader depends on the fish species.

Fifty yards of 36-pound dacron will fill a 200-foot spool, which should be adequate for most fishing situations. You won't have trouble landing even a 20-pound pike on 200 feet of line. If you fish waters where there's a chance to hook a huge lake trout, king salmon, brown trout or steelhead, you may want to use 500-foot spools.

Quick-Strike Rigging

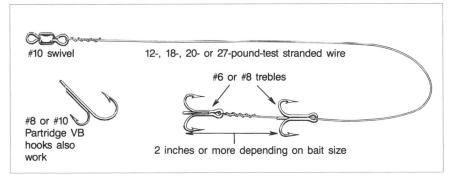

#10 swivel   12-, 18-, 20- or 27-pound-test stranded wire

#6 or #8 trebles

#8 or #10
Partridge VB
hooks also
work

2 inches or more depending on bait size

A basic quick-strike rig consists of two hooks rigged in tandem several inches or more apart depending on the size of the bait. For pike, often the hooks are small #6 or #8 trebles, or #6, #8, or #10 Partridge VB hooks from Cabela's or Bait Rigs. For pike, the hooks are rigged on 12-, 18-, or 27-pound-test stranded wire from Sevenstrand (or order from Cabela's).

Using small hooks for big fish is new to many American fishermen. It will take but one fishing session to convince you how well they work.

Smaller hooks instantly break free from live or dead baits, and the smaller barbs and sharper hooks sink in easily. You'll rarely lose a fish because you haven't set hooks properly. Indeed, in most cases, a hook set is little more than a lift.

Quick-strike rigging is applicable to fishing for almost every fish species.

A first-hand look!

Terminal Tackle

Terminal rigging depends on the fish species you're after. For crappies, smaller trout, largemouth and smallmouth bass, perch, big bluegills and many other species, try 4- to 6-pound-test monofilament leader and a #6 hook with a small minnow. Dave Genz tackles down to 1-pound-test line and smaller baits to score on crappies when they're tough to catch. Add lead shot a foot up your line for weight and hook the minnow near the dorsal fin or through the lips.

Another option is to add a 1/16-, 1/8-, or 1/4-ounce plain (no hair or feathers) leadhead jig (it may have a fluorescent head) to the end of your monofilament. Hook a minnow through the lips or near the dorsal fin. The leadhead jig serves as an attractor as well as an anchor. Teardrops also work well to anchor minnows. You may need to add extra shot with this option.

For walleyes, use 8- or 10-pound-test line. Terminal rigs include the same single hook, leadhead jig, or teardrop as for crappies. For larger predators, however, small treble hooks often significantly increase hooking percentages.

Although to many anglers, big hooks equate with big fish, nothing could be farther from the truth in most situations. Use #12, #10, or #8 trebles for walleyes, bass, and most trout; and #10, #8 or #6 for lake trout and pike. Embed only one of the small barbs in the bait. When a fish takes the bait, tighten the line and hand-over-hand the fish—no hookset.

Small trebles find flesh. On toothy predators like pike and walleyes,

Making Quick-Strike Leaders with Wire

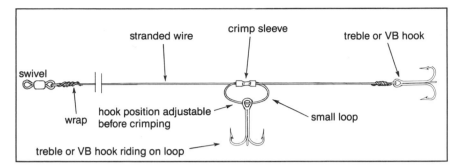

(Note: The final wire wrap will be much tighter than illustrated here.)

they slip between teeth to catch hold. On soft-mouthed predators like trout, they're a sure thing unless you set the hook too hard or put too much pressure on fish while playing them. With a treble, your hooking percentage will improve and so will your landing percentage.

"You can do even better than a small treble, though," Doug noted. "Use two trebles rigged in quick-strike fashion to even further increase hooking percentage. A quick-strike rig let's you set immediately after a fish takes a bait.

"Quick-strike rigging is a modification of an old idea first popularized in Europe. *In-Fisherman* magazine began coverage of Euro-tactics in the early '80s. Hooks rigged in tandem from 2 to 4 inches apart with hooks exposed, not totally buried in the bait's flesh, are an important ingredient in the success enjoyed by European pike, catfish, and zander fishermen.

Adjustable Alternative

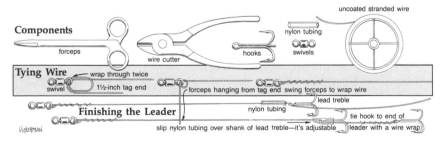

The most recent advancement in adjustable quick-strike rigging requires only the addition of a crimp sleeve. Slide the wire through the crimp sleeve, add a treble hook, make a small loop and run the wire through the sleeve a second time, and then finish the rig with a second hook. The loop makes the position of the looped hook adjustable.

"We gave the rigging its name after our first experiments with it. We hooked 44 straight fish—pike, catfish, walleyes—on 44 takes. No waiting and wondering when to set. The two hooks pretty well cover the important points on a bait; so when a fish takes, the hooks are in position to be set into the predator's mouth.

"Although trebles are easier to find and work well, some of our most successful fishing has been with the Partridge VB hook that sports a small hook attached to the back of a slightly larger hook. Insert the small hook into the bait while the large hook rides exposed. These hooks are available in North America from Cabela's and the Bait Rigs Company."

But let's assume that for the moment we're using treble hooks. For walleyes, tie a #8 or #10 treble to the end of your line, leaving about a 4-inch tag-end beyond the knot. Tie another treble onto the tag-end. The final length of the tag-end depends on the size of your minnow. Place one hook on the first treble into the bait a bit in back of the dorsal fin. Place one hook of the trailing treble in back of the bait's head.

The amount of hook in the bait is small, and it breaks free quickly to set into the predator. Besides, 4 of the 6 hooks are always exposed toward fish flesh. But don't set too hard. Odds are your hooks will sink in because your rig covers a major portion of the bait.

"For pike, use stranded wire," Doug instructed. "Pike cut even the heaviest monofilament and wire doesn't reduce strikes. Indeed, the right wire is much less visible than monofilament. It's so wonderful I often use 8-pound-test wire for walleyes, too."

Standard wire is available from Sevenstrand in break strengths of 8-, 12-, 18- and 27-pound test. Berkley also markets a 27-pound stranded wire. Sevenstrand wire is available from Cabela's.

Commercially tied quick-strike rigs are available from Bait Rigs and H.T. Enterprises. The rigs from Bait Rigs sport Partridge VB hooks. Greg Bohn's Stinger Tackle also sells two-hook wire pike rigs. For these rigs to be legal in states like Minnesota, add a small spinner to the rig ahead of the hooks to make it a lure.

Where And When To Use Tip-Ups

"Tip-ups apply to most situations for predators," Al said. "Sure there are situations where you might only want to use tip-ups. In recent years, though, Doug and I almost always use a combination approach, providing it's legal to use at least 2 lines. If we're after pike, we'll usually set out a tip-up apiece and then also move, jigging from hole to hole. Same for walleyes, trout, bass, and other predators.

"Say we're after big crappies, for a change of pace. We've just explored the outside of a major rock point that drops off into 40 feet of water. Crappies often frequent the water off the point, but they aren't there now. We might set a tip-up with a minnow off the point while we jig over the weed flat on the point. If crappies move along the outside of the point,

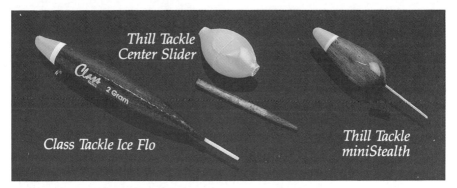

Thill Tackle Center Slider

Class Tackle Ice Flo

Thill Tackle miniStealth

the tip-up will let us know. Then we'd probably move out there to jig for them."

In this scenario, jigging is the primary approach, and the tip-up is used to alert you when fish move into another area. This approach works on many fish species in many situations.

Try jigging while you present a live or dead bait in the same area. Offer fish two distinctly different presentations, and the fish will tell you which they prefer.

Check state regulations for the distance you can be from a tip-up. Sometimes you can fish two bars at once by setting out tip-ups as far apart as 1/2 mile. Check the tip-ups with binoculars, and race over to a flag that pops. Tip-ups can provide mobility while you sit snug in a shack. Set them away from the shack to increase the area you cover.

How and where you use tip-ups is limited only by state regulations and your imagination. Experiment. You'll have more fun and catch more fish.

Floats For Ice Fishing

Floats today are streamlined—pen-shaped and straw-shaped. For bigger fish like pike and walleyes, cigar-shape floats work well, especially with bigger minnows. To be sensitive, a float must be almost neutrally

Rigging

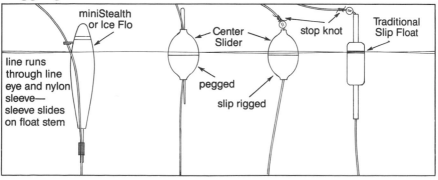

miniStealth or Ice Flo

Center Slider

stop knot

Traditional Slip Float

line runs through line eye and nylon sleeve— sleeve slides on float stem

pegged

slip rigged

buoyant and thin, so a fish can pull it under without sensing resistance.

The newest floats for icing panfish are scaled-down streamlined floats like the "Ice Flo's" from Class Tackle and "miniStealth" and "Center Slider" from Thill Tackle. These floats are made of balsa.

Slide your line through the small wire eye at the top, then through a silicone sleeve at the bottom. Push the sleeve onto the bottom stem of the float and you're ready. Adjust depth by sliding the float up or down the line.

Weighted properly with precision shot like Class Tackle's "English Soft Shot" or a similar product available from Thill Tackle, the float sits with just a "pimple" of the top showing above the surface. At the slight-

GETTING THE MOST FROM FLOATS ON ICE

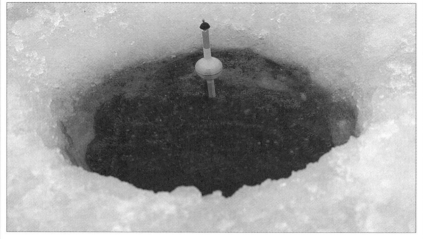

• A lead (clip-on) depthfinder lets you find the precise bottom. Start fishing three inches off bottom, and work your way up to the surface in 6- to 9-inch increments until you catch fish.

• Tackle down. Use the lightest line you can get away with for more bites and more fish.

• Learn to read a developing bite. Sometimes, hit the first tremor; other times, let the fish run.

• Don't rely on floats any more than you do on any other ice-fishing system. They're just one tool you need to master to be consistently successful.

Floats can lead to tremendous catches, even without sonar. In the Finnish National Championships, for example, where sonar is prohibited, the record catch was an astounding 72 pounds 6 ounces of perch in just four hours.

WHEN FLOATS ARE AT THEIR BEST

A "Carlyle" style float and one of those freshwater piranhas.

- For beginners.
- When fish are in a neutral or negative feeding mood, jigging or even the slightest hand vibrations can spook fish. If you're fishing outside with no shelter, even if you lay your rod on the ice, wind will affect spring bobbers or even line; a float lying just at or below the water surface is more stable and protected from wind.
- In shallow bays and river backwaters, fish often hold just below the ice and you catch fish in as little as 9 to 12 inches of water. Occasionally, even in deeper water, you may find fish suspended high in the water column, which may call for similar tactics.
- When fish are holding at one level and you need to quickly and easily return to that level. Sonar makes it easy to do this and to spot fish that move through at different levels. But floats are your biggest ally when you don't have sonar. When you pinpoint a certain depth that holds a concentration of fish, you can fish it quickly with a float.
- A slow-sinking float overbalanced with just enough lead shot so it won't stay on the surface will show you the depth fish are feeding. Slow-sinking floats, or "suspender floating" as Doug calls it, can also be deadly any time fish are triggered by a slow falling bait.

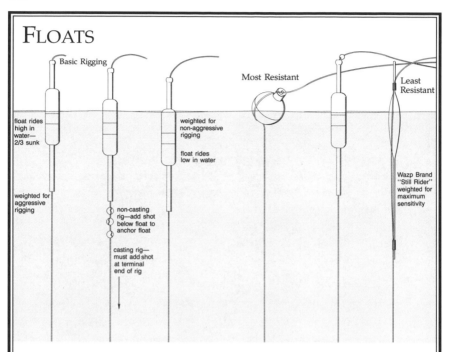

Floats

Floats should be weighted to match your terminal rig. Match an aggressive, relatively large minnow with a float that rests high in the water. An aggressive fish won't mind the resistance offered by a high-riding float, and the minnow won't pull your float under so often. If this happens, switch to a larger float.

Match a rig for nonaggressive fish with a low-riding float, because resistance spooks picky fish. Adding shot immediately below a float is easier than dragging your terminal rig to the surface to make adjustments, and it won't mess up the sensitive terminal system you're trying to match to the activity level of the fish.

Long, thin floats offer less resistance. Round floats designed to rest on top of the water have limited practical use in livebait fishing. Modified designs may perform well with large, actively swimming baitfish. But in most situations, the thin design is best.

est bite, the float moves and it doesn't take much to haul it under. This in turn means it's easier for a fish to inhale a bait.

Although not quite as sensitive, Class Tackle's "Still Rider" performs adequately in some light ice-fishing situations. Many anglers cut off most of the bottom stem, leaving only enough to thread on the silicone sleeve.

"Floats," Doug added, "are a great light-bite indicator in the hands of an experienced fisherman. Europeans made float fishing an art form. Fishing in North America will get better and better as anglers become more familiar with European-style systems for both ice and open water."

"Floats do an acceptable job of transmitting subtle strikes, but they aren't the perfect answer to winter fishing," cautioned Dave. "Their primary purpose is for easily letting line down to the same depth after you catch a fish or put on new bait.

"But floats have to balance perfectly to the weight of the hook and bait. And floats make it harder to change depths quickly—such as when you see suspended fish come through on a depthfinder. I constantly raise, raise, raise my line as I jig, and then slowly jig it back down. Once you start using a locator on the ice, it's easy to put a bait at the same depth time after time without a float.

"Floats are nice, especially for a second rod; but for your primary rod, there are better ways."

One guy who thinks floats are "better than nice" is Mick Thill, the only American to top Europe's best in the World Freshwater Championships, winning gold and silver medals in 1982. Thill is one of the world's masters at fishing with sophisticated float systems.

According to Thill, who now lives in Illinois, finding active, aggressive fish with electronics has been a major breakthrough in ice fishing. He encourages serious ice anglers to use electronics. But he also insists on becoming effective on the ice without their help. Floats are the best tool for teaching a beginner who doesn't have access to sonar.

Floats show all the different types of bites, and trial-and-error teaches when and how to strike. More on this in a moment.

As we mentioned, both Class Tackle and Thill Tackle offer specialized ice-fishing floats that cover the range from less than 1 foot deep down to more than 60 feet, for everything from small panfish to large lake trout.

Thill Tackle's miniStealth series (4 sizes), and Class Tackle's Ice Floes are primarily for water less than 15 feet deep. The smallest miniStealth (#1), for example, is just 1¾ inches long and needs one shot (equivalent to about a 1/64-ounce jighead) to balance it correctly. Each succeeding larger size needs twice the lead to properly balance. So a #2 takes two BB, a #3 takes four, and the largest, a #4, properly balances with eight BB.

If a slip-float is necessary (or if you just prefer them), try the Thill Center Slider. Designed to resist freezing to the line, it comes in 8 sizes. Intended mainly for water deeper than 15 feet, the float lets you play big fish with a reel.

Float fishing basics for ice fishing and fishing open water are the same, according to Dave. "If you're going to use a float, use the smallest float possible, to reduce the resistance fish feel when swimming off with your bait, or even just trying to suck it in. Add lead shot, or trim your jighead until the float will just hold the surface without sinking. With baits like lively minnows, the float must be buoyant enough to resist the bait's strongest surges.

"The perfect setup is as neutrally buoyant as possible. In fact, except

Suspender Floating—Minnow Line Settings

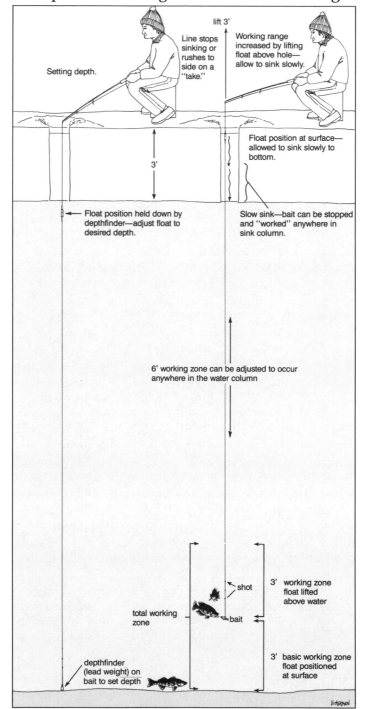

Shot Setting

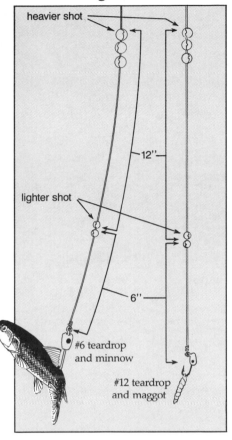

heavier shot

12"

lighter shot

6"

#6 teardrop
and minnow

#12 teardrop
and maggot

when you're using minnows, no part of the float should be resting above the surface. Even the tip should rest slightly under the surface, so a fish can easily inhale the bait, even from a distance."

Suspender Floating

Suspender floating often is a productive presentation during mid- and late winter. First-ice is long past. Fishing's more difficult. Better times are coming, but . . .

Suspender floating often turns a tough outing into success; that is, a few panfish when you would have caught none, and a few more when you would have caught some. Rarely, though, does it mean lots more fish when you're already catching lots of fish. When the fish are cracking, you should be cracking them with a different technique.

Suspender floating requires a float coupled with a bait and line weighted with lead shot so the rig is barely heavier than neutrally buoyant. Drop the bait and shot down the hole. As the bait settles, place the float daintily on the surface. Water tension on the surface of the float will keep it from sinking. When you move the float, however, water on the float will cause it to slowly sink. Shotted properly, it may take a minute for your float to sink from the surface to the bottom of your hole.

That's the idea. Your bait's sinking slowly, almost suspended in the water column. Any rod tip movement adds enticement to the bait.

Say you're using an ultralight graphite rod, 1- or 2-pound-test line, a #12 teardrop packed with two maggots, and a small float. Coupled with a matching reel, you have a deadly system for any panfish species.

Barely tip (a tip is less than a twitch) your rod tip and the bait will explode momentarily upward before slowing suddenly, stopping, and then gradually sinking again—Pooph!—like a good pitcher's change-up. You expect a fastball, see the fastball motion, but suddenly find a piece of styrofoam floating toward you at half speed. Even when fish have been pressured for several months, some of them will usually respond.

Components

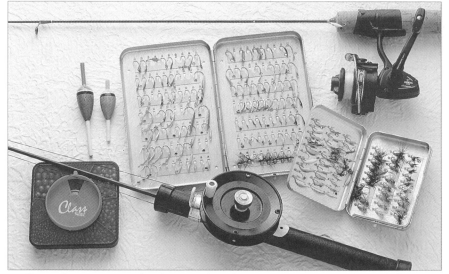

Basic Components for Suspender Floating—*Wazp Brand or Thill Tackle "Carlyle" floats, "Class" shot, and baits of your choice. These baits are from Upper Midwest Marketing (Jig-A-Whopper) and Comet Tackle. The tackle boxes are also from Comet Tackle.*

Minnow Hand Line—*27-pound-test Gudebrod dacron on an H.T. Enterprises graphite rod.*

Reel Up-and-Down Line—*1-, 2-, or 4-pound-test clear or grey (Berkley XL or Wazp "Class" line) line; Shakespeare 025 reel; and H.T. Enterprise CJL-26 rod.*

Another deadly move for picky panfish is to barely circle your rod tip a time or two and stop. Let the bait sink an inch and repeat the circles. Or twitch, twitch, twitch your tip. It's the closest you can come to imitating a jumbo grass shrimp or some other crustacean that panfish love to eat.

Neutral BuoyancyTips

The key to this system is to achieve near neutral buoyancy. Shot determines success when it's time to tune a rig toward neutral buoyancy.

Class Tackle offers the variety of shot necessary to tip the scales subtly toward and over neutral buoyancy. Particularly important are their "micro shot." While you're at it, grab a fistful of their "Carlyle" slip floats.

If you're inside a shack and can use a slip-float rig coupled with a rod-and-reel system, begin weight tuning by adding shot 18 inches above your lure. Add enough shot to almost achieve neutral buoyancy. Then fine tune by adding micro shot 6 inches above your lure.

Place the lightest shot nearest the bait to prevent tangling when you jig,

Dacron Hand Line On Ice

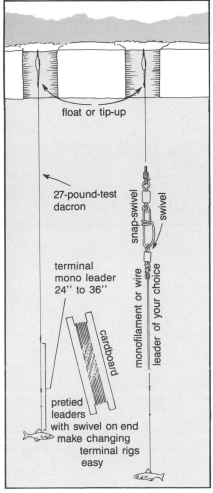

float or tip-up

27-pound-test dacron

snap-swivel

swivel

terminal mono leader 24" to 36"

monofilament or wire

leader of your choice

cardboard

pretied leaders with swivel on end make changing terminal rigs easy

and also so fish feel little weight when they take the bait.

Minnow Lining

An overlooked option for crappies and perch is a plain (no dressing) leadhead jig like the 1/64-ounce Heron "Mini Jiggler." For this presentation your jig should weigh 1/16 ounce or less. Pack the jig with maggots. We don't know what it looks like to fish, but it works from Ohio to the Dakotas to Canada.

At times, however, crappies and perch prefer a minnow presentation. Use black dacron line or plastic-coated ice line. These lines are essential to doing this quickly and efficiently.

Hand-over-handing monofilament is difficult, yet many fishermen think dacron spooks fish. Perhaps it does if you tie directly to your bait. Instead, tie a stop knot and slide it up a tad. Add a small bead and slip a "Carlyle" float on the dacron. Then tie about a 3-foot section of 2- or 4-pound-test clear or grey monofilament on the swivel at the end of the dacron as a leader.

I usually prefer to "anchor" the minnow with a wide-gapped teardrop like the Jig-A-Whopper #6 "Flasher" or #6 "Flutter Bug." A teardrop adds attracting color to the minnow, but more importantly, makes it difficult for the minnow to swim, therefore easier for fish to catch.

Barbs aren't necessary to land fish. File most of the barbs from your hooks to make minnow hooking and hook setting easier. Leave only enough barb to hold the minnow on the hook.

With the minnow facing away from you, barely nick the hook under the dorsal fin with the hook pointing away from you—toward the minnow's head. This lets the minnow swim seductively and also increases your hooking percentage. Bending hooks out about 10 percent or so makes it easier to hook the minnow and probably helps hook more crappies and perch, too.

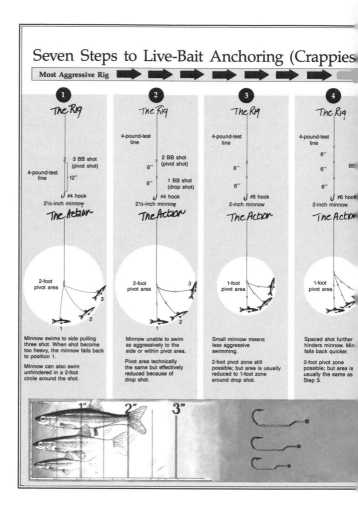

Seven Steps to Live-Bait Anchoring (Crappies

Step 1—*(most aggressive rig) 2-inch minnow hooked on a #4 hook tied on 4-pound line with 3 BB shot placed together a foot up the line.*

Step 2—*(slightly less aggressive rig) The same rig but with one of three shot (called a drop shot) slipped 6 inches toward the bait; thus, one shot 6 inches above the minnow and two shot placed together (the pivot shot) 12 inches above the bait.*

The minnow still has a 2-foot pivot area, but the drop shot reduces and slows swimming within the zone. This is the aggressive rig we use most often.

Step 3—*The same rig with a 2-inch minnow hooked on a #6 hook with the same shot placement as Step 2.*

Step 4—*The same rig with the top shot moved up 6 inches; thus, shot spread at 6-inch intervals starting 6 inches above the bait.*

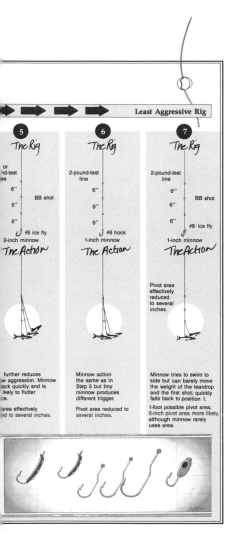

Perch usually prefer the bait within 3 feet of bottom. Crappies may be anywhere from top to bottom. Say crappies are coming through 5 to 10 feet off bottom in 30 feet of water. One approach would be to set your float so the bait is suspended 8 feet above the bottom. This lets you fish the float from the surface down 3 feet—your bait from 8 feet above bottom to 5 feet above bottom.

Cover more water by including a lift 2 to 3 feet above the water. After lifting (an attracting maneuver), drop the float slowly as you follow it down to the surface of the water with your rod tip. When a crappie takes, the line hesitates as it sinks. The addition of the lift means you can cover 5 to 6 feet of water instead of about 3.

Anchored Bait For Big Fish!

How much freedom should you give livebait to roam and wiggle? Doug Stange has developed a series of anchoring sets that allow you to adjust bait activity to the feeding mood of the fish you're after.

Walleyes, catfish, crappies, pike, trout, perch, bass, muskies. Name it. If it'll bite livebait suspended

Step 5—*The same rig, but further hinder the minnow by replacing the plain hook with a #6 Flutter Bug ice fly. Bend the shank of the Flutter Bug slightly out before hooking the minnow. At this point, consider dropping to 2-pound line.*

Step 6—*A 1-inch minnow hooked on a #8 hook with shot spread at 6-inch intervals starting 6 inches above the bait. Use 2-pound line.*

Step 7—*(least aggressive rig) Further hinder the tiny minnow by replacing the plain hook with a #8 ice fly; thus, a 1-inch minnow hooked on a #8 or #10 ice fly with shot spaced at 6-inch intervals starting 6 inches above the bait.*

If this 7-step system seems a bit too complicated, eliminating steps 2, 5, and 7 may not hurt a thing.

below a tip-up or float, you'll catch more of them with this simple, sensible baitfish anchoring system.

"One key to fishing livebait is anchoring it to match the feed mood of the fish you're after," Doug instructed. "This applies to casting or trolling livebait, as well as to ice fishing."

Larger, more lively baitfish usually work better for active, aggressive

Hooking

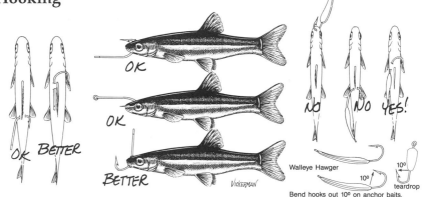

Walleye Hawger

Bend hooks out 10° on anchor baits.

Basic Rigs for Walleyes and Pike

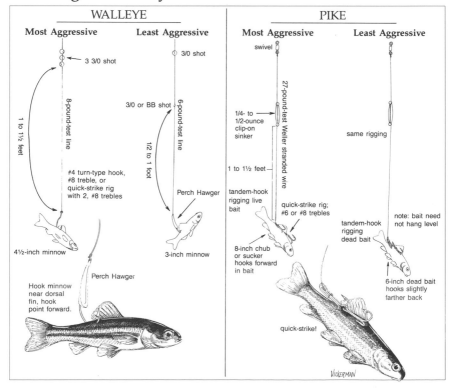

predators. Smaller, less active baitfish usually work better for less aggressive, inactive fish. Between those points lie the great abyss—fish in a hundred different feeding moods or activity states. Fishermen usually term this huge group of fish 'neutral.' And most fish are in a neutral mood most of the time.

Crappies are a fine fish to use as an example to explain the anchoring concept. Equipment components include Class Tackle lead shot; #4, #6, and #8 teardrops; 2- or 4-pound-test monofilament line; and stick-style European floats and float (bobber) stops from Class Tackle or Thill Tackle.

"Class Tackle shot are the softest shot available," Doug continued, "and they pinch on easily. I prefer Aberdeen-style hooks for crappies, and I'm convinced that off-set turn-style hooks increase hooking percentages. The tears are for anchoring baits. Supple lines ensure that what a crappie sucks at, he sucks in. Don't use fluorescent line in this situation. European-style floats are more sensitive. Finally, the Class Tackle float stop is one of the slickest fishing aids to arrive in years."

Rig Parameters

A series of terminal rigs for crappies? On the most aggressive end of the scale is a 2-inch minnow on a #4 hook tied on 4-pound line with 3 BB shot placed together a foot up the line.

On the least aggressive end of the scale is a 1-inch minnow hooked on a #8 teardrop tied on 2-pound line with individual BB shot spaced 6 inches, one foot, and 12 feet above the bait.

Successful presentations must include an attraction phase and a triggering phase. A fish first must be attracted to live bait by movement and then be triggered by the same movement when it gets closer. Match the attracting and triggering qualities of your presentation to the mood of the crappies. Do this with live bait by switching the size of your bait, hook, and line, and by spacing shot appropriately on your line.

Aggressive, schooled, and competitively feeding crappies usually try to eat what they see. Lots of attraction is important. The three shot hinder the minnow only from moving beyond a two-foot zone. The shot act as a pivot point; but within the pivot area, the minnow can swim unhindered. Occasionally lifting the minnow and letting it fall keeps it swimming and attracting crappies.

Less aggressive crappies, on the other hand, may or may not be schooled, but are not feeding competitively. They may react to a properly presented bait, though. A big, wildly swimming minnow will attract them, but it may also intimidate them when they get within triggering range. It's too much of a good thing. A rig for less aggressive fish should be less of almost everything—line test, hook size, minnow size.

The best way to totally anchor a minnow is to anchor it with an ice fly—weight right on the minnow. Secondarily, anchor it and the ice fly with shot. The shot are spaced above the bait to progressively hinder the already hindered small minnow from swimming anywhere quickly. Reduce the bait's pivot area; tighten the reins, you might say. Most small minnows flutter almost in place. Coupled with an occasional lift-fall to catch a crappie's attention, a stationary, fluttering minnnow provides triggering power for less-active fish.

To fill the gap between rigs for the most aggressive and least aggressive fish, progressively decrease hook and minnow size, increase shot spread, and at times, use an teardrop to anchor your minnow. Most fishermen probably use tears as attractors, but it's anchoring that counts.

The system can be easily modified for fishing live bait for other species. Go with bigger shot and bigger minnows or chubs for walleyes or lake trout. Add stranded wire to your terminal rigging for pike. In place of a tear, try anchoring bigger baits with a jigging spoon like a Jig-A-Whopper Perch or Walleye Hawger.

It's the progressive anchoring idea that's important. Aggressive fish require bigger baits that swim more actively, while less-aggressive fish require smaller baits that swim less actively. To get the right presentation as you go from aggressive to less aggressive fish, progressively decrease bait size, increase shot spread (weight), and use a terminal lure to further anchor a bait. Proper anchoring guarantees improvement in your catch when you fish with live baitfish.

Active jigging presentations are often the best choice. But in the situations we've outlined, tip-ups and floats will often put more fish on the ice. That's one reason you're there.

CHAPTER 6

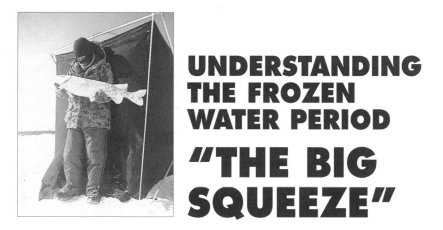

UNDERSTANDING THE FROZEN WATER PERIOD "THE BIG SQUEEZE"

"Never met a body of water I couldn't figure out given a little time. Understanding how a body of water changes throughout the winter season is a missing element for most fishermen."
Doug Stange

A hard frost announces the passage of summer into fall. The sun's rays weaken. Days shorten. Leaves blush, fade, and fall. The first snow of the season serves a final warning. Winter's icy grip hardens, staking claim on the earth.

A frozen lake, river, reservoir, pit, or pond remains a "living" body of water. The solid surface appears a mirror image of a glass-calm summer day. Waves frozen in time. Water stopped . . . cold.

"The In-Fisherman calendar divides the year into 10 Calendar Periods based on seasonal environmental conditions and fish response," Al began. "The Winter Period, which encompasses the frozen-water season, is best viewed as three discrete segments—early-ice, midwinter, and late-ice. The changing physical environment forces fish to shift locations and behavior. Anglers must adapt and adjust to conditions, just as fish do.

"Laws of physics affect all creatures, but at no time is their effect stronger than winter. By late fall, thermal stratification has been eliminat-

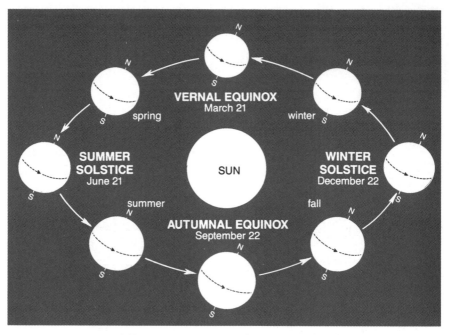

Inside the figure:

N

N

N

VERNAL EQUINOX
March 21

spring

winter

SUMMER SOLSTICE
June 21

SUN

WINTER SOLSTICE
December 22

summer

fall

AUTUMNAL EQUINOX
September 22

Spring, summer, fall, winter. The pendulum swings between seasons, bringing obvious changes on land, but more difficult-to-define changes underwater. Photoperiod (length of daylight) influences the tempo of the environment, from microorganisms to top-of-the-line predators. The intensity and duration of light in a yearly cycle influence fish migrations, spawning, and feeding.

ed by turnover. Water temperature and oxygen content are almost constant from surface to bottom.

Immediately after turnover, water temperatures range from the mid-40°F to low 50°F. As late fall progresses, water temperatures dip into the 39°F to 40°F range.

Once water reaches about 39°F, another turnover begins. Water is most dense—heaviest—at 39°F. Therefore, when the air temperature reduces the temperature of surface water to less than 39°F, that water remains at the surface and the 39°F water sinks.

Eventually, of course, the surface temperature is reduced to freezing (32°F) and ice forms. Ice floats, being less dense than water.

"One of my favorite late-season fishing options," Doug offered, "was to fish until freeze-up on a certain spot and then try to fish the same spot within a few days—occasionally the next day—through the ice. Did this at least half a dozen times on West Okoboji Lake in Iowa when I lived nearby.

"A deep rock bar runs across the entrance to a big shallow bay that holds walleyes in fall. By the end of November, the shallow bay would be frozen over. By the first week in December, the ice would be thick

The Ten In-Fisherman Calendar Periods

1	2	3	4	5	6	7	8	9	10
Prespawn	Spawn	Postspawn	Presummer	Summer Peak	Summer	Postsummer	Turnover	Cold Water	Winter

In-Fisherman divides the fishing year into 10 basic Calendar Periods of fish response. A general characterization of each period includes:

Cold Water: *Occurs during late fall and very early spring.*

Prespawn: *Fish are on the way to or in the vicinity of spawning areas.*

Spawn: *A brief variable period linked to the range of preferred spawning temperatures for each fish species.*

Postspawn: *A brief transition period with length depending on water and weather conditions. Fish begin feeding strategies and move toward areas they'll use for much of the rest of the year.*

Presummer: *A continuing transition period. Fish search for areas to spend the summer and begin to establish summer patterns.*

Summer Peak: *Fish establish a pattern in a habitat that can sustain them for summer. The sudden presence of other fish usually spurs competitive feeding and good fishing.*

Summer: *Usually a long period when fish remain in habitat areas established during the Summer Peak. Fish activity and location are predictable.*

Postsummer: *Cooler weather lowers water temperatures, and fish move toward wintering areas.*

Fall Turnover: *Occurs in lakes, ponds, and reservoirs that stratify into 3 distinct water-temperature layers during summer. As fall progresses, colder weather lowers surface water temperatures, the colder water sinks, and stratification breaks down, allowing fish to use the entire column of water.*

* Winter: *Coldest water of the year. Frozen water occurs in northern regions.*

The Calendar Periods In Practice For Crappies

Normal Calendar	Jan.	Feb.	Mar.	Apr.	May	June	July	Aug.	Sept.	Oct.	Nov.	Dec.
Northern Range		10		9	1	2 3 4 5	6	7 8		9		10
Mid-Range	10	9	1	2	3 4 5	6			7 8	9		10

*Coldest water of the year—frozen water in northern regions.

1. Prespawn   4. Presummer   7. Postsummer   10. Winter
2. Spawn   5. Summer Peak   8. Fall Turnover
3. Postspawn   6. Summer   9. Cold Water

Calendar Periods, including the Winter Period, vary in length from year to year. Unusually warm or cool weather affects the length of the periods. Periods aren't based on the Gregorian calendar, so they don't occur on specific dates each year. Instead, Calendar Periods are based on nature's clock.

This example shows how periods might vary for crappies in two regions of North America.

132

Winter Calendar Periods

Northern Wisconsin

| Nov. 15 | Dec. 15 | Jan. 15 | Feb. 15 | Mar. 15 | Apr. 15 |

◄────────► ◄──────────────────────────────► ◄────────►
Early-Ice   Mid-Winter   Late-Ice

Northern Iowa

| Dec. 7 | Jan. 7 | Feb .7 | Mar.7 |

◄──────────► ◄──────────────────► ◄──────────►
Early-Ice   Mid-Winter   Late-Ice

The ice season can be divided into three basic periods: early-ice, midwinter, and late-ice. These periods vary based primarily on the local climate. On a local level, though, small shallow lakes experience freeze-up faster and ice-out sooner than large shallow lakes; and large shallow lakes experience freeze-up faster and ice-out sooner than large deep lakes. The dates suggested here, therefore, are for comparison to illustrate a basic seasonal principle.

The Squeeze On Basic Types Of Waters

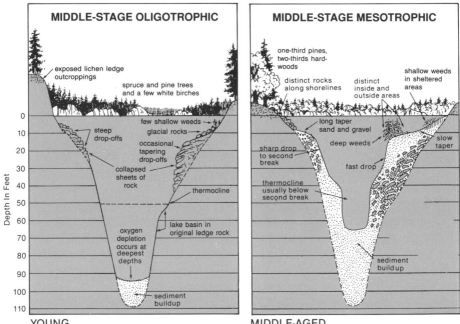

The big squeeze. The tendency for fish under ice to move deeper because of reduced oxygen and colder temperatures in shallow water.

This shift is most pronounced in shallow lakes (eutrophic) or lakes with a lot of shallow bays. Shallow lakes tend to be more fertile and oxygen conditions deteriorate more rapidly as weeds decompose. In shallow lakes, the bulk of the fish population move to the open basin even if the water there isn't deep.

Movement to deeper water is less significant in deep, relatively infertile lakes

enough to slide a small duck boat across to open water in the main lake. The rock bar protruded into the main body of water—a huge section of deeper water. Wind would typically keep it ice-free for at least another week.

"Eventually I'd be out there in my duck boat in the evening catching walleyes when the wind calmed after several days of blowing. The lake literally began to freeze around me. I'd row in through 'gelling' ice.

"By morning, ice on the main lake would often be 3 or 4 inches thick. When a lake's ready, this happens quickly. The water probably had been cold enough to freeze for a week or more. When the wind went down, the surface froze and I was sometimes out ice fishing on the same spot the next day—the same spot I'd fished from a boat the evening before. The fish were still there. Only the physical environment and the tackle had changed."

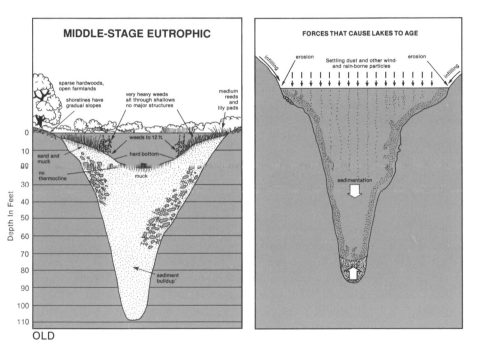

(oligotrophic). This movement is also less significant on large medium-fertile lakes (mesotrophic). The tendency to move deeper in midwinter remains, but is less pronounced because no compelling oxygen or temperature reason forces fish to move to deeper water.

Exceptions? Sure. For one, in years with little snow, fish tend to hold in shallow water longer (some stay the winter) and typically return to shallow water earlier. Inflowing water such as a stream or warm-water discharge also draws fish.

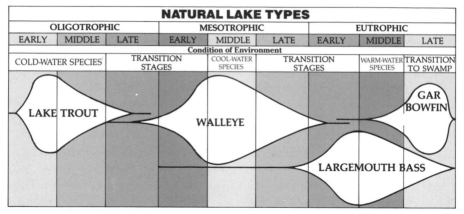

NATURAL LAKE TYPES								
OLIGOTROPHIC			MESOTROPHIC			EUTROPHIC		
EARLY	MIDDLE	LATE	EARLY	MIDDLE	LATE	EARLY	MIDDLE	LATE
Condition of Environment								
COLD-WATER SPECIES	TRANSITION STAGES			COOL-WATER SPECIES	TRANSITION STAGES		WARM-WATER SPECIES	TRANSITION TO SWAMP

Oligotrophic waters. *Lake trout water, although pike, walleyes, and white fish are probably also present. Infertile water in pits and ponds may also host stocked trout. And the Great Lakes host salmon, brown trout, brookies, splake, steelhead, and rainbows.*

Mesotrophic waters. *Prime conditions for everything from walleyes, pike, bass, and muskies, to panfish species like crappies, bluegills and perch.*

Eutrophic waters. *Early-stage eutrophic lakes often host robust populations of the same species present in mesotrophic waters. Eventually, fish like bullheads become predominant.*

Ice Facts

• Current slows or prevents the formation of ice. This is illustrated most vividly in a shallow fast-flowing stream where ice called "anchor ice" forms on the bottom. Moving surface water often doesn't freeze all winter in these bodies of water.

• Ice is lighter than water, so 10 to 20 percent of it rests above the surface of the water. For example, with 10 inches of ice, about an inch will be above water level. The weight of snow, however, can force ice down.

• Lakes protected from wind freeze over sooner than those exposed to wind. But by midwinter, the exposed lake will have thicker ice because wind reduces snow cover that acts as an insulator. Frigid air temperatures continually add more ice to the bottom of the ice pack, but as the ice thickens, the rate of increase declines.

• Ice serves as an insulator between the warmer water below and the cold air temperatures above.

• Snow is also an insulator. Too much early snow, especially before ice is thick enough to safely support fishing traffic, can make ice unsafe all winter on the fringes of ice-fishing territory.

• Impurities lower the freezing point of water. Salt in ocean water, for example, lowers its freezing point to 28.5°F instead of 32°F.

First-Ice Feeding Binge?

"Most folks still seem to believe," Doug said, "that first-ice triggers fish

Classic's The Key At First Ice

Hardcore early-ice anglers don warm clothes and waders, step into float tubes, and shuffle across ice no more than two inches thick. If they break through, they bob for a moment before using an ice pick to pull themselves back onto the ice.

Too dangerous to encourage, but it shows how serious some anglers are about first-ice fishing. Their enthusiasm isn't unfounded. First-ice produces some of the best fishing of the season. Not only good fishing, but it's easy. Classic fish location and presentation are keys at first-ice. Understand that and you're in for a fish-catching good time.

An explanation of first-ice activity might not seem important, but it's a major step in defining one stage fish progress through during the Frozen Water Period.

Classic? The ordinarily expected. It's bacon and eggs, pork and beans, and taxes. It's also walleyes and deep-breaking rock and rubble points, bluegills and weedflats, and pike and remaining standing weedgrowth.

Classic fish-attracting areas offer a combination of food, shelter, and security. Whether it's oxbows, natural lakes, reservoirs, or river backwaters, primary fish attractors are constant. Focus your effort on bars, current areas, and bays.

to go on a feeding binge. Having often fished on open water right up to freeze-up and then returned to the same spots to ice fish within a day, I don't believe the feeding binge theory. Fish don't suddenly go on a feeding binge. Ice cover, though, makes it easy for anglers to take advantage of fish that have been actively and consistently feeding there before ice-up."

"Right," Al emphasized. "Most anglers can't compare fishing at first-ice to fishing right before freeze-up. As fall progresses and weather becomes colder, most anglers stop fishing. Fish that aren't pressured by anglers tend to move into preferred habitat and feed predictably.

"Consider a virgin fishery," Al continued. "Fish may be so numerous that they're everywhere, but they certainly are on obvious (classic) points and inside bends, bars, or bays. Fish location is predictable."

"Vital point," Doug offered. "The principle's much the same during late fall and extending to the first-ice period. Fish move to classic locations where they school. They're ready and waiting when anglers begin fishing for them shortly after ice-up. Anglers are getting in on the tail end of the sustained fall bite, instead of an ice-triggered feeding binge.

"Another reason fishing is so good is that most anglers tend to fish more effectively through the ice than on open water. That's especially true during late fall when wind makes boat control difficult; and cold, often wet conditions intensify the problem of presenting a bait effectively. But fish are on obvious spots and are catchable on effectively presented baits. So ice cover allows anglers to present baits effectively to grouped fish that are feeding predictably."

Yes, fishing is good at first-ice. Our main point, though, is that at first-ice, classic spots produce good fishing. At first-ice, fish are exactly where they were immediately before ice-up.

Classic Spots

"The explanation of activity at first-ice might not seem important," Al noted, "but it represents a major step in defining the stages fish progress through during the Frozen Water Period. You're treading on new ground (frozen water) along with us. Yet the situations are obvious and easy to understand."

Classic fish-attracting areas offer a combination of food, shelter, and security. Primary fish attractors remain constant, whether they're oxbows, natural lakes, reservoirs, or river backwaters. Focus on three fish attractors—bars, current, and bays—although we could include many more.

Bars in various forms—dominant shoreline points as well as subtle projections, sunken islands or humps, wing dams—are the most obvious and most important structural element. Bigger bars generally gather more fish; productive bars, however, offer a variety of fish-attracting conditions.

Productive bars often have many types of cover. Weeds or fallen timber, for instance, attract small fish as well as larger predators. Many species also feed efficiently over clean bottoms, although such areas are often near major drop-offs. Each species has priorities, and fish congre-

Murphy Flowage

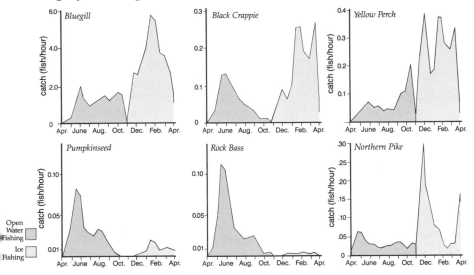

In Wisconsin, people ice fish with religious fervor. For many decades, biologists there have studied the behavior of fish under ice and how well they bite. Over a 15-year period, Howard Snow of the Wisconsin Department of Natural Resources described angler catch rates in Murphy Flowage, a 160-acre eutrophic lowland impoundment.

Graphs of catch rates (number of fish caught per hour) showed faster fishing for pike, bluegills, yellow perch, and black crappie during the Frozen Water Period than during any other time. Early-ice peaks were more pronounced for some species, but anglers evidently moved with the fish for good catches all winter.

gate in an area that fulfills their needs during the fall Cold Water Period, remaining at first-ice.

"Amount of 'edge' often affects whether bars host fish, too," Doug said. "An edge exists where one distinct area meets another. Thus, a spot where deeper water butts against shallower water (a drop-off) is an edge. Areas where rock meets sand or gravel, where muck meets sand, or where weeds or timber meet open water are also edges. Small points or dips (inside turns) in the edge of a bar, weedbed, timberline, or rock pile often funnel fish into small areas."

Current is another classic gathering point in any body of water. Current in lakes and reservoirs is most often associated with incoming feeder creeks or rivers. Current is also often created between narrow necked-down lake areas.

"Of course," Doug added, "other elements are necessary before current can perform its magic. For example, walleyes are usually drawn to current flowing over a rock-rubble bar near a major drop-off. Most walleyes use the drop-off at first-ice. But remove the drop-off or the bar and the current area won't draw walleyes consistently. You see, current's the key ingredient, but not the only ingredient."

The prerogatives for each species change, but current is generally a major fish attractor at first-ice. But current can result in thin ice; be careful!"

Bays are the third major fish attractor.

"Small shallow bays occasionally draw fish," Al said, "but aren't of overall importance. Moderate-size to large bays with enough deep water to support fish life year around are important. These bays (creek arms in reservoirs and backwaters in rivers) are often more fertile than the main body of water.

"Bays host predators and prey. Moderate-size bays often draw some fish species even when a major structural element like a bar isn't present. In most bays, however, bars or current areas congregate fish. It often helps to view bays as a separate lake."

Oxygen content is an increasingly important factor in fish location as winter progresses. Oxygen is no longer added by wind or atmospheric absorption, and photosynthesis by aquatic plants is virtually nil once snow builds.

At first-ice, oxygen content is nearly the same (about 9 parts per million—ppm) from top to bottom. But by midwinter, oxygen may be reduced to about 3 ppm. It drops faster in shallower, more eutrophic waters without inflows or springs.

The Big Squeeze

Highest oxygen concentrations are found at the surface throughout the winter because colder water holds slightly more oxygen. And organic decay that removes oxygen occurs on the bottom.

Doug: "By mid-February, fish may move right up under the ice in shallow fertile lakes and ponds. Winterkill can occur in northern lakes with little water deeper than 15 feet, no inlet, and snow cover blocking sunlight. When a lake is winterkilling, as you drill holes, fish swim into them and you can scoop them up. Placing an aerator in one of these lakes, same story. Instant fish accumulation. A natural spring or inlet will also draw fish."

Low temperatures and oxygen depletion in shallow water can become stressful by midwinter. Deeper water tends to contain less oxygen, but is warmer. Surface water has oxygen, but is frigid. In combination with thickening ice, we refer to these two constraining forces as "the squeeze."

"In shallow lakes, fish move to the open basin even if the water isn't deep," Doug explained. "It's common to catch a mixed bag of fish roaming basin water.

"Movement to deeper water is less significant in 'lake trout' water—deep, relatively infertile lakes. This movement is also less significant on fairly large mesotrophic lakes. Fish still tend to move deeper in midwin-

Early-Ice Conditions

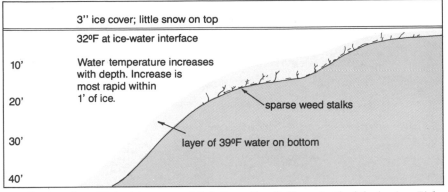

3" ice cover; little snow on top

32°F at ice-water interface

10'   Water temperature increases with depth. Increase is most rapid within 1' of ice.

20'

sparse weed stalks

30'   layer of 39°F water on bottom

40'

Oxygen is sufficient to support fish from the shallows to the lake basin. Fish occupy habitats according to availability of prey and their own characteristics as a species. Remaining cover and warmer water may concentrate fish near the bottom. Some species shift vertically over a 24-hour period in response to prey migrations and light levels. Classic structure typically holds large numbers of fish.

Midwinter Ice Conditions

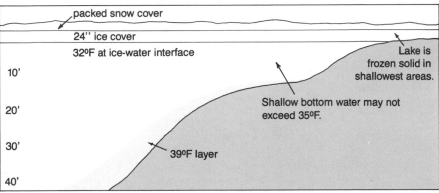

packed snow cover

24" ice cover

32°F at ice-water interface

Lake is frozen solid in shallowest areas.

10'

Shallow bottom water may not exceed 35°F.

20'

30'   39°F layer

40'

Fish may be squeezed off flats by thickening ice, cold water, and low amounts of dissolved oxygen. Water adjacent to ice holds more oxygen because it's colder and farther from the bottom. In lakes where winterkill occurs, fish may hold directly under the ice and create indentations by constant finning.

Dissolved oxygen declines in deep areas, but not as quickly as in the shallows where abundant organic material rapidly consumes oxygen.

Late-Ice Conditions

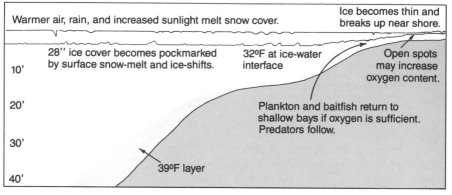

It's not clear whether the layer of warmest, densest water always hugs bottom contours or slides off drop-offs and concentrates in the main lake basin. Bottom shape and environmental factors seem to affect the location and width of this layer.

ter, but it's less pronounced because reasons to move aren't as compelling.

"Exceptions exist, as you might expect. In years with little snow, fish stay in shallow water longer and return to shallow water earlier. Inflowing water such as a stream or warm-water discharge also draws fish.

"Before the squeeze, a wider variety of fish-catching patterns have potential, and most species are more active than they'll be later," Doug

Lake Within A Lake

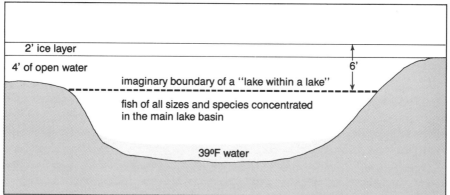

During midwinter, bowl-shape lakes often form a lake within a lake. Warmer, denser water is pushed or slides off shallow flats into the main lake basin. All fish may be concentrated in this interior lake where temperature and oxygen conditions are most inviting. It's common to see suspended fish with sonar, but action may be slow because of reduced metabolism in the fish.

continued. "As the squeeze tightens, most action occurs in deeper water. During midwinter, fish may be more consolidated, but aren't feeding as heavily."

This is the time you'll see suspended fish on your flasher that refuse even tasty maggots. Their metabolism seems to be dulled. Panfishermen must rely on delicate presentations with a sensitive rod and tiny flies. Fishermen after walleyes need to fish deeper and concentrate on the twilight periods. Everyone needs to be satisfied with reduced catches.

Late-Ice

As late winter daytime temperatures rise above freezing, ice melts from the top of the ice pack. As it melts, the reverse of ice-up occurs. Snow cover melts. Then surface ice melts and water seeps into the ice, pock-marking it.

Along the shoreline, open water appears well before the main lake opens, due to the warming land mass. At last-ice, anglers often must cross planks to get to fine fishing. Safety first, though. Finally, the ice becomes black and rotten—waterlogged and unsafe, even though it may still be quite thick.

"Fishing gets good in shallow bays at late-ice, but the reasons are rarely talked about," Al commented. "At late-ice, the food chain moves back into the shallows, especially shallow bays. During the one or two months when fish leave shallow water for deeper bays or the main lake is a respite time when plankton populations rebound.

"At late-ice minnows return to feed on the abundant plankton, panfish feed on the minnows, and large predators feed on the minnows and panfish. It's a party or a war, depending on whether you're prey or predator. I think I fall into the predator category."

CHAPTER 7

ABOUT PANFISH

Depending on your viewpoint and the size of your pan, just about anything smaller than a hammerhead shark can qualify as a panfish.
Dave Genz

Panfish. Bluegills, crappies, perch, white bass. Major panfish species pursued during winter. Doug, Al, and Dave proceeded with general observations about panfish, given having discussed equipment for panfish in Chapter 2, and having covered a fishing system for panfish in Chapter 3. Those chapters are the basis for their discussion here, just as this chapter becomes an additional part of the panfish puzzle.

"Panfish feed on vaguely similar prey, so you can use some of the same equipment, baits, and lures to catch them," Doug said to Al and Dave. "Jumbo perch, for example, are found in bluegill habitat in shallow water, though they may also reside 80 feet deep in a lake basin. Crappies, too, are often found in bluegill habitat, and vice versa. Yet crappies more likely suspend and use open water than do bluegills or perch, although big bluegills (Dave calls them "no-nosers" because their head grows right onto their snout) often roam open water with crappies. Big 'bull' bluegills hold in deep water around rocks; while small bluegills rarely do."

"The reason fishermen don't catch more big bluegills suspended with crappies," Al observed, "is because they're fishing through them with big minnows. Plus, most people who fish that zone fish after dark when bluegills don't bite well."

"Yes, and if more people believed they could catch crappies with maggots on an ice fly," Dave advised, "they'd catch more crappies—more bluegills, too. Maggots outproduce minnows most times."

"Perch, though," Doug said, "are different from other panfish. They're closely related and more similar to a walleye than to other panfish. So lure size and location may change more drastically than when you switch from bluegills to crappies. Perch fishing is more like small-scale walleye fishing."

OK, guys. Slow down. Let's keep this organized. Panfishing, we can say, differs based on where you find fish, their size, and their aggressiveness. Perch can be found both deep and shallow. Panfish are similar and panfish are different. Take a deep breath. Focus first on an overlooked relationship vital to panfishing.

Micro Food

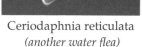

Daphnia *species*   Ceriodaphnia reticulata   Cyclops varicans
(*water flea*)   (*another water flea*)

Micro animals (zooplankton) like Daphnia, Ceriodaphnia, *and* Cyclops *are the bulk of panfish diets during some periods. Besides their different appearance, each animal has characteristic movements and lifestyle. Daphnia swim slowly in a bobbing fashion and tend to slowly migrate upward in a column of water at dark and downward in daylight. Copepods are built for bursts of speed and can also swim erratically. They often hold an established position regardless of light conditions, although general movements up or down or left or right may take place on a daily or weekly basis.*

Plankton And Panfishing Success

"Zooplankton are microscopic animals that feed on phytoplankton—one-cell plants capable of food production," Doug offered. "Phytoplankton are the base of any aquatic food chain. Zooplankton comprise the next step. The following step includes panfish like bluegills, sunfish, crappies, and perch.

"Zooplankton, therefore, influence the location of crappies, bluegills, perch, and sunfish, as well as the presentations needed to catch them. Indeed, panfish feed on zooplankton and may even wipe out entire segments of a zooplankton community. During most yearly periods, zooplankton provide a continual source of nutrition for panfish. Winter's no exception".

Of the hundreds of zooplankton species, we'll focus on two general types, *Daphnia* and copepods. *Daphnia* are about the size of a pinhead. They look like a compact rubber ducky with skinny wings.

Copepods, on the other hand, may be 1/10 of an inch long. They look like small bullets, with long sensory projections at the head of their bodies and one or several fuzzy swimming organs at their tail end.

"Using positions on a football team for comparison, copepods are the halfbacks," Dave said. "They sense and evade predators and also attack prey. *Daphnia* on the other hand, make slow, subtle locational changes to avoid predators and contact food. *Daphnia*, though, are no less successful than copepods, only different."

Selective Predation

FACT: *Bluegills, crappies, perch, and sunfish practice size-selective or vulnerability-selective predation on zooplankton. In a given group of zooplankton, panfish usually choose the largest. And they usually focus on the most vulnerable—least evasive or easiest to see.*

"Yes, I know small ice fishing lures are much larger than zooplankton," Al noted. "But they represent the zooplankton that panfish often feed on. A properly presented teardrop dressed with a grub probably looks like a huge, succulent *Daphnia*. Panfish feed heavily on zooplankton during winter, so it's no surprise that teardrops, small jigs, and other ice flies—lures that look like zooplankton—work well."

"The type of ice fishing lure and the jigging motion you choose," Doug said, "depends on the type of zooplankton panfish are feeding on. In most cases, imitate the more vulnerable, slow-bobbing *Daphnia*, rather than darting copepods.

"*Daphnia* exhibit an almost constant subtle fluttering motion. They rarely move horizontally, so a bobbing 1/16- to 1/8-inch motion is a proper presentation of a *Daphnia*."

Dave calls this presentation "pounding." He makes a nervous movement. His hand barely moves, yet his rod tip vibrates up and down.

As we've noted, most ice fishing presentations should be a combina-

Basic Jigging

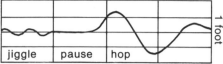

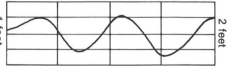

A *good* Daphnia *jigging imitation* is a slow or fast subtle bobbing (fluttering) movement (about 1/16 or 1/8 inch). But one easy way to feel when a panfish slurps up the bait requires the bait to be still. A fish can't eat what it can't see, however. Larger hops attract panfish from a distance. The final result is a subtle jigging movement interspersed with pauses and hops.

The basic jigging imitation becomes a *jiggle, jiggle, jiggle, pause, jiggle, jiggle, jiggle, pause, hop, hop. Illustrated on a horizontal line, it might look like this:*

Copepods are darters. They're more difficult for bluegills to catch, but are available, especially during the middle of the day when Daphnia move deep. The basic darter-imitating jigging movement is a hop, hold, hop, hold. Illustrated on a horizontal line it looks like this:

Experiment with other variations of these two basic patterns.

tion of "attraction" to get the fish's attention and "triggering" to encourage fish to strike. Distinct jigging movements draw attention to your bait. Then frequent pauses allow bite detection. The basic jigging motion becomes jiggle-jiggle-jiggle (1/16- to 1/8-inch moves), pause, jiggle-jiggle-jiggle, pause, hop, hop (1 foot moves). Repeat the procedure.

"I like to start with a basic presentation—pounding—starting near bottom or wherever I see fish on my locator," Dave offered. "I slowly raise, raise, raise up from the fish, always maintaining that pounding motion. Then I slowly lower the bait back toward bottom, still pounding.

"Bites are easy to detect once you get tuned to the feel of the ice fly. The bite often is the absence of weight when the lure should come to the bottom of its drop when you're pounding. If you don't feel the lure, a fish has sucked it in. Set!"

"Experiment with that basic pattern," Doug added. "Lengthen the pause. It's almost impossible to hold a bait perfectly still; but such slight movement may be a trigger on some days. A small

For consistent jigging without a bobber, rest your ice fishing rod on your knee. Use your finger or small wrist movements to bob the bait.

float suspends a bait as still as possible. Studies show, however, that pan-fish seldom take dead *Daphnia*; rarely should *Daphnia* imitations be fished perfectly still."

Certain baits better represent certain zooplankton at certain times. Carry a variety of different size teardrops, some with long-shank hooks, others with short shanks; some with thick bodies, others with thin bodies.

Stock at least three basic color themes: (1) subdued colors such as black, purple, or green; (2) bright colors such as fluorescent orange or chartreuse, plus phosphorescent (glow-in-the-dark); and (3) subtle colors such as white or yellow. Colors probably are more for attraction than close-up triggering.

Also carry single hooks (#4 through #14) and lead shot. Sometimes a single grub on a hook is the best bait. Single hooks weighted with wraps of lead wire (available at fly-fishing shops) also produce fish, sometimes even without bait. So do small blank leadhead jigs packed with grubs or maggots. Flash lures such as the Acme Kastmaster or Jig-A-Whopper Rocker Minnow, and swimming lures such as the Jigging Rapala or Wisconsin Tackle Swimmin' Ratt should also have important places in your arsenal.

Let the fish decide which lures or jigging movements best represent the plankton forage they want. Experiment when you're on fish and they're not popping. Your knowledge of zooplankton can help you duplicate what panfish want.

Location, Pursuit, Attack, And Capture

FACT: *The activities of panfish feeding on zooplankton can be broken into 4 categories: location, pursuit, attack and capture.*

"About location and pursuit," Doug began. "Zooplankton suspend. The depth they suspend at is influenced by factors including light intensity and defenses to evade panfish. To keep from being easily detected, *Daphnia* often migrate, rising when it's dark and descending when it's light. Copepods don't descend into murky depths to hide. They depend instead on evasive darting maneuvers.

"Zooplankton are found over open water and near structural elements such as bars. Most panfish, though, have an affinity for structural elements. They usually combine the presence of zooplankton with an attractive structural element.

"Panfish, however, pursue zooplankton in open water when structural elements don't provide enough zooplankton. Panfish commonly suspend off bars during midday, often searching for *Daphnia* that have descended in open water. *Daphnia* on bars drop into bottom vegetation and are almost inaccessible."

Because panfish pursue *Daphnia*, and because *Daphnia* change location based on light intensity, panfish location often changes during the day. Panfish move because zooplankton move. They often feed heavily at

The depth panfish hold at often is determined by the location of their forage, including zooplankton.

daybreak when *Daphnia* haven't yet dropped in the water column. And some fish from this concentration may linger in shallow water all day.

Anglers who continue to fish an area that was productive in early morning may find that jigging techniques necessary to trigger fish change as the day progresses. A subtle jigging technique imitates the *Daphnia* panfish often pursue during early morning. At midday, when fish may seek darting copepods, aggressive jigging may catch more fish.

"The way I see it," Al said, "some zooplankton are always shallow, so some panfish are almost always shallow. Other zooplankton are deeper, so some fish, especially crappies and perch, are usually deeper, too. At midday, panfish are more often scattered—roaming. Snow cover, thick ice, dark skies, or dingy water modify vertical zooplankton movement, and thus panfish movement and location."

"Right," Dave agreed. "Panfish roam until they find zooplankton or other prey. Where panfish are concentrated and holding, zooplankton are usually plentiful. Panfish concentrations remain high until they reduce zooplankton numbers. When zooplankton numbers are reduced, panfish begin to roam again until they find other zooplankton concentrations.

"A weather change, a change in barometric pressure, or the approach of predators like pike also move panfish. Search until you find an area panfish are using. But don't expect them to stay there."

Having covered location and pursuit, what about attack and capture?

The Big Squeeze

" It seems he didn't want anyone to see he was catching fish, so he just piled them up inside and, well... they froze and he couldn't get out."

Panfish recognize the difference between *Daphnia* and copepods, and they attack based on the escape ability of these prey. Understanding this can help you catch more fish.

"When panfish attack and capture *Daphnia*," Doug offered, "they may casually swim up, hesitate, then suck one in. When they attack a copepod, however, they carefully position themselves and then aggressively swim into the prey, sucking it in when it's close enough—before it can scoot away. Success rates for panfish attempting to capture *Daphnia* are 3 or 4 times higher than for capturing copepods."

Knowing that zooplankton species swim and react differently reinforces the need to find the jigging technique that best imitates the zooplankton fish are feeding on at that moment.

When panfish strike a bait vigorously, it may be because of competition; several fish may be vying for the same morsel. But it may also indicate they're after copepods. If that's the case, a more aggressive jigging approach with pauses might produce more fish.

Reactive Distance

FACT: *Panfish see and react to zooplankton within a given area. The distance involved, called "reactive" distance, is influenced by zooplankton size and movement and the amount of available light. Reactive distance influences presentation.*

Panfish Reliability

Good news. Panfish usually continue to feed throughout the day. While weather conditions and other factors affect panfish, they're more reliable than larger predators. Even if you fish during the middle of a winter day, you usually can catch a tasty meal of panfish. Many anglers fish for walleyes during low-light periods, then switch to panfish during midday when walleye fishing can be tough.

"Zooplankton are small and panfish spend a lot of time searching for them," Doug noted. "Ice fishermen peering down at panfish through a hole in the ice see a bluegill swim into view, stop, ever-so-slightly fan its gills and fins, move a foot or two, and stop again. The bluegill is searching for zooplankton. At each stop, it scans the water. Having found a *Daphnia*, the 'gill swims to it, ever-so-slightly tilts its body and sucks in the morsel. The attack would be different if the morsel were a zooplankton with evasive capabilities."

Studies indicate that crappies can detect 1/32-inch zooplankton from a distance of 5 inches. Bluegills see small tidbits slightly better than crappies, and both crappies and bluegills see small tidbits much better than do larger predators like pike, walleyes, lake trout, and bass.

But panfish don't easily distinguish large or distant objects; so much of their time is spent focusing on things close-at-hand. Panfish live in their own little world, and zooplankton are a vital part of it.

Larger size, increased movement, and good light increase reactive distance. But many of our fishing choices depend on subtle tradeoffs where one choice is barely better than another. For instance, larger lures are almost always easier to see, but after a certain size, they lose their triggering effect.

"Remember," Dave said. "Panfish have difficulty seeing even large zooplankton during low-light periods, especially if the zooplankton aren't moving. During low-light periods, fish larger vigorously moving baits and perhaps add flash. During high-light periods, fish smaller realistic lures and use subtle movements.

"Remember, too," Dave continued, " even though large, perhaps flashing, vigorously moving lures may attract fish, they may not trigger them. On the other hand, a small, realistic morsel like a grub on a #14 hook isn't adequate for searching out scattered fish in open spaces. Too small takes too long to drop and is too tough for fish to see."

Attraction And Triggering

Lures must first attract and then trigger fish. Few lures both attract and trigger equally all the time. No perfect lures exist for all conditions.

A Search Lure

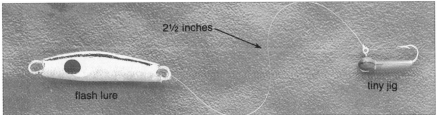

A combo lure popularized by Doug Stange is an effective compromise that's good when you're on fish and especially effective as a search lure when you're searching for fish.

Remove the treble hook from a lure like a small Rocker Minnow. Then tie a small piece of light line on the bottom split ring and add a 1/32- or 1/64-ounce leadhead jig or a small teardrop to the end of this line. Bait with grubs, a minnow, fish meat, or a fish eye. The baited lure should hang 2½ to 3 inches below the flash lure. If the line's too long, it tangles when you jig the lure. If it's too short, the flash seems to distract fish after attracting them.

A search lure offers flash for attraction and a small morsel as a trigger. It gets deep fast and can be effectively fished at most depths.

For crappies, add a minnow hooked under the dorsal fin. Grubs, though, are good for all panfish species. Once you find fish, try a teardrop and grubs, a minnow on a teardrop, or a minnow on a blank leadhead jig (especially for perch or crappies). A single grub on a plain hook, a lead-wire hook, or a blank leadhead jig packed with maggots or grubs work well.

The key is recognizing which lures offer the right measure of attraction and triggering, given the situation.

"Generally, small live minnows work for crappies and perch, but rarely for average-size bluegills," Al noted. "Trophy 'gills are another matter. Flash lures tipped with grubs or a piece of fish work for perch, but rarely for crappies, bluegills and sunfish. Teardrops, depending on their size and shape, dressed with grubs work for bluegills, sunnies, crappies, and perch.

"Flash lures are attractors. Add livebait—grubs or a small piece of fish meat (perhaps an eyeball)—to provide the trigger.

"On the other end of the spectrum, an individual grub fished on a small hook has great triggering ability, but little ability to attract. Add attraction by vigorously jigging the bait.

"Teardrops probably are the best compromise lure for panfish. Teardrops dressed with grubs provide attraction, depending on the size, color, and flash of the head. Vigorous jigging also adds attraction."

No matter which lure you use, increase attraction especially in low-light conditions by adding movement and increasing size. To increase the triggering quality of a bait, add livebait, fish with smaller lures, and use less movement.

More On Lure Selection

Dave, Doug, and Al divide panfish lures into 2 groups. One group includes light lures that can only be worked slowly. The second group includes heavier lures that can, but don't have to be worked aggressively.

Generally, leadhead jigs and spoons fit into the heavier category, while teardrops fit into the lighter category. Leadhead jigs, however, can be light; and teardrops can be heavy.

Teardrops—Whether teardrops fish light or heavy depends on their shape as much as their weight. Wider, flatter teardrops drop slowly and fish light, while longer, thinner teardrops fish heavy and can be fished fast. These two types of tears are often referred to as "Minnesota" (wider and lighter) and "Wisconsin" (thinner and heavier) teardrops.

Whatever you call these two types of teardrops, they fish differently. Minnesota-type teardrops drop slower and must therefore be fished slower. Wisconsin teardrops can be fished fast or slow. Many different varieties of each exist for different fishing conditions.

"Rocker jigs" (Wisconsin) and "flipper jigs," (Minnesota) are variations of Wisconsin and Minnesota teardrops. Rocker jigs are a type of thinner, heavier Wisconsin-type teardrop usually with a long-shank hook and a bend in their backs. When jigged aggressively, they ride horizontally.

Flipper jigs usually have a wide, flat Minnesota-type body with tiny spinner blades (usually 2) attached to the hook eye. Flipper jigs are gaudy—good fish attractors. They're too much, however, for most neu-

Lotsa Lures!

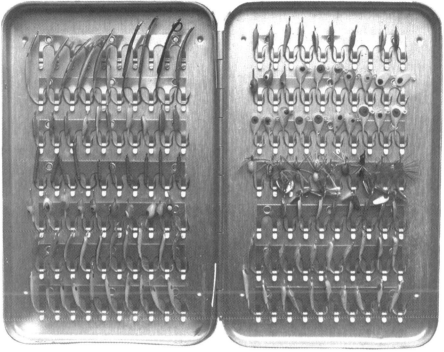

One of the most perplexing parts of panfishing can be picking a lure style and color to turn fish on. Does it make a difference? It does!

Row 1: Six "Dipper" spoons and 4 "Firebug" spoons.

Row 2: Minnesota-type (relatively wide, flat and light) teardrops.

Row 3: Bounce jigs (hooks wrapped with lead wire).

Row 4: Various ladybug-type leadhead jigs.

Row 5: Various rocker jigs, an off-shoot of the Wisconsin-type (relatively long, thin and heavy) teardrops.

Row 6: Various small "Dipper" spoons.

Row 7: Another assortment of Minnesota-type teardrops.

Row 8: Several ladybugs followed by 5 "minnow jigs" and 2 Daphnia jigs.

Row 9: An assortment of minnow jigs.

Row 10: Spider jigs have rubber legs; ants have hackles.

Row 11: Flipper jigs.

Row 12 and 13: Glow-in-the-dark jigs. Various Minnesota- and Wisconsin-type jigs with phosphorescent paint.

tral fish.

Leadhead jigs—Ladybug jigs (Dave's panfish favorite, a larvae bug from Wazp) are small, slightly flattened portions of lead placed slightly below the eye of a #8 or #10 long-shank hook. Painted one color or two-tone, with small contrasting dots, they look like a ladybug.

Ants and spiders are leadhead jigs, too. Ants have two small body segments with a hackle tied between them. Spiders may have one or two body segments with rubber legs between the segments or a hackle in front of the first body segment. Trim the rubber legs and hackle so panfish don't nibble at them.

Leadhead jigs with the head flattened vertically or horizontally, or rounded in standard fashion are "minnow jigs." Although they're jigged vertically, they rest horizontally and can be made to quiver like a finning minnow.

Bounce jigs, plain #6 to #12 hooks wrapped with lead wire from a fly-fishing store, are also considered leadhead jigs. Bounce these lures vertically. They're often effective without livebait.

Spoons—Lures like the Acme Kastmaster, Jig-A-Whopper Rocker Minnow, and Custom Jigs and Spins Stinger are favorite choices for jumbo perch. But they're a good search lure for all panfish, including bluegills.

Russian spoon-type lures like fire bugs and dippers are more common sunfish fare. The dipper features a willow leaf blade, bent to create a diving or swimming action. Firebugs, on the other hand, have a wide notched head and dart erratically when jigged.

Most ice-fishing lure manufacturers are small localized operations. While the lures we've discussed may not be available in your area, something similar probably is.

Color

Once you know the bait panfish are after and the depth they're at, the next question is color.

Match the hatch? Then a subtle black, brown, green, or grey, with maybe just a teeny squiggly bit of attracting hot pink might be your choice.

Going gaudy? Then a blindingly bright chartreuse or hot orange is tough to look at and just as tough for panfish to turn down.

Carry both ends of the color spectrum, plus intermediate colors like soft yellows, whites, and golds, and you're set.

Don't forget phosphorescent baits, the glow-in-the-dark option. The advantage to phosphorescence is visibility, much more visibility than any of the hottest, brightest colors you're used to fishing. Colors fade in deep or dingy water and during twilight and after dark—just where and when panfishing is often best.

Fishing phosphorescent isn't magic. It isn't guaranteed. It's just anoth-

Color

Color and Bluegills

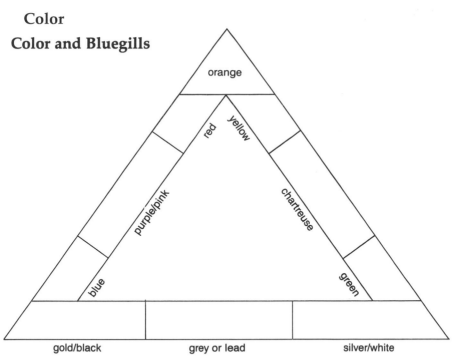

We don't claim to know which colors panfish see or respond to best. Ken Matheson has devised a handy system for deciding which colors panfish see best at any given time. He uses a simple color spectrum based on several decades of winter fishing experience.

Highly visible orange is at one end of the spectrum; grey at the other end. Matheson terms baseline colors natural or neutral colors; besides grey, there's black, gold, silver and white. The colors placed in descending order down the legs of the triangle represent two distinct groups of opposing visible colors.

er option, another step toward ensuring consistent fishing.

Fishing phosphorescent is a proven step, however. In the right place at the right time fished in the right way, phosphorescent baits can be the difference between lots of fish and some fish, or some fish and no fish.

"Phosphorescence is achieved by the paint on lures. To activate the glow, the paint must be exposed to light," Dave offered. "Light intensity equals glow intensity and duration. Bright sunlight produces more glow longer than filtered sunlight, for example. And intense artificial light can produce more glow that lasts longer than sunlight."

Dave and his friends were some of the first to use a camera flash to activate phosphorescent baits. Of course the occasional application of glowing baits is only a small part of Dave's approach to panfishing.

Try phosphorescence in dingy or deep water, at twilight or after dark, and when the ice is thick or snow-covered and fish are near bottom.

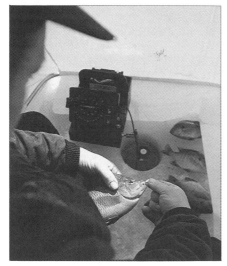

Inside your portable shack with a fat bluegill taken from 15 feet of water below 3 feet of ice. Sure there's light down there. But it's probably just dark enough so glow will make your bait more distinguishable.

Sunlight or a 35mm flash? Natural light or artificial? Sunlight works, but intense artificial light may be better.

Drop the jig in and zap it!

The result? Panfish! Sometimes bluegills; sometimes perch, crappies, or white bass.

Perch, crappies, bluegills, and white bass will respond.

Baits

In 1987, Doug wrote an article for *In-Fisherman* magazine about fishing with phosphorescent baits. At the time, he was familiar with phosphorescent products from primarily two companies. While we're going to review the contents of that article here, note that today most companies, most notably Wisconsin Tackle, K and E Tackle, Comet Tackle, and Northland Tackle sell phosphorescent baits.

Note too that Doug's comments about the bait styles from these two companies apply to similar bait styles from other companies.

Custom Jigs & Spins—*Rembrant*—A spoon-jig tipped with a plastic-glow covering. It's particularly productive fished bouncing and flashing on or near bottom. Smaller fish often don't get a good mouth grip on the bait, but it's a sure hooker for bigger fish.

Rembrant

As is true with most of the jigs mentioned here, smaller sizes with #8, #10, or #12 hooks work best for bluegills. Sizes #8 or #10 may be necessary for wary perch or crappies, although those species usually respond better to #6 hooks. White bass like a bigger bait, say #4 or #6.

When jigged, the Rembrant is an active bait; that is, a bait that's visible because of it's larger profile and spoon shape. The spoon shape gives it lots of flash and action. Not a subtle bait, you say? Right. Even in small sizes, the bait's for active, aggressive fish.

Purist—A bent-bodied teardrop with a flat leadhead. The plastic body and the lead head glow. It's a wonderful imitator of two prime panfish forage types—*Daphnia* and freshwater shrimp. It may just be one of the most productive ice jigs of all time. Use #8s and #10s for bluegills and go with larger baits for perch and white bass. A #6 or #8 is a good bet for multiple species. The Purist fishes best with a subtle, slight bobbing motion.

Purist

Rat Finkee—A standard horizontal-riding leadhead jig with a glow body and head. Standard leadhead jigs are an overlooked option for panfish in deep and shallow water.

Rat Finkee

Fish them with a lift-fall movement, or bob them.

2 Spot—The most traditional teardrop design—a flat lead body anchored on a hook just below the eye. One side of the lead body glows. Although the bait presents a small profile and fishes stiffly without much action for less-active fish, it's a versatile bait that can also be jigged aggressively for active fish.

2 Spot

Willow Spoon—A small, thin-bodied vertical-riding

Willow Spoon

spoon with a glow body. Fishes somewhat like the Purist, but provides a longer profile.

Demon—A teardrop with a bug-shaped body—small head, and larger body that glows. Presents a different profile than a standard-bodied teardrop like the 2 Spot.

Demon

Rocker

Rocker—A traditional vertical-riding bait with a long, thin body (which glows) on a long-shank, slightly bent Aberdeen hook. Again, the bait is a teardrop with a slightly different profile and action. It couples well with a minnow nicked lightly under the dorsal fin. The hook point should ride toward the head of the bait and parallel to the dorsal fin.

Stinger—A flash jig with a glow body for aggressive fish. A treble hook is connected to the body with a small split ring. It's primarily a perch and white bass bait, although larger models are a fine option for walleyes.

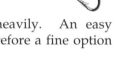

Stinger

Striper Special—A teardrop with a thick body (which glows) on a straight, short-shank hook. Fishes stiffly and heavily. An easy teardrop to read in deep water, therefore a fine option for perch and crappie.

Striper Special

Jig-A-Whopper-UMM Holdings—*Flutter Bug*—A thin plastic glow body set on a rocker-type (bent) hook. Another of the finest panfish producers of all time. A fine imitation of *Daphnia*, grass shrimp, and other tiny water critters. Fishes subtly.

Flutter Bug

Glow Fry

Glow Fry—A short-shanked jig with a heavy, glow body shaped like a football. The jig hangs vertically, however, and fishes heavy for its size. A fine jig to couple with light line for deep water. The weight lets you maintain contact with the jig; the small size triggers panfish.

Flasher Rocker

Flashers—Flat-bodied, long-bodied tears on a slightly bent hook. Offers the combination of various color choices (one side of the body) with glow (the other side). Available in a #12. The jig fishes heavy, but with slightly more action and profile than the Glow Fry.

Tear Flasher #12

Flasher Rocker

Super Dot Rockers—Same basic design and function as the Custom Company rocker. Combinations of standard color choices on one side of the jig and glow on the other side plus various eyespot patterns present different triggering effects.

Perch Hawger

Perch Hawger—A long, heavy-bodied jig on a bent hook. Often tipped with maggots or a fish eye and used as a lift-fall "flash jig." Usually fish the bait in combination with a minnow hooked parallel to the dorsal fin for perch and white bass. A good walleye option, too. One side of the body glows, with various color options on the other side.

Rocker Minnow—A lead-bodied flash lure. Great for all aggressive perch or perch in deeper water, plus big crappies and white bass. The entire body glows. Another fine walleye lure.

Rocker Minnow

Hawger Spoon—A bent-bodied metal slab spoon provides lots of flash and action. Prism strips provide the glow. The 1-inch size is dynamite on perch and white bass, or use a larger size for perch in deeper water.

Hawger Spoon

Various Tears, Rockers, and Bugs— Choices of many tiny baits with slight design variances offer slight differences in triggering power.

Glow Bug

Points To Remember

•Phosphorescence isn't magic, but neither is it a gimmick.

•Phosphorescent baits should be incorporated into an efficient fishing system. Phosphorescence, however, won't make up for basic location and presentation problems.

•The principal advantage to phosphorescence is visibility—fish more likely see your offering. Often, however, natural colors or standard bright colors trigger fish better.

•Phosphorescence isn't guaranteed to double your catch or revolutionize panfishing through the ice. But you never know.

CHAPTER 8

MORE ABOUT PANFISH... BLUEGILLS, CRAPPIES, PERCH, AND WHITE BASS

Never met a panfish I didn't like, in the water or in the pan.

Doug Stange

E quipment's important (Chapter 2). The system's vital (Chapter 3). You won't catch many fish without understanding attraction and triggering with a jigging approach (Chapter 5). Understanding changing environmental parameters are important, too (Chapter 6). But location remains the first step in catching fish. And panfish location is principally influenced by forage (Chapter 7).

"Thing is," Doug suggested to Al and Dave, "panfish are more numerous than predators like walleyes, pike, and bass." Dave and Al nodded, "Obvious!" So where was Doug leading?

"An energy pyramid illustrates an important idea that influences fish location," Doug continued. "The broad base of the pyramid is formed by micro plants (phytoplankton) that use energy from the sun to produce food. The next step includes micro animals (zooplankton) that feed on these plants. Another step includes minnows and other small fish that feed on the plankton. Bluegills, crappies, and perch, another step up, feed on zooplankton and minnows. The top spot's for predators like pike.

"The original energy from the sun is transferred from step to step. But as it's transferred up the ladder it's also lost. Less energy supports less life, so organisms on top of the pyramid are less numerous than those on the bottom. Middle-steppers like bluegills and crappies are more abundant than top-line predators. Most of the time, only a couple key pike patterns will be going in an entire lake, because there aren't that many pike. But 4 or 5 bluegill patterns may be going on the same bar because there are so many bluegills."

"Good point," Dave emphasized. "But even with many panfish patterns cracking, several usually are better than others."

"And big panfish are another story," Al interjected. "Big panfish are more like top-line predators. If you're going to find the key pattern, the pattern that means the most fish, or the pattern that means the biggest fish, you have to search. That's why 'the system' we discussed so thoroughly in Chapter 3 is so important."

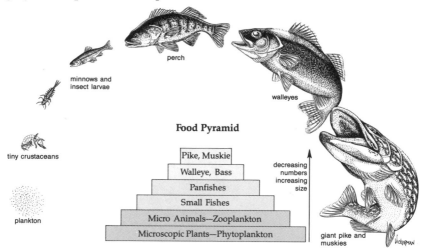

Food Pyramid

"But let's talk reality for a moment," Doug offered. "Truth is that most 'good' catches are the result of taking a few fish here and there from scattered smaller concentrations. Scattered concentrations are part of the pattern. Often you don't seem to be catching much, but like magic, the ol' bucket gets heavy by day's end."

And what does it take to improve chances for heavy buckets?

"If this is beginning to sound like a broken record, we're making headway," Dave said, preparing to answer the question. "Again, consistent fishing success is the result of applying an efficient approach to searching areas where panfish should be. We've already said that panfish feed on vaguely similar prey, so you can use some of the same equipment, baits, and lures to catch them. It's also not unusual to find bluegills, crappies, perch, and white bass on the same areas of a structural element.

"But each fish is different, too, and at times that means they may be on

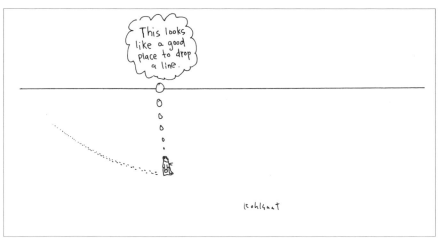

much different portions of a structural element—or even on different structural elements."

"And even in different lake areas," Al interjected.

"With fishing experience," Al continued, "you have an idea where fish will be and when. But let's discuss specific examples later. Let's stick with the idea that you need to search major structural elements. Say you're going to fish a major main-lake bar. Search shallow, search the edge of the shallows (drop-off), and maybe the base of the bar in deep water. And if you're after crappies, you may need to search open water beyond the edge of the bar."

"But you're already getting a step too specific mentioning the crappies off the edge of the bar," Doug said. "Stick with the bar."

"Granted, every main-lake bar won't hold lots of fish. But most major bars will. Search right, and by the end of the day you may discover a variety of patterns.

"Lots of bluegills of various sizes, plus a few big crappies and perch might be roaming shallow along remaining pockets of weedgrowth. Bigger crappies might be suspended at mid-depth along the edge of the bar, while a few big bluegills might be in deep water near a small rock pile close to the base of the bar. As evening approaches, you're ready to make a judgement about where you should fish during prime time."

But what specifically should fishermen look for when they're searching?

"Cover," Al said. "Particularly edges in cover. Edges are formed where two distinctly different areas or conditions meet. Major edges include (1) where deep water and shallow water meet along the edge of a bar, especially if weedgrowth, timber, or brush extend to the drop-off; (2) where distinct weedgrowth on a flat meets an open area where weed pockets have formed; and (3) where sand or sandy muck meets gravel or rock, especially when weeds are present.

"Cut holes and look with sonar, so much the better if you've fished the structural element during open water. When you find fish, fine tune. Small teardrops or tiny leadhead jigs and grubs or maggots are good options to begin your search with because everything will eat them. A search lure's (Chapter 7) a good choice, too."

"Fine tuning—right," Dave said, continuing the discussion for Al. "Might need to switch colors. Might need to go smaller or larger. Might need to switch lure types. Might need to increase or decrease the number of maggots on your lure or how you hook them. Might need to try different depths—different jigging motions. And on and on. Fine tuning is based on the species, where they're holding, and the feeding mode they're in."

"Get specific for a moment," Doug told Al. "Say you begin searching with something fairly heavy and visible like a #6 ant—chartreuse with red dots, dressed with a lively maggot. Say you run into a bunch of good-size perch holding near sandgrass patches on a sand flat. Say you're catching an occasional fish, but it appears many more fish aren't going for the ant."

"First thing I'd assume is that maybe the presentation isn't big enough or flashy enough to be visible to enough perch to attract them to bite," Al said. "Most folks would assume the opposite, that the fish are off, and therefore try another color or smaller bait. And that may be right. But lots of times when perch are cracking they ignore small in favor of larger. Or they just don't see smaller items. They can't eat what they can't see.

"I'd probably try a small flash lure like a Kastmaster, Swedish Pimple, or Rocker Minnow, or a small swimming jig like a Rapala or a Swimmin' Ratt tipped with maggots. Sometimes a fish eye or a minnow head works

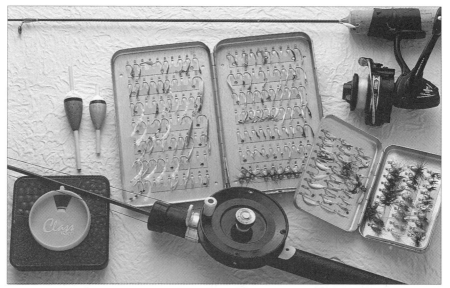

Start searching with something all panfish will eat. Then fine tune .

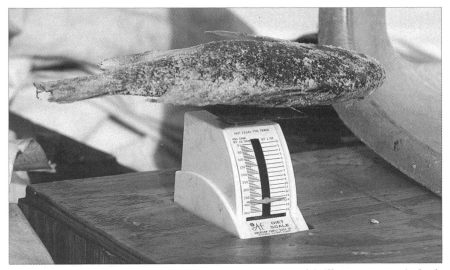

Think you've landed a big one? Honest one-pound 'gills are scarce; indeed, on-the-scale 12-ouncers are big fish anywhere in North America. Weigh 'em with a dietary scale for an honest weight.

better than maggots; consider that option if the fish didn't go on maggots. I'd soon know how active the fish were. If they seemed to go after the flashier bait, I might indeed try a swimming bait, especially once I'd caught some perch and the fishing slowed.

"Another option," Al continued. "Drop a small blank leadhead jig packed with maggots. It's the kind of bait lots of fishermen overlook; a bait that has a swimming movement when steadily jigged; a bait that can represent either a minnow or tiny crustacean. It's an easy bait to bounce on the bottom, too. Perch love that at times. It's just one of the best perch baits.

"Finally, if the fish are really touchy, I might try small teardrops or jigs, maybe even a #8 or #10 hook weighted with lead wire—tipped with maggots. Subtle colors, too—cream, gray, maybe black."

"No minnows in the equation?" Doug asked.

"Oh yeah, minnows. Forgot," Al replied. "I rarely find it necessary to use minnows. But they can be the deal for perch in a few situations. When fish are off, drop a tiny minnow on a teardrop jig or leadhead jig. Reverse the minnow, though."

"Of course, the presentation you begin searching with is dependent on the species and habitat," Doug said. "We presumed to search shallow, not knowing which species we'd find. We found perch and we adjusted our presentation to find the key to catching as many as possible. Take a different tact now. Say we're after perch in 40 feet of water at the base of the drop-off. What do we begin with? And what might we switch to after we contact fish?"

"You have to get down quickly," Al said. "It'll take 45 seconds to drop a #6 ant without shot to the bottom; and adding shot to a small presentation doesn't fish well in deep water. You need a compact presentation with flash, like a 1/10- or 1/16-ounce Kastmaster or Rocker Minnow tipped with a minnow head or fish eye. Sometimes you might even begin with a bigger flash lure, like a 1/3- or 1/4-ounce Northland Fire-Eye Minnow or a Kastmaster or a Rocker Minnow.

"Cracking fish good? Stick with the bait. Fish slowing down? Try a swimming lure like a #3 Swimming Rapala (tipped with a fish eye or minnow head). Or if the fish are touchy, switch to Doug's search lure."

"No minnows this time?" Doug asked.

"Too much trouble to fish in deep water," Al answered.

"Back to the bar, Dave," Doug instructed. "Say you run into 6- to

Eurolarvae

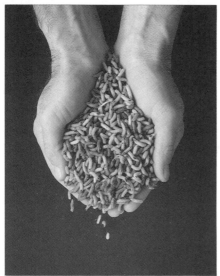

Eurolarvae or maggies, one of the deadliest all-round live baits for panfish, are living, wriggling maggots in colors ranging from blue to orange to yellow or red to white. Most anglers don't know how to properly hook them. To trigger reluctant panfish, hook the maggots through their little fannies.

Pick one up and you'll see a pointed end and a fat end. You'll see two black dots on the fat end. Roll the fat end between your thumb and index finger so it bulges. Now place your hook through the tip of the fat end. A sharp hook will slide through without injuring vital organs.

A clear liquid will ooze out of a properly hooked bait. Hooked too deeply, liquid the color of the maggot oozes out. They still work hooked this way, but not as well.

Maggot Tipping

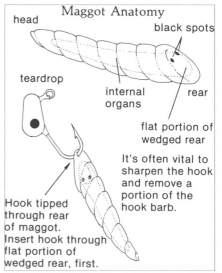

Maggot Anatomy

head

black spots

teardrop

internal organs

rear

flat portion of wedged rear

It's often vital to sharpen the hook and remove a portion of the hook barb.

Hook tipped through rear of maggot. Insert hook through flat portion of wedged rear, first.

Maggots will stay alive for hours if they're hooked so their internal organs aren't injured.

10-ounce bluegills instead of perch. Remember you began with the ant. Fine tune."

"The #6 ant is a good search lure, Doug," Dave began, "but it's on the large end of the scale for 'gills. Fine tuning almost certainly calls for a smaller bait. Before I'd go smaller, though, I might try something gaudy like a flipper jig (Chapter 7).

"Then I'd stick with a bright color, but drop to a #8 ant with one maggot. I might try dropping extra maggots down the hole, too—a steady stream of maggots dropping slowly through the water column to get fish interested or keep them interested. You can see the maggots drop on your depthfinder. You can also see how the 'gills react to them.

"Time to experiment with color. Try another bright color—hot pink or orange. Try phosphorescence. Try a subtle color—grey, cream, or black. Try a different lure style—a basic tear. Finally, go smaller. Lots of days during midwinter, #10s, #12s, and #14s will take fish when nothing else will."

Although the guys could have gone on with other panfish species in dozens of other situations, the point had been made. Search for patterns in obvious areas. Fine tune, given the species and the habitat they're in.

BLUEGILLS

Bluegills are widely distributed in ponds, reservoirs, river backwaters, and natural lakes across the U.S. and into southern Canada. And they bite well all winter. Sure, tough days occur. And fishing for huge 'gills—honest 1-pound fish—is as tough as catching a 30-pound muskie. But 'gills of average size usually cooperate if you use a mobile fishing system, and they're a treat on the table .

Chapter 7 keyed on the importance of plankton in the diet of panfish. While bluegills often depend mainly on plankton, other panfish often target other forage. Being grazers, bluegills need to be active longer than other panfish in order to take in enough food. It's the reason they bite so well, and it's the reason they're probably the most popular winter panfish.

Widely distributed. Willing biters. Pound fish are a challenge. That's bluegills.

The expansive shallow and deep weedgrowth that attracts bluegills usually harbor lots of plankton.

Knots for Ultralight Line

Line is the focal point for ultra-light fishing, and as lines get lighter, knot tying becomes critical. You must know four basic knots to work with extra-light line.

TRILENE KNOT: A general-purpose knot for attaching an "eyed" hook to your line.

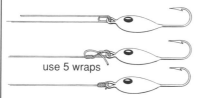

use 5 wraps

BACK SNELL: A general-purpose knot for attaching a spade-end hook to your line. It's easier to tie, but provides less knot strength than a nail knot.

5 back wraps and back through loop

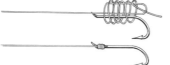

NAIL KNOT: A knot for attaching line to your shock tippet.

NAIL SNELL: A general-purpose knot for attaching a spade-end hook to your line. More difficult to tie, but more consistently strong than the back snell.

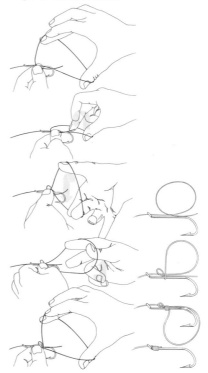

1. Make a loop in the line in front of the hook shank.
2. Pinch the front of the loop to the hook shank with one hand. Insert your thumb and index finger from your opposite hand in the bottom and top of the loop, respectively.
3. Keeping the loop open with your fingers, lift a portion of the loop with your thumb moving up and toward you as you drop the opposite portion of the loop by moving your index finger away from you. Wrap the loop around the hook shank and the end of the tag line. One wrap is completed as the thumb reaches the top and the index finger the bottom. The tag end of the line must always point straight back.
4. Twist your fingers back to Position 1 and make 5 more wraps. Pinch each successive wrap in place with your opposite thumb and index finger.
5. To finish the knot, your hands first must trade positions; that is, the fingers making the loops must now pinch the loop wraps to the shank of the hook. Remove the large loop at the bend of the hook by gently drawing on the main line. Again, trade hand positions. Remove the tiny loop at the head of the hook by biting the tag end and gently drawing on it with your teeth. Trim the knot.

Sometimes these plankton are visible. Cut a hole in the ice and plankton may kick and bob in it. Powerful depthfinders, too, particularly the Vexlar FL-8 (new version of the Micronar FL-8 and Hondex FL-8), will show tightly grouped plankton packs. Bluegills often are at the level of the plankton. During midday, this usually is at the bottom.

"The most productive areas usually are shallow," Dave offered. "And cover generally increases productivity. Shallow bays, creek arms, river backwaters, and ponds tend to produce lots of plankton and in turn attract bluegills. This is especially true if these areas offer cover—weeds, brush, or timber. Shallow bars or humps with cover on main-lake areas or flats in reservoirs and ponds also harbor 'gills. But they may also sus-

Setting Euro-Style Ice Floats

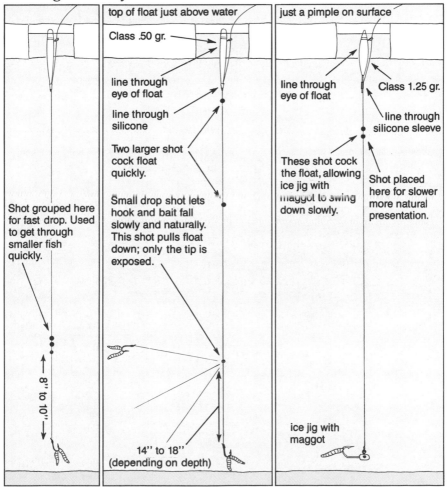

Randall Akin, European tackle expert, suggests these settings for Euro-style ice floats.

pend in open water or lie near deep-lying rock piles."

Current moves plankton and attracts minnows that perch, crappies, and white bass feed on. But bluegills, which tend to focus on plankton, have a difficult time with drifting plankton. The most productive areas for bluegills usually are away from current.

"Another point," Dave offered. "While shallow areas periodically host scores of 'gills during winter, the most consistent midwinter spots usually are near deeper water. A 5-foot river backwater with an 8- to 10-foot hole has potential to produce 'gills all winter. The deeper water holds fish during major weather changes. Check deeper areas with a depthfinder after a weather change, and you'll usually find suspended fish."

CRAPPIES

The crappie's flat compact body allows quick, responsive turns in and around weeds and brush. Its sleek head-to-tail shape permits successful, but limited use of open water—usually confined open water.

Deep water is a large expanse of water where fish relate to light penetration, water stratification (thermoclines), forage, and occasionally the bottom. True open-water fish are powerfully built and streamlined, so they can easily travel long distances and quickly charge into roaming schools of bait. Chinook salmon and stripers are open-water fish.

The nite-bite often is the right-bite for crappies.

Confined open water, on the other hand, is open water on a smaller scale. Confined open water always is near structure. In large bays, for example, confined open water often is present in the center. But the bottom, surface, shorelines, and weedlines always are close by.

"In large bodies of water, confined open water extends off weedlines, timberlines, or points," Doug instructed. "At some point, though, association with the weedline, timberline, or point is lost. At that point, open water begins. Water relatively close to a weedline, timberline, point, or inside turn may be confined open water.

"Crappies often use confined open water, but rarely use true open water. One exception occurs at late-ice when crappies roam the basins of lakes or reservoirs (or portions thereof) relating only to forage."

Much like bass, crappies are "ambush" predators only when at rest and in a negative or neutral feeding mood. When crappies are feeding, they're hunters.

The hunt usually takes them to areas where zooplankton and min-

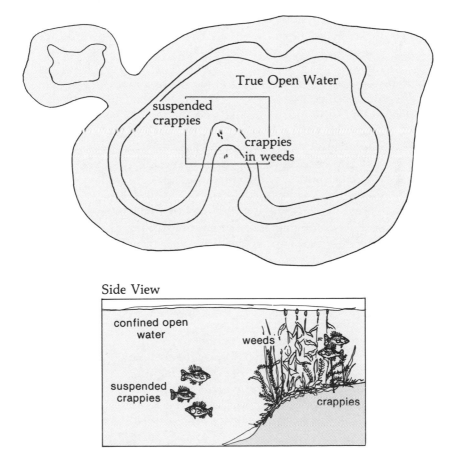

nows—preferred forage—are concentrated. Resting crappies often suspend in confined open water or near obvious cover. Crappies, like most predators, are opportunists. Their tendency to suspend and their body construction lets them function in cover or confined open water.

"Crappies are light sensitive," Al reminded. "In clear water they often bite best during twilight, after dark, or in deeper water during early morning and late afternoon. The heavy ice and snow cover of late season, however, often reduces light penetration and may allow midday feeding. During first-ice, crappies holding in or near weed or timber cover commonly bite during midday.

"In lakes with dingy water, crappies often bite consistently in shallow water right through midday. Even on these lakes, though, crappies tend to bite best at twilight; changing light intensity stimulates feeding. Our experience, though, is that night bites aren't consistent on lakes with dingy water."

Crappies at Early-Ice

At first-freeze on relatively large shallow bays or creek arms, some minnow life begins to move from the bay or creek arm toward the main body of water. At late-ice, bait often moves back into the bay or creek arm.

Bait moves from the shallows to hold in the first main lake or reservoir cover encountered, such as:

- Weeds, timber, or brush on an adjacent main-lake or reservoir flat.
- Weedlines or timberlines near the edges of the flat.
- The drop-off area at the edges of the flat.

"When bait begins to move out, crappies move in," Al said. "Not into the shallow bay or creek arm, but into areas adjacent to the mouth of the bay or creek arm.

"Perhaps first-ice causes a plankton bloom," he continued. "First-ice often is clear ice, allowing more light penetration than open water. Whatever the case, plankton in bays or creek arms seem to move via water currents, probably caused by the slight water temperature contrast between the deeper main body of water and the shallower bay or creek arm."

Prominent structural elements attract more baitfish. The bay or creek arm must be shallow enough so freeze-up or cold weather prior to freeze-up causes a bait migration from that area.

A bay or creek arm with a deep hole or channel may upset this pattern, because the bait may not move toward the main lake. Still, the flat or drop-off at the mouth of the bay is worth fishing. In the creek arm, try the flat or drop-off next to the channel. And if the hole inside the bay or the fringe of the creek channel concentrates forage, it'll attract crappies.

"The narrower the mouth of a bay or creek arm, the more bait and crappies will likely channel into a specific area," Al observed. "In a wide

"Bait Out, Crappies In"

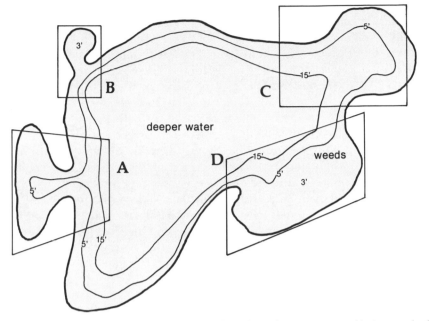

The "bait out, crappies in" pattern is based on the movement of bait out of relatively shallow bays into main-lake areas where they are intercepted by crappies. The best crappie fishing usually occurs outside large relatively shallow bays with narrow main-lake openings. The narrow main-lake opening should lead to a fairly deep and moderate-size flat, with cover extending to the drop-off.

Area A—A relatively shallow bay with a narrow opening to a cover-filled main-lake flat. Everything you're looking for except a distinct area on the flat or drop-off to concentrate fish. One of the best (perhaps the best) first-ice areas on the lake.

Area B—The bay is too small to hold much bait, and the flat is too small to hold many crappies. But any crappies attracted to bait moving out of this bay will be in the clearly defined area of the inside turn just outside the bay. If this inside turn was at the mouth of Area A, you'd have a tremendous spot!

Area C—The opening at the mouth of the bay is too large, and the flat outside the bay is too large to concentrate fish, but crappies will be here. The drop-off is a plus. The 15-foot water juts into the bay and creates a holding area.

Area D—Plenty of bait and crappies, but everything's spread, making fishing more difficult.

Fish Area A first, followed by Area C. Check Area B quickly before moving to Area C. Areas C and D would probably offer the most sustained crappie activity all winter.

bay or creek arm mouth, bait may leave the shallows at many different points. Crappies roam and are hard to pinpoint. The best fishing occurs when structure funnels baitfish and predators into confined areas.

"Later, as bait leaving a bay or creek arm contact the first main-lake or reservoir flat, crappies congregate there. A good flat should have cover, usually remaining stands of leafy pondweed (cabbage), timber, or both. A flat without cover won't hold fish. The flat should also be as deep as the bay or creek arm adjacent to it. Better if it's deeper.

"In a lake, the best scenario is a 7- to 15-foot-deep flat adjoining a 3- to 7-foot-deep bay. In a reservoir, look for a 7- to 15-foot flat and creek channel adjacent to the creek arm. Inside the creek arm, the flats would be 3 to 7 feet deep and the channel no deeper than 7 to 10 feet.

"These are optimum conditions, though. Depths of bays and flats vary depending on where you fish. The key is a contrast in depth between the shallower bay or creek arm and deeper adjacent structural elements."

The size of the main lake or reservoir flat makes a difference. But it's not so simple as "large flat, lotsa fish—small flat, few fish." A small flat adjoining a big bay can mean dynamite fishing. Once bait leave and crappies move in, few locational choices exist for crappies.

But small flats don't hold many fish for long. Big flats with cover adjacent to big bays or creek arms, on the other hand, may hold crappies for a long time. They may roam, though.

If the flat portion of a major main-lake or reservoir bar holds crappies, the adjacent drop-off will too. But even when flats hold few fish, drop-offs may still hold them. Expect the most consistent crappie activity to take place : (1) in confined open water just outside the drop-off; (2) immediately along the drop-off; or (3) on the portion of the flat adjacent to the

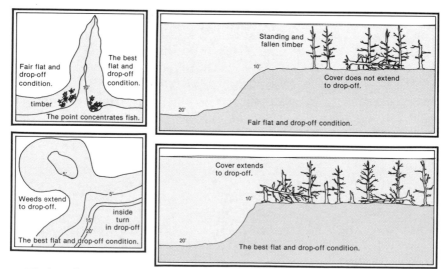

The best flats outside relatively large shallow bays offer plenty of cover extending to the drop-off. The best drop-offs have points or inside turns to concentrate fish.

drop-off.

"The drop-off area must be distinct, although it doesn't need to fall into the deepest water in the area," Doug said to Al and Dave. "A distinct drop-off has a quick depth change or an abrupt halt to cover. The best drop-offs have a depth change and cover extending to the drop-off. In a reservoir, look for a timber-covered flat adjacent to a drop-off into the main reservoir. In a lake, look for weedgrowth extending to the drop-off.

"Add the score so far. Good fishing usually occurs outside large relatively shallow bays or creek arms with a narrow main-lake or reservoir opening. The opening should lead to a fairly deep and moderate-size flat with cover extending to the drop-off.

"In early winter, crappies relate to major structural elements. Key your search around bars, humps, and sunken islands. Check shallow flats; the outside edges of weedbeds; pockets in weeds; or confined open water slightly away from weeds or other cover."

Midwinter and Late-Ice Crappie Location

As winter progresses, many crappies vacate the shallows and school outside weedbeds or in basin areas. Even at late-ice, most crappies are in these areas, although some may again roam shallow flats.

Crappie schools often become "basin drifters," moving a lot, staying with sources of food—zooplankton and minnows. These crappies may be difficult to find and to stay on.

"Again, though," Doug added, "a few obvious spots tend to gather basin drifters. Any indentations in the drop-off, like inside turns, especially if they're located at the end of a lake, collect randomly moving crappies. Also check inside turns along the drop-off that forms the main basin of the lake."

Lures and Baits

The traditional rig for crappies through the ice includes a small minnow on a #6, #8, or #10 hook, held in place by lead shot. The rig is suspended below a bobber.

Dave believes you'll catch more crappies on an ice fly and Eurolarvae (maggots) than on a tiny hook with minnows. "Not only that," he says, "you'll catch more bluegills along with crappies when you use tiny baits."

Even large crappies often feed on tiny zooplankton no bigger than a pinhead. Teardrops and other ice flies, hooks weighted with wire, and small leadhead jigs dressed with grubs imitate zooplankton.

Leadhead jigs are a fine option when you're searching for fish. You can easily move a jig dressed with a grub or two from hole to hole; no hooking and unhooking minnows or sticking your hand into a bait bucket. Once you find fish, continue with the jig and grub or switch to a teardrop and minnow, a plain minnow, or another jigging lure.

"My theory," Dave offered, "is that you often catch fish in shallow

Breakline Panfish

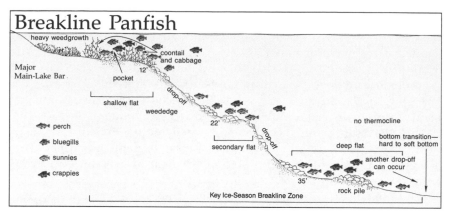

Find a major main-lake bar or point. Now find the key breakline zone that runs from the edge of the shallow flat to the transition from harder to softer bottom at the base of the deep flat. Panfish territory.

The weededge at the end of a shallow flat is one key area. Perch, bluegills, sunnies, and crappies use this edge, although crappies also suspend just away from it during morning and evening. Panfish also often tuck into weedgrowth on the flat or suspend just above it during the day. Look for pockets on the flat or in the edge of the weeds.

Panfish generally don't hold on quick-breaking drop-offs. They use the gradual drop-offs, however, in some shallow lakes.

Secondary flats between major shallow and deep flats can attract perch, bluegills, and crappies if the flats are large enough. The basin area is a better bet.

A deep flat begins at the bottom of a distinct drop-off and usually is part of the lake basin. Here bottom content usually softens.

In deep lakes, deep flats may be 40 to 60 feet deep. Other drop-offs may occur beyond the first deep flat.

Lakes with large adjacent bays often have basin areas with comparatively different depths. Perhaps the basin flat in a large bay begins in 25 feet of water, while the basin flat in the main lake begins in 40 feet of water.

Occasionally, bluegills are attracted to basin areas with rock piles. These bluegills often are some of the largest 'gills in a body of water.

Crappies also use basin flats, especially the immediate base of the flat when the drop-off is rock. Crappies also relate to rock humps beyond the base of a drop-off.

Perch love deep flats and often scatter on them. Perch concentration points usually are near the base of the deep flat or near a bottom transition from harder to softer bottom. Often the two coincide.

water without minnows, because they're sight feeding. It's harder to catch fish without live bait in colored or deeper water because those fish are tuned more to vibrations. Their sense of smell and taste and vibration help trigger the strike. The thing has to smell, taste, and feel like prey."

Morning, Noon, or Night

Doug began, "Can't tell you exactly when crappies will bite in the bodies of water you fish, but we can talk tendencies. Consider four major fishing zones: (1) the flat, (2) the small slice of flat immediately adjacent to the drop-off, (3) the drop-off, and (4) the confined open water off the drop-off. Crappie activity's possible in all 4 areas during the twilight periods (morning and evening) when changing light intensity often triggers crappies."

"In dingy water, though," Dave added, "crappie activity usually occurs during the day in any of the 4 areas. But the zone in confined open water is a marginal zone because crappies tend to relate to something definite. We also haven't done well at night on these waters, but that may not be the case everywhere."

Al continued, "In clear water, look for daytime activity only on flats with good cover. Even then expect fishing to be sporadic because the fish are likely scattered. Look for schooling fish off the drop-off or the flat immediately adjacent to the drop-off. Confined open water usually holds more fish. Expect intense night feeding on the drop-off and flat. Although night activity may occur in confined open water, it's more common there during midwinter late-ice."

Crappie activity often occurs at evening twilight, then shuts off abruptly and begins again an hour or two later. Doug theorizes that crappies have a vision advantage over minnow prey during twilight hours and after dark. Perhaps activity usually slows for a short time just after dark because crappies need time for their eyes to adjust to darkness.

PERCH

Arguably the best fish on the table.

In the water they're a challenge, especially jumbos of a pound or more. On the table you're flirting with perfection. And they're fun to catch.

Yellow perch are opportunists. Some perch may hold near rock and gravel, while others are on sand or muck; some may be deep, while others are shallow. Perch usually relate to the bottom, but they also suspend. And perch love weedgrowth, too.

Perch feed on zooplankton, larvae, and other tiny foods. But because they have a fairly large mouth, they can feed on a range of prey sizes. Their food may be shallow, deep, on the bottom, or even suspended. You'll find perch wherever their food is.

Key Locational Patterns

Even though many fishing patterns exist for perch at any time, one basic pattern usually can be used to find them. Perch activity usually centers around one type of spawning area, especially during first-ice and just before ice-out—two consistently productive periods for perch.

Recognizing a perch spawning area is easy. Some perch usually use shoals (bars) in about 2 to 8 feet of water. These shoals usually are composed of rock-rubble or rock and gravel mixed with sand. Perch, however, lay their eggs in long adhesive strings and attach them to weedgrowth. So hard-bottom bars with some weedgrowth are good perch

Basic Perch Patterns

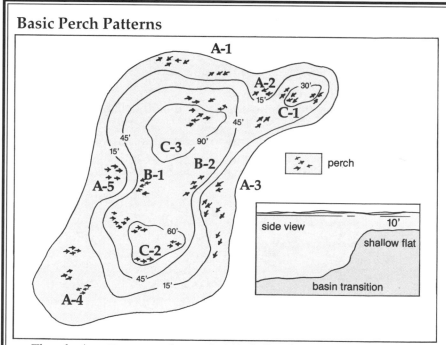

Three basic pattern areas for perch: (A) shallow bars; (B) basin transitions; and (C) basins.

Bar A-1—*Indistinct bars like A-1 often are overlooked, but may attract as many perch as obvious bars if they offer characteristics that attract perch forage. Generally, look for harder bottoms in conjunction with weedgrowth. Perch, however, often use bars without weedgrowth during some winter periods. Search. Perch often are grouped in general areas.*

Bar A-2—*Obvious. Not difficult to search quickly. At the mouth of a fertile shallow bay, therefore a prime gathering point for wandering perch.*

spawning areas. Shoals vary in size, but expect larger bars to produce the most consistent activity.

"So one basic way to find perch any time of year," Doug said, "is to locate a large bar—very large if possible. The more varied the structural elements or options, the better. Again, though, the bottom will typically be hard, but vegetation remains a key factor. When perch are shallow, they tend to function like sunfish and crappies; they're attracted to areas with lots of zooplankton and minnow forage.

"In lakes without many bluegills or crappies, shallow weedy areas are primary perch spots."

Fish of Flats

"It's seldom considered," Doug suggested, "but perch are fish of flats,

---

Bar A-3—*An obvious main-lake bar with characteristics to attract perch. Should hold perch all year. Start at the edge of the drop-off and work shallower while another fisherman works deeper along the basin transition. A top spot, although perch often are scattered.*

Bar A-4—*An interior flat. Overlooked, but a big deal for perch so long as hard bottom coincides with weedgrowth. Remember that weeds don't always have to be standing tall. Matted coontail and cabbage, or even sparse sandgrass holds perch forage. Perch may be scattered, but you aren't likely to have competition. Bonanza time when you get on them*

Bar A-5—*Same as A-3 on paper. Gotta fish it. May be much better than the other bars. Any bar may also hold perch for unknown reasons while seemingly similar bars are devoid of fish.*

Transition B-1 and B-2—*The obvious transition areas will be off obvious main-lake bars. But transitions exist around the lake wherever hard bottom becomes soft bottom in deeper water. Other key areas to check include off any areas where you find perch shallow during early or midwinter. Check the zone off A-2, also.*

Basin C-1—*Potentially a hot spot all winter, but particularly at late-ice. Smaller, shallower basins in bays tend to offer more fertility and therefore more forage to attract perch. Such areas are easier to fish and to find fish too.*

Basins C-2 and C-3—*On paper it's difficult to say which basin might be better. C-2 is within a fishable depth range, while you have to fish edges around the 90-foot water in C-3.*

Narrowing the search in basins: Begin by checking basin areas in the ends of lakes. In C-2, begin in the south portion of the basin. In C-3, begin in the basin area of the bay.

Once perch drop into basin areas, so many fish often are present that it isn't difficult to catch fish.

not drop-offs. Perch rarely use drop-off areas. Small groups of perch might hold along a drop-off, especially where it leads onto a small flat. But most perch usually hold on big flats.

"Perch may be shallow and perch may be deep, but they're almost always concentrated on flats. Shallow fish will be looking for minnows along or in weedgrowth or along rock edges.

"On the other hand, small minnows in deep water are attracted to areas with lots of tiny crustaceans, fry, and insect larvae. In deep water, that means softer bottom areas which are away from drop-offs. Drop-offs usually have hard bottoms."

At first-ice, the most consistent activity usually is in shallow water (3 to 15 feet) near standing or matted weedgrowth. Look for edges in cover on flats. Weededges, pockets in those edges or in weedbeds, and the transitions where sand meets rock, gravel, or mud may attract fish.

During late-ice, jumbos often roam shallow water again. But too many anglers fail to focus on perch in deeper water off spawning areas. Perch hold near transition areas where the bottom type changes from harder to softer material. This transition may be as shallow as 8 feet in a fertile shallow dishpan-shape prairie lake, or as deep as 50 feet or more in moderately infertile lakes with distinct drop-offs and maximum depths over about 70 feet.

"The squeeze moves perch consistently deeper during midwinter," Al noted. "At late-ice, hard-to-soft bottom transition areas on deep flats at or beyond the base of a drop-off consistently attract the most perch. To find this transition, find the portion of the bar that drops into the lake basin. On shallow lakes, look for a major hard-bottom bar—more likely a huge flat that gradually drops and extends to the lake basin. Expect a major concentration of perch near the bottom transition where sand and clay become softer."

"Same process works for finding a transition zone in a deeper lake," Doug offered. "There, however, a basin doesn't have to be the deepest water in the lake. Say a big bay exists off the main lake, with a shallow flat extending to 12 feet before breaking quickly to 18 feet. A small shelf runs from 18 to 25 feet and then a secondary drop-off breaks to 35 feet before flattening out. The transition point between hard and soft bottom will be at or beyond the base of the 35-foot break.

"By comparison, a main-lake bar may gradually extend to 15 feet before dropping directly into 50 feet of water. The transition point here may be at or beyond the base of the drop-off, even though the deepest water in the lake is over 100 feet deep. How deep will perch go? We've caught them to 70 feet, and they're certainly deeper at times, but fishing becomes difficult that deep.

"The transition point is rarely distinct and rarely are perch concentrated in such areas. They'll more likely be scattered on a deep flat. They won't swim like robots following a precise transition point, even when one exists.   Instead, they're foraging—grazing—on tiny crustaceans, worms, insect larvae, and fish fry. The only consistent way to find them is to fish the general area. So many perch gather in such general areas that

The Perch Search

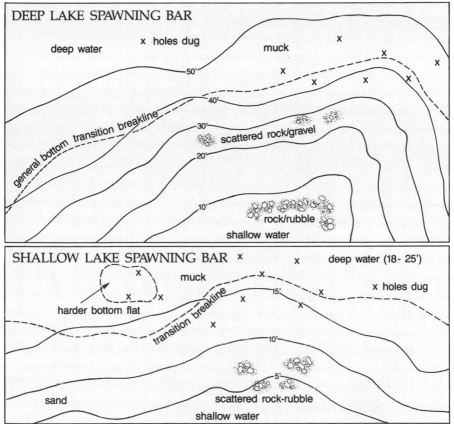

Perch may be in many different lake areas, but one consistent pattern centers near large bars where perch spawn shortly after ice-out. Look for hard-bottom shoals with remaining weedgrowth in 1 to 8 feet of water. But key your fishing deep, where the bottom transition from harder to softer bottom begins.

To find this transition area, fish the drop-off that leads to the lake basin. Find the base of the drop-off; the transition usually begins somewhere on the flat beyond the base of the drop-off. Sometimes the transition is detectable with a depthfinder (distinct bottom reading becomes indistinct) or with a heavier lure (a thump becomes a sticky thud when the lure is bounced on the bottom).

Perch don't key on the exact transition line, but on the general area that often attracts perch forage. Probe the deep flat around the transition area. Once you've found them, they aren't as likely to move as the perch in shallower water. A deep-water pattern may hold for weeks unless too many fishermen are working the area.

you'll often have fast fishing."

One interesting late-season predator-prey relationship occurs in shallow eutrophic perch lakes. Red worms live in the softer bottom areas. The bodies of these worms are built like small accordions. During most periods, the worms burrow into the bottom and are unavailable to perch. But during late-ice, oxygen levels decrease and the worms do their accordion act, extending their bodies above the bottom to absorb more oxygen. That's when perch feed on them, even though you'd think the low oxygen levels would turn perch off.

Perch in Bays

"Okay," Al said, after thinking about what we'd covered. "We've talked about finding perch on major bars, points, humps, and basins. The rest of the story is that you'll find 'em in major bays with plenty of harder bottoms—large bays relative to other bays on the lake. Not a little bass spawning bay, but a bay area that's like a little lake.

"Say you have a 5,000-acre lake with a 100- or even 200-acre bay. Say the bay has the same patterns as the main lake, only on a smaller scale. But in this 100-acre bay, you'll find more shallow than deep water and typically a lot more vegetation than in the rest of the lake. Vegetation patterns in the bay, therefore, are a lot more important."

"Shallow's more important in bay patterns," Doug added. "But big bays can have deep water, too. And just like the general tendency for fish in larger bodies of water, including perch, to move deeper as the winter progresses, perch in a big bay with deep water, say 30 feet or more, also move deeper.

"So at first-ice, key on shallow flats on a main-lake bar, and shallow weedy flats in the bay. But as winter wears on, the deep basin of the main lake could hold a lot of perch; likewise the basin of the bay."

Gear and Tackle for Perch

In shallower lakes where finesse is needed, try a rod like HT Enterprises HT Lite, a Jig-A-Whopper Panfish Rod, or Berkley's Northern Lite. Tape a small closed-face spincasting reel like Zebco's UL4 Classic, or a spinning reel like a Shakespeare 025 to the handle.

Most of your fishing will be in 10 to 25 feet of water. But in water deeper than 35 feet, use a longer and slightly stiffer rod—helps set hooks and maintain a tight line

Fill one reel with 2-pound-test line and another with 4-pound. Use the 2-pound option to present smaller ice flies and the 4-pound for tiny flash lures.

For shallower water: Try flies like the Jig-A-Whopper Flutter Bug or the Flash Rocker. The Flutter Bug is molded plastic with small bulges that contrast in color to the rest of the body. "Closest thing I've seen to live zooplankton," Doug remarked. "And it imitates the tiny fish fry and cad-

Nothing like a graphite rod-and-reel combo for fast, efficient, and fun fishing for perch.

dis larvae or blood worms that live in the soft basin mud of many lakes. Favorite color patterns for perch include yellow dots on hot red; hot red dots on yellow; or pink on white and black on green."

Four-Dot Rockers are solid-bodied jigs on bent hooks. They attract perch and are deadly hookers. Another option is tiny leadhead jigs like Custom Jigs and Spins' Rat Finkee or Heron's Jiggler. Lots of other companies make appropriate lures. And don't forget to try additional attractors like Wisconsin Tackle's Jiggle Skirt or Uncle Josh's Ice Flecks.

You can't beat Eurolarvae (maggots) for a companion live bait. Minnows, of course, often are deadly on perch, too. Try them on a plain hook anchored with shot or a teardrop. Run the hook parallel to the dorsal fin with the hook point toward the minnow's head, instead of the traditional method of hooking them perpendicular to and below the dorsal fin.

Flash lures for shallower fishing should be smaller than those you'd use for deep water. Favorites include 1-inch Acme Kastmasters, Custom Jigs and Spins' small Stinger, Worden's Skinny-Minny II, and Jig-A-Whopper's smallest Rocker Minnows.

For deeper water: Use slightly heavier Kastmasters, Rocker Minnows, and Walleye Hawgers. Try the two smallest Jigging Rapalas too, as well as 1/10- or 1/4-ounce Reef Runner Cicadas, and 1/16-ounce Wisconsin Tackle Swimmin' Ratts.

Tip these lures with maggots or a perch eye. "Do me a favor," Doug said. "Dispatch perch quickly before using their eyes for bait."

These baits will often be effective by themselves, but when fishing gets tough, try a search lure. The heavy lure gets deep fast, the flash attracts perch in deep water, and the small jig-and-maggot combo triggers reluctant fish.

WHITE BASS

White bass provide some of winter's fastest fishing when you find a school. Location and behavior varies with white bass population levels in the lakes or reservoirs you fish.

"Where large populations exist," Al remarked, "at times it may seem like whites are everywhere—on bars, along bars, in open water, deep and shallow.

"But white bass also roam when they're looking for food. Sometimes 80 percent of a population will congregate in a small portion of a body of water. In waters that get lots of pressure, someone usually finds fish— soon everyone knows. Patterns usually develop, too; the fish return to given areas during certain winter periods.

"White bass aren't classic structure-oriented fish. Even when they're in a general area and you catch some, they don't stay in specific spots for long. They find forage efficiently in open water, over shallow bars, or along the outside of bars."

No faster action when you find them.

High Percentage Location

High-percentage spots are similar to areas where you'd look for crappies. Check obvious structural elements like points and other areas that tend to congregate fish; check current areas or necked-down areas, too.

Causeways and narrow channels are another possibility.

A causeway, long point, or inside turn in the shoreline drop-off act like "catcher's mitts" to collect forage and whites. These spots tend to hold more food than open water holds, so white bass often remain until their food temporarily thins.

During early-ice, whites tend to be shallower than they are later. Even during midwinter, though, they rarely stay deep for long. Forty feet's deep.

"Most fish," Doug added, "function better in shallow water early in the winter, so white bass use areas like major structural elements in major bays and creek arms.

"Later, in reservoirs, white bass use points where creek arms enter the main body. They're rarely found in extremely shallow portions of creek arms or very shallow in bays.

"In reservoirs and natural lakes," Doug continued, "white bass will move through open water until they're gathered by a structural element that sticks into the lake basin. Or they might run into an inside turn that temporarily holds them. As they move along and around it, if they find forage, they'll stay. Once they're in an area, they may roam the shallow edge of a bar, moving at times up over the bar.

"They tend to be deeper later in winter, but may still hold 10 feet down over 35 feet of water."

Catching White Bass

Generally choose larger lures that fish more aggressively than typical panfish lures. Try flash lures like 1/4-ounce Jig-A-Whopper Rocker Minnows or Hawger Spoons; Northland Fire-Eye Minnows; #3, #5, and #7 Jigging Rapalas; 1/16- to 1/4-ounce Wisconsin Tackle Swimmin' Ratt Fools; or leadhead jigs (1/8 ounce) tipped with maggots or minnows.

Use an aggressive jigging presentation most of the time. "A small 1/4-ounce Airplane Jig," Al said, "hasn't been tried much for winter whites, but it would probably be a great bait."

White bass often compete aggressively for food. "Catching white bass," Al offered, "is a matter of the fish seeing a bait that represents something to eat. When the fishing gets tough, try smaller Jigging Raps or smaller minnows, and work them less aggressively. But you rarely need to use something as small as an ice fly."

CHAPTER 9

LARGEMOUTH AND SMALLMOUTH BASS

Not only can they be caught, but at times you can catch a bunch. But I haven't seen one jump, yet.   Doug Stange

I ce fishing for bass. The conversation was hesitant at first, as though we were tampering with a sort of grail, treading on the thick, hard waters of tradition.

In many respects, you see, Americans treat bass fishing with a reverence reserved for baseball; that is, the law of harmonious consumption decrees that bass fishing goes inflexibly with certain other things, and that among these are plastic worms, beads of sweat, and electric trolling motors. Above all, the playing field is not to be frozen over.

Times change. Years ago, in defiance of the bass fishing gods, Doug Stange and Dave Genz began catching bass through holes in the ice. And recently, Al has cracked his share, too.

Maybe bass don't have the greatest reputation under ice, precisely because much of their trademark drawing power—heart-stopping surface strikes and aerial leaps—are left behind when ice forms.

"I don't know why," said Dave, "but almost all the frozen-water bass catches I see or hear about seem to happen by accident while fishing for something else. Even my group—and we catch a lot of bass when we're fishing for panfish—rarely fish for bass."

Largemouth Bass

"More people might target largemouths if they realized how concentrated and cooperative they are at early- and late-ice," Doug noted. "They

Good fishing peaks at early-ice and late-ice, but may happen any time you're cutting lots of holes and searching efficiently with a depthfinder.

can become unpredictable during midwinter, but so are many other species.

"Fortunately, largemouths feed actively at first-ice; unfortunately, once they feed successfully, they may not feed again for a week. Keep your expectations within bounds. Turn to panfish for mass catches. But good news. Largemouth, bluegill, crappie, and perch concentrations often coincide, although bass aren't everywhere panfish are found.

"Finding bass under the ice is easy if you begin with a location principle. Largemouth bass in most natural lakes and in many reservoirs that ice over spend much of their time shallower than the lip of the first major drop-off. In natural lakes, look for bars close to spawning areas, usually shallow bays with lots of submergent vegetation.

"Say we have 100 bass on a major bar with good weedgrowth," Doug continued. "During summer, those fish are spread out. Some relate to weedgrowth in 2 to 3 feet of water, while some spread across the flat in 5 to 8 feet. Still others relate to the deep edge of the weeds in 8 to 12 feet.

"During fall, weedgrowth, especially shallow growth, deteriorates. Bass are pushed deeper, off the tops of major flats to the edges. There they congregate in small areas with remaining weed cover—inside turns and points. Inside turns, though, are the classic collector of large concentrations of winter bass.

"In principle, the same happens in reservoirs," Doug continued. "Lots of bass accumulate in spots that are easy to identify. Natural lakes contain more weedgrowth than most reservoirs do, but when weedgrowth is available, bass use it in reservoirs as much as they do in natural lakes. In reservoirs that don't contain weeds, bass drift from inside creek arms toward the mouth of the creek arm. Again, cover—brush or timber—concentrates bass.

"Look for cover near a creek channel. Maybe 50 bass were spread around a shallow flat in summer. By ice-up, 25 of those 50 fish may be concentrated in one prime spot, especially where cover meets deeper water.

"Wood functions like green weeds in natural lakes. It becomes an 'oasis of life'—a collector of baitfish and other fish food. Again though, inside bends seem to be better than points."

"Same basic idea goes for ponds and stockdams," Dave said. "Bass drop from shallow areas into leftover weedgrowth, or in the absence of weeds, to other cover. In shallower ponds where the basin is only 15 to 20 feet deep, they retreat to the basin area. Midwestern pits and ponds probably offer the best ice fishing for bass.

"Don't forget to harvest selectively. Biologists usually recommend removing from 5 to 10 times as many pounds of bluegills as bass from ponds and small impoundments."

Pre-ice scouting helps locate largemouths. Fishing open water late in the fall provides cues to winter bass location, according to Doug. If you find 'em a couple weeks after turnover, they'll usually be in a similar pattern and location at early-ice.

Ice fishing for bass can be good because the fish are tightly grouped in predictable spots. If only 10 percent of the bass in a group are active, the action can be memorable. "If 10 percent of 10 bass are active, your chance of catching that one bass isn't so good," Al said. "But now we have 10 percent of 100 or so bass active. Even though they're not as active as during summer, action can be steady, sometimes even fast.

"After 4 or 5 days of unusually warm weather, higher percentages of bass may be active and biting. The action's phenomenal, but don't expect it too often."

Classic spots we've described are potential areas to catch bass all winter. But high-percentage times are only at first-ice and late-ice. Activity decreases as winter wears on. We speculate that the following factors may be responsible:

Location in Principle

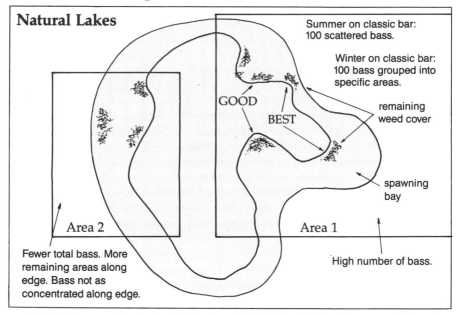

This lake map illustrates the basic principle for finding largemouth bass in natural lakes in winter.

Area 1 *offers two bars at the entrance to a spawning bay. Bass scatter in the bay and along the two bars during summer. By late fall, they concentrate along points and inside turns on the bars, holding primarily in remaining weed cover. Inside corners with cover tend to hold more bass than points with cover.*

Area 2, *another major bar, holds fish, too, but probably not as many. Also, because points and inside turns are less distinct, bass are more scattered—harder to find.*

•The metabolism of largemouth bass, a warm-water fish, perhaps slows so much they rarely need to feed when water temperatures fall to the low 30°F range.

•They may move to other areas where we lose track of them, possibly in response to shifts in prey location; or declines in dissolved oxygen, water

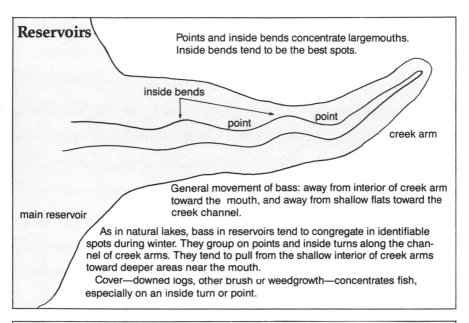

Reservoirs

Points and inside bends concentrate largemouths. Inside bends tend to be the best spots.

inside bends

point

point

creek arm

General movement of bass: away from interior of creek arm toward the mouth, and away from shallow flats toward the creek channel.

main reservoir

As in natural lakes, bass in reservoirs tend to congregate in identifiable spots during winter. They group on points and inside turns along the channel of creek arms. They tend to pull from the shallow interior of creek arms toward deeper areas near the mouth.

Cover—downed logs, other brush or weedgrowth—concentrates fish, especially on an inside turn or point.

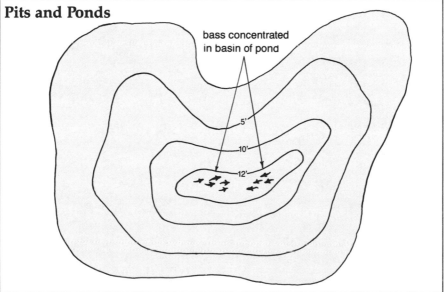

Pits and Ponds

bass concentrated in basin of pond

5'

10'

12'

temperature, or current. We feel that location shifts are more likely in river backwaters or oxbows, or in fertile lakes and impoundments. In most lakes, bass probably remain in a general area during winter.

"But bass can be roamers during midwinter," Dave added. "In a darkhouse, you'll see 'em swimming, passing through usually right along the bottom. Even if you're using what should be a decent bass bait, like a small minnow on a plain hook, the bass seem willing only to swim up for a closer look.

"In early and late winter, they're along weedlines and up in the weeds; and they're more active. In midwinter, they seem to just go on patrol."

"Perhaps some fish roam while others stick tight," Doug responded. "Whatever the case, it's not prime time to fish for bass."

Largemouth Location

Under ice, largemouth bass location is theoretically simple, but that doesn't mean easy. Search for key spots.

Largemouths typically occupy water shallower than the lip of the first

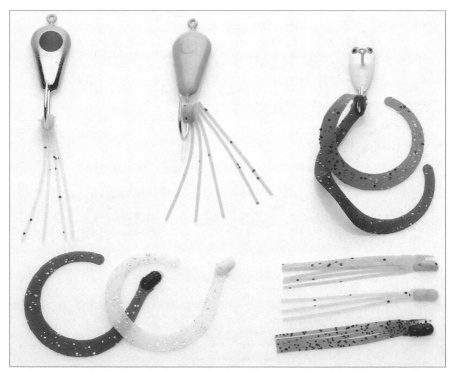

Reverse a Jiggle Ratt Tail on a Lunker Tear or add a Ripple Ratt Tail to a Swimmin' Ratt. Tip both lures with a minnow.

The Lunker Tear is from Jig-A-Whopper/UMM Holdings. The Jiggle Ratt Tail, Ripple Ratt Tail, and Swimmin' Ratt are made by Wisconsin Tackle.

major drop-off, according to Doug. "In natural lakes, major bars close to spawning areas (usually shallow, protected soft-bottomed bays) hold bass if there's cover. In reservoirs, check edges of major creek arms. In ponds, look deeper than the shallowest shelf, into the main deep basin if it isn't deeper than 15 or 20 feet."

In every case, cover—green weeds or at least remnant stalks, deep stump rows, standing timber—consolidates bass. First, identify large flats that hold bass all year. Then identify patches of remaining weed-growth or other forms of cover on the edges of these flats. Inside bends are often productive, but don't ignore rather straight edges if cover is present.

Some spots look like they should hold high concentrations of bass, but they aren't productive. "Cover may be too sparse to attract numbers of bass," Dave said. "Try a good-looking spot several times before giving up, though. Bass can be finicky during winter."

Presentation

"As Dave mentioned, most bass are accidentally caught by panfish anglers," Doug said. "Teardrops and ice flies dressed with grubs or minnows certainly work, even where water's a bit murky. If you're catching bluegills, crappies, perch, and an occasional bass, great.

"But you'll catch more bass on slightly larger baits. My best action has

Anchoring A Minnow

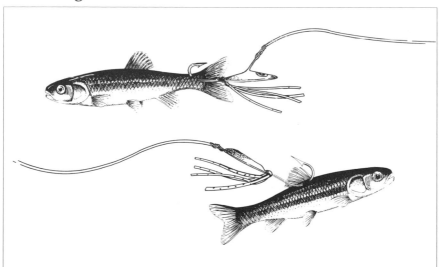

To anchor a minnow for bass, slip the hook of a large teardrop like the Jig-A-Whopper Lunker Tear parallel to the dorsal fin of a lively 3- to 4-inch minnow. If the minnow remains too active, further anchor the bait by adding shot 6 inches to a foot above the bait.

Species Caught During Ice Fishing Seasons

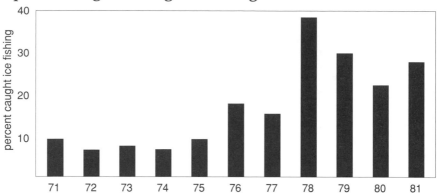

When In-Fisherman editor Steve Quinn lived in Massachusetts, he analyzed the results of the Massachusetts Freshwater Sportfishing Award Program, which gives bronze pins for the catch of trophy-size fish. Although ice fishing was possible only for two to three months in most parts of the state, a high percentage of largemouths over 7 pounds were caught through the ice, especially from 1978 through 1981.

During the 11-year period, percentages of other species caught through the ice were: pike—71 percent; yellow perch—63 percent; chain pickerel—47 percent; crappie—27 percent; smallmouth bass—6 percent.

been on flash lures like small (1/4-ounce) Jig-A-Whopper Rocker Minnows or Acme Kastmasters dressed with a 3-inch long lip-hooked minnow. Jig subtly to attract bass, ease the lure up a foot or two and let it flutter back. The struggling minnow triggers the strike, and bass inhale the bait during the pause. Jigging Rapalas (#5) get a lot of action, too. Tip the bottom treble with a fish eye or minnow head.

"I also like a large (at least 1/32-ounce) teardrop like the Jig-A-Whopper 'Lunker Tear' coupled with a lively, struggling back-hooked minnow about 3 inches long," Doug continued. "Bend the hook out about 10 degrees—lets you present the minnow better; you also hook more bass. File off most of the barb and then hone the hook to needle sharpness.

"Slide the hook through just under the minnow's skin parallel to its dorsal fin, not crosswise under the dorsal fin, which is the traditional way to hook minnows. This lets the minnow struggle forward naturally until the weight of the lure makes him drop back. The hook is also in a better position to hook a bass no matter how he takes the bait. Add leadshot about 6 inches above the hook if the minnow swims too aggressively."

Failing to change bait is the biggest mistake you can make, according to Dave. "After a while, you'll know how long certain types of minnows last

Bass Options

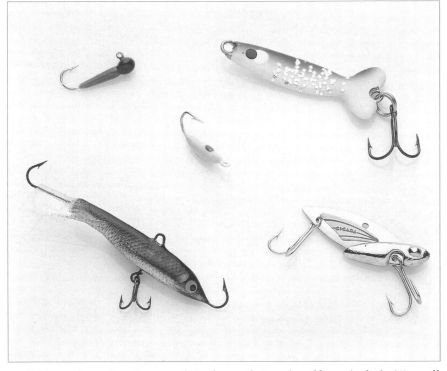

Other options attract wary winter bass. Categories of lures include (1) small leadhead jigs like the Rat Finkee (Custom Jigs and Spins); (2) small teardrops like the Glow Fry (Jig-A-Whopper/UMM Holdings); (3) flash lures like the Fire-Eye Minnow (Northland Fishing Tackle); (4) swimming lures like the Jigging Rapala (Normark Corp.); and (5) blade baits like the Cicada (Reef Runner).

before they quit working," he said. "Change 'em, whether you've had a bite or not.

"Then, too, consider that it might take a very small bait to get bites. Often times when we're fishing for crappies with small minnows, we'll get into largemouths and catch a bunch. And as many panfishermen know, bass will certainly strike a tiny teardrop and grub, such as Eurolarvae (maggots) or wax worms."

Use 6- or 8-pound-test line if you're specifically fishing for bass; heavier than that if cover is thick and tangly.

"You can even land big bass on 4- and 2-pound line," Doug said. "You won't consistently land bass on panfish tackle, but it's great sport to try."

SMALLMOUTH BASS

Smallmouth bass are another overlooked quarry that are catchable at early-ice and late-ice. They're notoriously difficult to catch during mid-winter, although exceptions occur, especially in lakes where smallmouths are the dominant predator. Without competition from other species, smallmouths seem more inclined to bite all winter.

"Sure we can theorize why that might be," Doug said. "But why bother when the number of lakes I've found like that can be counted on one hand. Then, too, most of this handful of lakes hadn't been pressured before we fished them. So however you look at it, they're an exception we find most often in remote southern Canadian waters.

"But four to six weeks before ice-out is a different story," Doug continued. "Smallmouths become more active again, often in the same areas you catch 'em at early-ice. Circumstantial evidence suggests they don't move much during winter. And they apparently don't feed much until late-ice."

"This isn't a scientific observation," Doug noted. "And smallmouths I catch in spring don't appear skinny or in poor condition. That suggests they feed throughout winter. In most lakes, however, it's difficult to catch smallmouths during midwinter."

And anglers who hunt smallmouths often have trouble finding them because they're subconsciously fishing for walleyes. The two species prefer a distinctly different habitat.

Smallmouths and walleyes both relate to rock drop-offs; rock humps; or deep rock, clay, or sand flats. But walleyes relate to rocky drop-offs associated with the deepest water in a section of a lake, while smallmouths relate to rocky drop-offs only in moderately deep sections. Smallmouths are usually in only a few distinct spots.

Similar to locating largemouths, the best approach is to locate smallies in open water during late fall. They remain in the same areas once ice forms.

"Smallmouths congregate in specific areas along bars," Doug said. "The key is pinpointing subtle turns, and humps. You'll catch several fish if they're active."

Smallmouth Location

During fall, smallmouths move into deep water and remain there after ice forms. They hold close to the bottom in areas with bottom substrates composed of rock or clay, generally in 25- to 50-foot depths. They generally avoid the shallows and tend to move as far from shore as bottom configuration permits.

Focus on this general principle and promising areas are easy to identify on a lake map. "Smallmouths seem to be attracted to deep areas of transition from hard to soft bottom—rock and clay to muck, for example," Doug commented. "They're often lying close to this edge, inactive but still catchable."

Smallmouths in lakes tend to be homebodies, remaining in the same area from birth to death. Unusual conditions, like limited spawning habitat or forage fish roaming over wide areas, force them to wander. And in rivers and riverine impoundments, they're migratory.

Accurate lake contour maps help identify potential smallmouth groups. A prime smallmouth home area must have three characteristics: (1) a suitable rock and gravel area for spawning; (2) access to moderate-depth basin areas; and (3) features that attract and hold forage.

Lake areas that provide better combinations of these three characteristics are major populations areas. But marginal populations also exist. Major population areas produce most fish, but they're often fished hard. At times, marginal areas can be better.

LOCATION

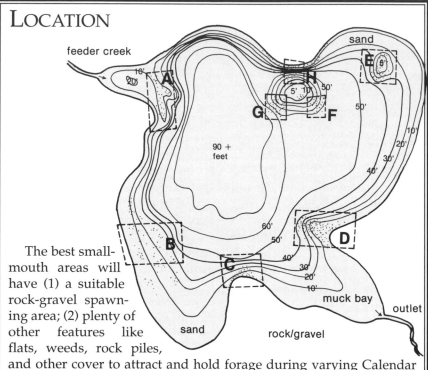

feeder creek

sand

90 + feet

muck bay

outlet

sand

rock/gravel

The best small-mouth areas will have (1) a suitable rock-gravel spawning area; (2) plenty of other features like flats, weeds, rock piles, and other cover to attract and hold forage during varying Calendar Periods; and (3) suitable moderate to shallow lake basin areas for use during Cold Water Periods. Keeping this in mind, we'll evaluate the potential of Areas A thru H:

Area A—A fine looking spot that's likely to attract many anglers. Area A will not be home to large groups of smallmouths because it lacks enough shallow to moderately deep basin water.

Area B—Provides diverse smallmouth habitat, but the fish probably won't be concentrated because turns and drop-offs aren't distinct.

Area C—This bar would probably hold a few smallmouths, but not a large group.

Area D—Provides characteristics for a great smallmouth area. Note in particular the 40- to 50-foot basin water off the tip of the bar.

Area E—Has characteristics to hold smallmouths, but limited spawning area. Some shore spawners could be attracted to the island.

Areas F, G, and H—An attractive fish-holding area. Even though walleyes and smallies might mingle, Area F will probably attract more smallmouths and Area G more walleyes.

Areas A and G, are high-percentage walleye areas; while D and F are better for smalljaws.

In some lakes, smallmouths occupy different areas at early- and late-ice. In these lakes, at early-ice, smallies remain in their late-fall habitat—deeper water, typically as far from shore and as close to moderatly deep basin areas as possible. At late-ice, they still spend most of the time in deeper water, but usually closer to shore, near potential spawning grounds.

The best drop-offs aren't all rock, but have rocks scattered along the drop-off. Outcroppings and boulders concentrate fish, making them easier to locate and catch. In rock-covered areas, look for distinct breaks like sharp drop-offs, particularly large rocks, or some other distinct feature.

Smallmouth anglers often neglect to fish transitions from harder to softer bottom. Key transitions may be from: (1) rock to gravel or clay, (2) rock to muck, or (3) clay to muck. Most mesotrophic lakes have a general hard-to-soft-bottom transition point in the 25- to 50-foot range. This concentrates smallmouth bass during the Frozen Water Period.

Smallmouth As A Middleman

As well as a homebody, smallmouths are a "middleman" fish, according to Doug. "Comparing smallmouths to walleyes is necessary in order to understand the middleman concept," he said. "Most smallmouth lakes also contain walleye populations, and the two species interact although each occupies a particular niche. During fall, both species spend time near the lake basin, but they don't relate to the basin in the same way. This difference is important.

"A lake basin is the softer bottom of a lake that's deeper than harder-bottom areas such as bars or humps. The basin starts wherever a drop-off ends and a relatively soft bottom begins to flatten out. The basin isn't necessarily the deepest water in the lake. Some basin areas are deep, some are moderately deep, and some are shallow. Lakes may also have several basin areas, each with a different depth.

"As fall progresses, smallmouths shift deeper, finally spending much of the Cold Water and Frozen Water Periods near a lake basin transition from harder to softer bottom. During fall, walleyes in most deeper mesotrophic lakes hold near fast-breaking areas (often off a bar or hump) adjacent to a large area of deep water. The top of the bar must also have a large flat to provide forage. The two species use similar but divergent habitats when they have a choice."

Walleyes often relate to the deepest basin area during winter, while smallmouths prefer shallower or moderately deep basin areas. Basin depth is important in finding smallmouths. "I've seen a few smallmouth lakes where a soft, flat basin may start as shallow as 15 feet," Doug noted. "Spirit Lake in northwest Iowa is one example. But its maximum depth is only about 25 feet, so it's not typical."

Shallow basins usually begin at 25 to 30 feet; mid-depth basins can be up to about 50 feet. Exceptions occur, but the most appropriate basin depths for smallmouths in most lakes seem to range from 25 to 50 feet.

MR. MIDDLEMAN

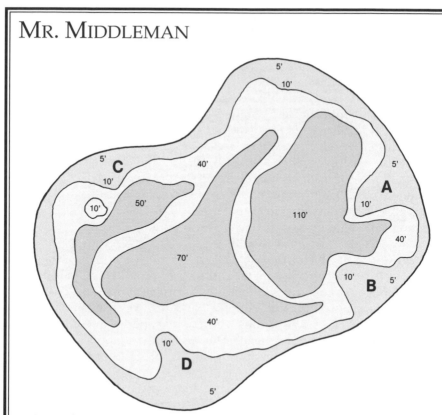

To understand the smallmouth "middleman" concept, focus first on the lake basin. A lake basin is the softer bottom of a lake, deeper than the harder bottom areas. Lake basins start wherever drop-offs end and the bottom begins to flatten out and turn soft.

"This 'middleman' concept is handy for reference," Doug commented. "But it isn't correct in every instance. In some Canadian Shield lakes, for example, smallmouths could be called 'Mr. Shallowman' because fish interactions and environmental conditions during most of the year place lake trout deep, walleyes in the middle, and smallies shallow. So while the 'middleman' concept is a partial misnomer, it can help anglers recognize the smallmouth niche."

With a good map, this concept can help evaluate the potential of smallmouth home areas. You can even evaluate the basic potential of natural lakes to produce smallies and pinpoint good ice fishing locations.

Presentation

Presentation options for smallmouths are similar to those for largemouths. "Say we're fishing a rock bar that drops from 15 to 35 feet of

The basin is not just the deepest water in a lake. Many lakes have more than one basin area. Some basin areas are deep, some are a moderately deep, and some are shallow. Smallmouths, in most cases, relate to shallow or moderately deep basin areas, while walleyes occupy deeper basins.

Although Areas A through D could serve as smallmouth home areas, Areas C and D have the most potential. C and D have shallow to moderately deep basin areas for use during fall, winter, and early spring.

Why isn't the 40-foot water surrounding Area A adequate to hold winter smallmouths? It will hold a few fish. But more smallmouths probably relate to lake areas with substantial shallow to moderately deep basin areas. The 40-foot basin water near the shoreline at A isn't as attractive because smallies are farther out into the lake during late fall and early winter. Substantial basin areas at the right depth must be available off the end of a bar. Area A doesn't provide substantial cold-water smallmouth habitat.

What about Area B? Even though B doesn't offer the potential of C and D, the southwest corner of B could be good.

One last thought that may help show you why the tip of Area A isn't good fall and winter smallmouth water. A basin is never a drop-off area, but a drop-off area can be in a basin. In other words, basins are flats. A 40-foot flat off Area A isn't large enough to constitute a true basin area. Neither is there enough 40-foot water off the northeast corner of Area C to constitute a basin. But there's plenty of 50-foot basin water, and that's within the range smallies seem to prefer. Thus, Area C is probably a good spot, depending on a number of factors, such as cover and food on the shallower flat.

The best smallmouth home areas have substantial shallow to moderately deep basin areas adjacent to them. Fishing these areas for smallmouths is playing percentages for the most and the best fish.

water," Doug began. "Cut at least 6 holes from the tip of the point, down the drop-off to the flat at the base of the drop-off.

"Start fishing the deep flat by dropping your lure— say a 1/4-ounce Jig-A-Whopper Rocker Minnow dressed with a fish eye—to the bottom. Smallies seldom hover far above the bottom, so lift the bait sharply a foot or so and let it flutter back. Hold the lure stationary for 5 or 10 seconds with an occasional twitch to wiggle the fish eye.

"Hook 3- to 4-inch chubs below the dorsal fin and rig them on tip-ups or bobber rods to increase coverage. Activity usually peaks early and late in the day, although smallies can be caught all day.

"Even though we've tried to separate smallies from walleyes locationally," Doug added, "an approach for smallmouths is similar to fishing for walleyes. Lures, though, tend to be slightly smaller.

"The #5 and #3 Jigging Rapalas are staple items. We've also caught a

Hovering off the deep edge of a major rock . . . a congregation of smallies. Find 'em and you can catch 'em.

lot of smallies on 1/8-ounce leadhead jigs packed with maggots all the way to the hook turn, but not covering the point. Ice flies with maggots and 1/8- to 3/8-ounce jigging spoons with minnows are attractive at times, too."

Smallmouths are vulnerable to fishing pressure. Hit it right and you can catch 10 or more fish an outing. Quickly unhook bass and redirect them down the hole. No immediate problems are obvious with fish pulled from 30 or more feet of water, but long-term effects are unknown.

If you fit all the biological, physical, and chemical pieces of the puzzle together and discover the mother lode of bass, catch a few to document your results. Then consider leaving the group to overwinter in peace. After all, you have three more seasons to go.

C H A P T E R   1 0

WALLEYES

They grow large and fight hard. They're challenging to find and get to bite. Finally, they're mighty fine filleted and fixed just about any way you can think of. No surprise that walleyes hold favored fish status among so many ice fishermen.   Al Lindner

"Location is the thing for most fishermen," Al said to Doug as we began to discuss fishing for walleyes. Previous chapters have discussed equipment and tactics inclusive of jigging and set-lining with minnow lines or tip-ups. Doug and Al's job here is to focus on finding walleyes and to offer specific observations about getting them to bite in certain situations.

"Presentation is so basic," Al continued, "that if you put most fishermen on walleyes, they'll catch some. Of course fine-tuned presentation means more fish—always does. But getting folks on fish is the critical first step."

"And it isn't difficult, although that's not to say fishing won't be difficult lots of times," Doug replied. "Hey, during midwinter, walleyes get tough. The squeeze puts fish down. And fishing pressure has an effect, too. First-ice is easy, though. And last-ice gets pretty hot, too."

"I love fishing at first-ice," Al said. "It just tickles me to have followed the fish throughout fall, right up to ice-up when almost no one's fishing in open water, and then get right back on them at ice-up. It's some of the best fishing of the year because the fish have had a chance to congregate on classic spots. Remember late last November when I found that big

WHERE?

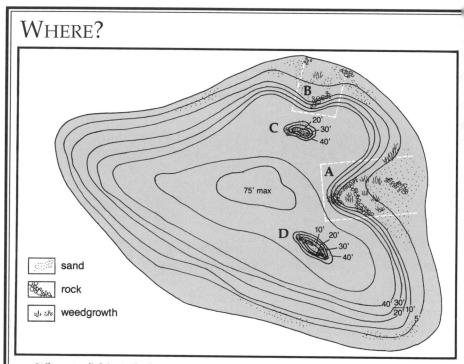

Where to fish? Ask these questions:

Is the bar or sunken island comparatively large? The bigger the bar, the more forage and walleyes it generally attracts. Likewise, does the bar protrude into the deeper portion of the lake? Walleyes like proximity to deep water during winter, and long, large bars help gather roaming walleyes.

Then, too, is there plenty of shallow-water shelf near the deep-water drop-off? Large shallow-water areas are like large pastures where forage can form. And a variety of bottom content—rock, gravel and sand—apparently helps fuel the food chain. *Bars A* and *B* and *Sunken Islands C* and *D* have good general characteristics for attracting and holding walleyes. Each is worth fishing. Yet *Bar A*, the largest bar, has a huge shallow shelf. *Bar C* has potential, too, however.

First choice: *Bar A*. Second choice: *Sunken Island D*. Third choice: Either *Bar B* or *Sunken Island C*.

school of fish using a deep saddle in a 10,000 acre lake near our office—and I told you we'd shoot that film just after ice-up?"

"Yeah, that's the way to do it. Sure-fire fishing," Doug said. "We just walked right out to the same spot in early December, chipped holes and caught fish that first night out—got one on the first drop. Too easy,

Focus on Bar A

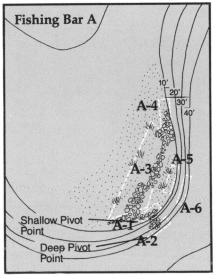

Fishing Bar A

Shallow Pivot Point

Deep Pivot Point

Where to fish on Bar A? Ask these questions:

Does the drop-off have a fishable basin as well as a shallow zone? The spot where the bar begins a major break into deep water is the shallow pivot point, a reference point in shallow water.

Likewise, the spot down the drop-off where it levels off and a major shelf begins in deep water is the deep pivot point. Increase your odds by having both a deep and shallow zone in close proximity.

Now, where's the quickest-breaking drop-off portion of the bar? Walleyes either like these areas more than other areas or are naturally funneled through them—so much the better if the fastest-breaking portions of the pivot areas offer a mixture of bottom content.

Other factors may influence your fishing location. For example, how many other anglers are using portions of the bar? Try to be the first angler to fish good portions of a bar. Move when the walleye-to-angler ratio declines.,

Now then:

Area A-1—Probably the best shallow pivot area because it offers several types of bottom content.

Area A-2—The best deep pivot area for the same reason.

Area A-3—Good shallow water for walleye activity at night.

Area A-4—Another good shallow pivot area. The adjacent basin zone may or may not hold fish.

Areas A-5 and *A-6*—Shallow and deep pivot points without the mixture of bottom content offered by *Areas 1* and *2*.

First choice: *Areas A-1* or *A-2*. Second choice: *Area A-4* or perhaps *Area A-3* at night. Last choice: *Areas A-5* or *A-6*.

though. Tougher's fun, too—when almost no one's catching fish during midwinter. The fish move to confined spots on classic structural elements, or they move off those same elements to less obvious areas nearby. That's the time to search for isolated structural elements that rarely get fishing pressure."

"Right," Al replied. "But don't fish those kinds of spots during prime time early and late in the season. You just can't expect to take many fish on such spots. But your point is well taken—during midwinter a good fish or two is a fine morning or evening on ice."

"Late-ice is fun, too." Doug said. "Aren't many places in the country where the fishing remains open then, but walleyes congregate near areas where they'll spawn immediately after ice-out. Current draws fish and so do the edges of shallow rock-rubble bars. Actually, you could fish 24 hours a day 365 days a year and be on fish every hour of every day. Well almost. Want to try that sometime?"

"Already have!" Al said, smiling at the thought.

Location

The first step in finding walleyes in lakes, reservoirs, and rivers depends on a hydrographic map. Look for large hard-bottom bars (shoreline connected or sunken islands) with big shallow flats that protrude into a deep basin area. The basin area doesn't have to be the deepest water available, but it must be a significantly large and comparatively deep portion of a body of water.

"The combination of elements is vital," Doug emphasized. "During cold-water periods, walleyes generally drift toward deeper water. That doesn't mean they'll all be found in deep water. Deeper drift is a general principle. Walleyes will still roam shallow flats, far from drop-offs. And walleyes will use weeds in shallow bays. But basic location still depends on a combination of factors that goes like this:

"Once you find a major bar (point) or sunken island, see if it intersects deeper water. Then see if there's plenty of shallow shelf near the deep-water drop-off. The shallow shelf helps draw walleye forage. And the larger the bar the more forage and walleyes it potentially will attract. Again, a small bar usually offers marginal potential."

"Now to get more specific about what makes a good bar," Al said. "A good bar usually offers a combination of bottom types—sand, gravel, and rock along with some weedgrowth. Variety attracts and holds forage and therefore fuels the food chain.

"Secondly, the bar should have a fishable deep zone as well as a good shallow zone. Follow the bar until it begins a major break into deep water. That's the key shallow zone—shallow 'pivot point' we call it. Then follow the break into deeper water to the point where it levels off and a major basin shelf begins. That's the deep pivot point.

"Is the deep shelf in less than about 60 feet of water? Sure walleyes use

Pivot Points

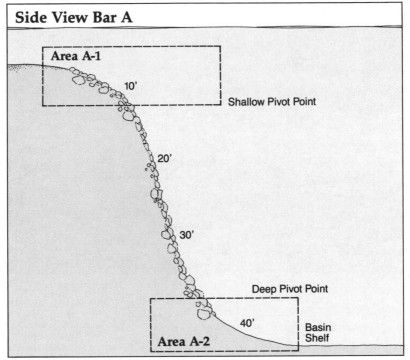

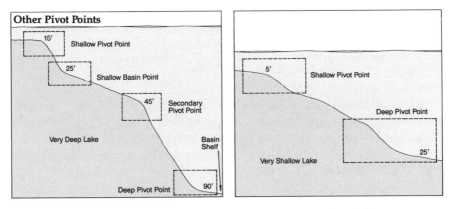

Pivot areas come in other forms. In a deep lake, the shallow fishing zone may include a "shallow pivot point" and a "shallow basin point." The deep fishing zone will be around a "secondary pivot point." These three pivot areas are most important because the "basin pivot point" is too deep to fish.

In a shallow lake, pivot areas may be hard to define because drop-offs often aren't distinct. The pivot areas still function as relation points for fish activity. As you might expect, pivot areas in shallow lakes aren't as defined and fish more likely roam. In deeper lakes, walleyes usually are in clearly defined areas.

Whether walleyes are deep or shallow, the two twilight periods produce the most consistent activity. Walleyes holding in deeper water more likely continue biting through midday.

90 and 100 feet of water. But those depths just aren't fishable. If the deep pivot point's too deep, check for a secondary shelf at a fishable depth below the shallow pivot.

"The final step is to look for the quickest-breaking portions of the bar. Walleyes often funnel through those areas—forage too, so sometimes walleyes also hold there. Identifying these spots often narrows your search for fish once you've found a good bar and know the depths of the shallow and deep pivots."

"I'd add another step, though," Doug suggested. "Fishing pressure plays such a consistently important role in fishing today . . . ask yourself how many fishermen are using the high-percentage portions of the bar. Only so many fish hold on any bar. And only so many fish are going to stay for long around a lot of commotion. Just keep considering the walleye-to-angler ratio on the spots you're fishing. Major areas hold more fish, but may also attract more anglers. Get on those areas first, but don't stay too long where there aren't any walleyes to want you."

Both Al and Doug emphasize that these principles apply to walleyes in reservoirs and rivers. Most walleyes move to the lower (deepest) third or half of a reservoir and relate to structural elements within that section.

In rivers or flowing reservoirs like those on the upper Mississippi River, the principles hold for fish that move to the general 5- to 10-mile section of river below a dam—the general tailwater area. Good backwater areas, too, usually are off a tailwater area near current.

Shallow or Deep Walleyes

Doug and Al tend to view walleyes either as shallow fish (those relating to the shallow area around a pivot point or first major drop-off); or deep fish (those relating to the deep pivot point or basin-shelf area).

"If more than about 25 feet of water separates the shallow pivot point from the basin pivot point, my walleyes don't mix," Doug emphasized. "Shallow fish are shallow fish. Deep fish are deep fish. And you can fish for either or both simultaneously.

"Walleyes generally are stimulated by two major daily periods—twilight periods. Although most anglers believe walleyes in deep water become active first, that's rarely the case. Walleyes in deep water seem to sense the change as easily and at about the same time as shallow fish. Assuming you fish these two major periods, you must decide which fish to go for."

Start by cutting holes shallow and deep—cover the pivot areas. When someone starts catching fish, move to holes in that area. Have plenty of holes cut so you don't need to cut more holes when the fish are going. Big

Typical Tactics

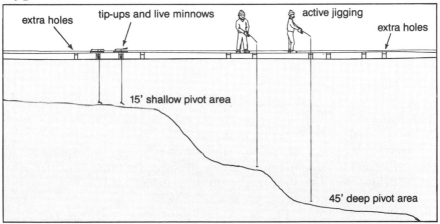

Most states allow at least two lines for ice fishing. A typical approach used by Doug and Al begins with cutting plenty of holes over deep and shallow areas where they believe walleyes could be. They set tip-ups shallow while they jig over deeper water.

Usually Al moves from hole to hole, never staying anywhere for more than 7 minutes. Occasionally he'll jig shallow, too, although the tip-ups are set shallow to allert him when fish move in.

Doug, on the other hand, will often sit over a good hole longer, waiting for fish to move in. No chance to miss them. Al's searching for groups of fish that they miss if they both stayed in the same spot. They believe this team approach is the most effective technique they've found for covering an area and consistently catching fish.

walleyes may or may not be bothered by noise when they're feeding, but don't take a chance.

"One option is to set tip-ups both deep and shallow," Al suggested. "Or jig shallow and set a tip-up deep or vice versa. Once again, shallow means either just up or down from or on the first major drop-off. Deep means just up or down from or on the basin pivot point. The best pivot areas usually are near the fastest-breaking portion of a bar, providing it's not right along shore.

"Walleyes using the shallow pivot area may scatter on the flat. That's one time to spend time searching a shallow flat during the day. Fishing at night is a story we'll cover later."

If the difference between the shallow and deep pivot points is only 10 to 20 feet, as is typical in a shallow body of water, the shallow and deep fish groups may mix. Still, view the two pivot points as major concentration areas. In shallow bodies of water, however, expect walleyes to spend more time scattered away from these points.

"Deeper fish are more likely, but not very likely, to continue biting through midday," Doug observed. "In most sections of the North Country—Canada, Minnesota, Wisconsin, Michigan, Pennsylvania, New York—too many walleye anglers spend too much time only fishing shallow. Walleyes are also in 40, 50, and 60 feet of water. Walleyes from deep water may not be releaseable, due to the great pressure change when you bring them to he surface."

Icing Night 'Eyes

Twilight comes early and night is long in the dim world of walleyes under ice. Both Doug and Al have spent lots of time sitting on frozen lakes after dark. But Doug's up first.

"Many an evening I'm bundled up butt on a bucket, back to the wind, straddling an ice hole and lifting, lifting, lifting a graphite rod to make the spoon below jump like a pathetic injured something-edible.

"Time? Gave up watches years ago. Satchel Paige, the old baseball pitcher, used to ask in response to questions about his age: How old would you be if you didn't know how old you were? So, what time would it be if . . . ?

"I know it's sunset. So do the walleyes. Some darkness later, 4 of them have hit the ice—one 24-incher, two 20s, and an 18. Tonight, I've released the 24 and 20s.

"The 18? That's life. Predators and prey. A perch meal yesterday sustained the 18-incher today. Tonight, I'm predator, but my harvest has been selective.

"Home. Kitchen. Dice four strips of bacon and fry it with a handful of chopped scallions. Drain on a paper towel. Reserve enough fat to fry two fillets. Add a touch of crushed garlic. Aroma!

"Crack a head of lettuce. Crumble blue cheese, add oil and vinegar, a

Although walleyes bite anytime , there's no time like twilight—particularly the 45 minutes before sunrise and after sunset. This is Camp Fish Director Reggie Thiel with a 12-pounder.

sliced tomato and sprinkle the salad with crumbled bacon and cracked pepper. Fillets done, rip off a piece of fresh whole wheat. Butter. More cracked pepper for the fillets.

"Grace: God, I have to tell you, tonight all is pretty well in this tiny corner of the world . . ."

Timing

Dark is a long time during winter in the North Country. At winter solstice on December 21 in northern Minnesota, we have 16 hours of dark, 2 hours of twilight, and 6 hours of daylight.

Twilight periods focus walleye activity. During twilight, walleyes have a vision advantage over prey such as perch and bluegills. So walleyes will more likely be active at twilight than during any other time of day.

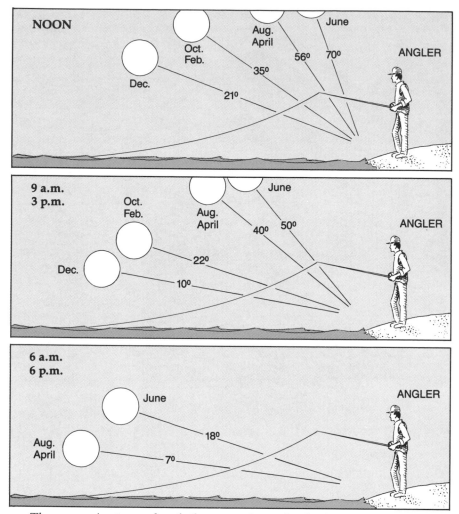

The approximate angle of the sun above the horizon at Minneapolis, Minnesota, on the 21st day of the month at various times of day throughout the year. Sunset occurs about 1¼ hours after the sun reaches 10° above the horizon in the afternoon.

"Fishing for walleyes only during twilight periods is a sensible approach given that patterning walleye activity during 16 hours of darkness can be difficult," Doug said. "A perfect day for walleyes would be fishing two hours surrounding sunrise and another two hours surrounding sunset. In between, fish for panfish or pike and take a break at noon for a bowl of homemade fish'n dumplin' soup.

"Of course fishing each morning and evening is impractical for most fishermen, even fishermen who live near lakes. But a point can be made regarding patterning walleyes during twilight.

"Say you're on a proven walleye spot, so much the better if the spot isn't being fished by other anglers. Fish each twilight period every day for several weeks in a row and you'll see patterns to the feeding. A few walleyes will always become active during twilight. But the number of fish that are active and the number of successive twilight periods that remain active probably depend on how successful those walleyes are at feeding."

"We can't support this scientifically," Al said, "but based on fishing experience, we believe a portion of the walleye population in most lakes become programmed to feed only during twilight periods. Fish that feed unsuccessfully during a morning twilight period shut off during the day and wait for the evening twilight period. They'll be even more aggressive.

"If, on the other hand, they feed effectively during a morning twilight period, they won't be active during the evening twilight period or for several succeeding twilight periods. Walleyes digest food slowly during winter."

"So even when you're on a good spot," Doug observed, "you may be there when the fish aren't cracking. The only reliable way to predict what's happening is to constantly fish and keep track of fish activity.

"Two or three hot bites out of 14 possible twilight periods a week is common. That doesn't mean the lake won't burp up a 10 for you on a day when the fish generally aren't cracking. But it suggests how difficult it can be to hit a good bite when you only hit a lake once or twice a week. You see, even with location and presentation under control, variables remain. That's fishing."

Weather, too. Intense cold fronts affect fishing, although they affect fishing at twilight and night less than fishing during daylight. The first morning or evening after an intense cold front, however, usually means fishing for stragglers. Stragglers can be big fish as well as small fish, though. Doug and Al sometimes move to a known big-fish spot and fish for one good fish.

Stable weather means a better chance for stable fishing patterns. Yet while several days of mild and stable weather improve chances for good fishing, that's not guaranteed. Factor in the "bite variable." Walleyes rarely bite every twilight or dark period, even during the finest conditions.

"Exceptions occur where walleye populations are so large that even when only a portion of a huge school is feeding it seems like a lot of fish," Al emphasized. "This often happens around the Bass Islands of Lake Erie; on the portion of Lake of the Woods off Baudette, Minnesota; and on portions of the Bay of Quinte, Bay de Noc, or Saginaw Bay. But these are some of the world's finest walleye fisheries."

To fish a twilight period, be ready to jig or "tip 'em up" at least a half hour before sunset. If sunset's at 4:30 p.m., drill holes to probe for spots at

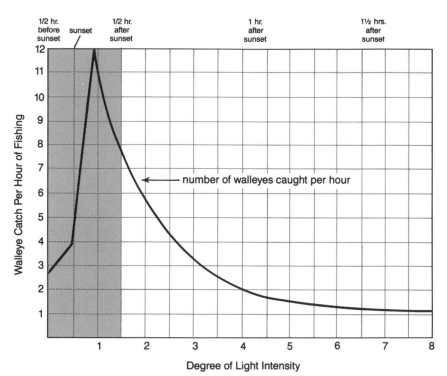

In 1962, Ontario fisheries scientist Richard A. Ryder began 15 years of research on walleyes. Ryder sought to prove that light was a primary feeding trigger for walleyes.

One aspect of Ryder's work showed the rate of change in light as the most important feeding trigger. Ryder found that fishing was better at certain surface light levels. For instance, as the sun's rays became more oblique (about 1 ½ hours before sunset to a half hour after).

Ryder concluded that amount of light has a bearing on walleye feeding, and under optimum light conditions, fish might leisurely feed throughout the day. But the main trigger for intensive feeding appears to be the fast rate of change in light at dusk, and to a lesser degree at dawn.

3:00 and be set up by 3:45. Because of the angle of sunlight hitting ice and water, sunset occurs at least 30 minutes earlier below the water. The evening twilight bite usually lasts for at least 45 minutes, until after sunset. Then fishing usually slows, although walleyes usually feed periodically through the night.

The key portion of the twilight periods, though, is the hour after sunset or before sunrise. Be on a good spot, deep or shallow.

After Dark

Doug continued with observations about the evening fishing period.

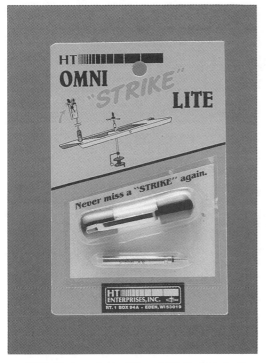

H.T. Enterprise's "Omni Strike Lite" clips to the flag on an H.T. Polar Tip-up. Insert the lithium battery. When the flag trips, the light flashes on.

"Twilight biters almost always quit biting after dark, probably because of their interaction with forage. During twilight, forage such as perch and bluegills become less active and walleyes have a distinct vision advantage over them as it gets darker.

"Prey continue to move during twilight until they settle into an area where they rest on the bottom for the night. While forage continue to move, walleyes continue to bite. When perch and bluegills settle in, walleyes often quit biting or settle into another feeding strategy.

"Are walleyes that begin biting after dark different fish, or are they twilight biters that have gone through a transition of sorts? Can't say. Can say that walleyes may bite anytime all night.

"As we've said, though, the after-dark bite is difficult to pattern. Pick a period and go fishing, from say dark to 10:30 or midnight. Or fish the night away in a cozy shack, catnapping occasionally. Do this several nights in a row and you may be able to pattern the bite in the area you're fishing."

But ther's more to fishing patterns than location. Lure's play a principal part too. And bait choice can also be a factor.

Jigging Lures

Flash lures—Lures like the Acme Kastmaster; Jig-A-Whopper Rocker Minnow, Knocker Minnow, and Hawger Spoon; Custom Jig and Spin Stinger; and Northland Tackle Fire-Eye Spoon.

Swimming lures—Lures like the Northland Air-Plane Jig; Normark Jigging Rapala; Acme Nils Master Minnow; and Wisconsin Tackle Swimmin' Ratt.

Standard leadhead jigs—Lures like the Northland Fire-Ball and Lip-Stick

Tip-ups are fine most of the time. But active jigging consistently produces more walleyes.

Jig; Jig-A-Whopper Drip Lip and Competition Head; Heron Jiggler; and Lindy-Little Joe Fuzz-E-Grub.

Comments

Flash lures: The Jig-A-Whopper Rocker Minnow is a versatile and productive bait. The leadbodied bait drops quickly and precisely while its flash and vibration attracts walleyes. Use the 1/16-, 1/8-, or 1/4-ouncer for perch or walleyes during daylight. The 1/3-ouncer works as deep as 50 feet; but beyond 40 feet, a 1/2-ouncer is probably better.

Try a Knocker Minnow if you want to add sound to your attack. And switch to Hawger Spoons for even more flash and vibration.

The Fire-Eye Spoon is much like the Rocker Minnow, except the finned tail adds vibration on the lift and flutter on the fall. The Kastmaster, on the other hand, is a "straight bait" that fishes with reduced flash and wobble. It fishes precisely.

Both Doug and Al prefer bigger baits after dark because they offer a lower-frequency wobble on the fall and a larger profile in dim light. Try baits like the #3 or #4 Jig-A-Whopper Hawger Spoon or the 3/4-ounce Kastmaster.

Basic Categories of Jigging Lures for Walleyes

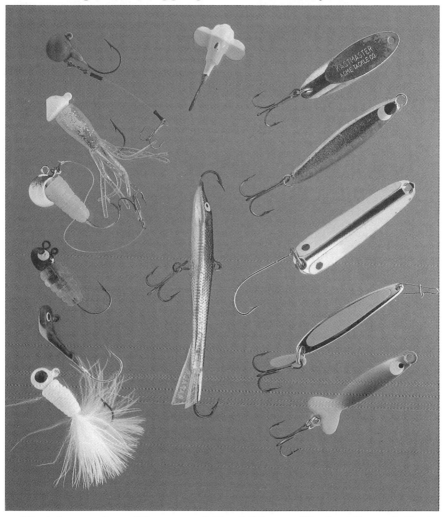

Flash lures—*Acme "Kastmaster"; Jig-A-Whopper "Rocker Minnow"; Jig-A-Whopper "Hawger Spoon"; Bay de Noc "Swedish Pimple"; Northland "Fire-Eye Spoon."*

Swimming lures—*Northland "Air-Plane Jig"; Normark "Jigging Rapala."*

Standard leadhead jigs—*Northland "Fire-Ball"; Northland "Lip-Stick Jig"; Jig-A-Whopper "Drip Lip"; Jig-A-Whopper "Competition Head"; Heron "Jiggler"; Lindy-Little Joe "Fuzz-E-Grub."*

Swimming lures: Doug has caught more walleyes and more large walleyes on the Jigging Rapala than on any other lure. Yet this lure, one of the best ice lures of all time, remains underused in many parts of North America.

In clear water during daylight, Doug usually begins fishing with a #7 Jigging Rapala. After dark, he switches to a #9 Jigging Rapala—more profile (visibility). In moderately clear or dingy water, he usually begins with a spoon. Eventually he lets the fish decide which bait they prefer. Often it's both.

Northland Tackle, by the way, has modified its Air-Plane Jig to include a stinger system. Fish the jig coupled with a minnow hooked nose-forward and stinger rigged.

Standard leadhead jigs: Al and Doug fish with flash lures or swimming lures about 75 percent of the time. They almost always begin fishing with them. The remaining 25 percent of the time, they use leadhead jigs tipped with minnows for inactive walleyes.

They tip a leadhead jig with a minnow hooked through the lips only when they're fishing in distinct current. Away from current, reversed minnows trigger more walleyes. Doug prefers to fish a reversed minnow on a light-line stinger system, the type that comes with Jig-A-Whopper jigs. Or tie your own light-line stingers.

Color

Fluorescent colors reflect more light at twilight; shades with gold or silver work particularly well then. Experiment to see which combinations work best on a given outing.

Try phosphorescent baits, too. Jig-A-Whopper, Northland Tackle, Custom Jigs & Spins, and Wisconsin Tackle offer phosphorescent baits. Doctor Jigging Rapalas with Firefly phosphorescent tape from Blue Fox or Witchcraft. The tape adds phosphorescence to any jigging bait.

Bring phosphorescent baits to the surface occasionally to recharge them. Subtle phosphorescent glow seems to work better than bright glow.

Jigging

"No need to change your jigging approach after dark," Al said. "Lift-fall flash lures and swimming lures about once every 10 to 15 seconds. If the fish are cracking, pause just 7 seconds before lifting again.

"The lift is a sharp lift of the rod tip about 1½ feet, with an immediate return of the rod tip to its original position (creating slack line), usually about 3 inches above the hole. I begin with the bait positioned 3 to 6 inches above the bottom. Tip baits with a minnow, chub head, or fish eye."

"You're as likely, though," Doug said, "to catch walleyes right on the bottom during twilight. Any lure can be bounced on the bottom to attract attention, then lifted slightly to let fish take the bait. Walleyes, however, many times love baits on the bottom.

"Try a jig like the Jig-A-Whopper Drip Lip. Tip with a 4-inch chub or shiner in reverse by slipping the hook just under the skin on top of the tail (see Chapter 4) so the head of the bait rides forward. Place the stinger

Phosphorescence! According to Al and Doug, so often the key to good catches.

hook just behind the head. The jig hangs horizontally off the bottom. On the bottom, a slight lift with your rod tip makes the jig rock forward to lift the minnow up off the bottom as it struggles in the fish's face.

"After dark, suspend baits 3 to 9 inches off bottom unless your depthfinder shows fish coming through higher. Lift-falls with leadhead jigs tipped with minnows should be gentle to let the minnow struggle as it falls and settles back in place. A tiny nudge with the rod tip makes the minnow struggle after it settles. Use as light a jig as possible to maximize minnow action."

Tip-ups

Jigging is so effective that Al and Doug rarely use tip-ups for walleyes. They're handy, however, in conjunction with jigging.

Quick-strike rigging with Partridge VB hooks.

While they're jigging over deep water, they set a tip-up near a shallow pivot point to let them know when walleyes move shallow. They cut extra holes so they'll be ready with plenty of spots to jig when the walleyes move in. "We jig deep and set a tip-up shallow, because it's more difficult to set a tip-up over deep water," Doug offered.

"Use a light indicator from H.T. Enterprises on your tip-ups to indicate bites after dark. The light's called the "Omni Strike Light." Clip it to the tip-up flat or tape it to the flat shaft. Insert the battery pin and as soon as the flat trips, it lights up."

"I'm glad you convinced me to use quick-strike rigging," Al said to Doug. "One of your favorite riggings consists of either two #10 Partridge VB hooks or two #8 or #10 Partridge "outbend" trebles rigged in tandem about 12 inches apart. As an alternative to the Partridge outbend treble, bend out the throat of a 'beaked' treble about 10 degrees.

"The lead hook on the end of your line should be near the dorsal fin of the bait," Al continued. "The tail treble should be near the bait's tail. Set immediately when you get to a tripped tip-up; no need to wait for the fish to swallow the bait."

"That's about it," Doug said as he took a moment to consider the ground he and Al had covered. "Applying the information from previous chapters with what we've covered here, should move anglers well on their way to fine-tuning approaches for walleyes."

"Right you are," Al said. "We've fished across the walleye belt using these approaches and they work. But stay loose out there. Nothing says every little detail we've touched on will apply exactly to the situations you face. And nothing says we've covered every little detail.

"For example. I suppose we should have discussed presentation in current. Going to use a Jigging Rapala in current? Tip a whole small minnow on the tail hook of the lure instead of using a minnow head on the treble hook below the lure.

"Things like that. Lots of them. Hey, get out there and have at it. It's up to you now."

CHAPTER 11

STOCKED TROUT

Trout! Stream trout! Stocking programs have made brook, brown, splake, and rainbow trout available in bodies of water ranging from small pits and ponds to the Great Lakes. Dave Genz

Stocked trout are active during winter, and each year more fishermen pursue them. You'll find hot action on reclaimed lakes, two-story lakes, and bays of the Great Lakes. Trout location varies in each case, but similar presentation tactics will take them in each environment.

"Designated" trout lakes are lakes stocked with stream trout—brookies, browns, and rainbows, plus splake, a cross between brook trout and lake trout. These species grow fast and survive well; and fishermen who know how, catch them. Because stream trout rarely spawn in lakes, regular stocking sustains each fishery.

Frank Pratt, a Wisconsin DNR fish manager from Hayward, Wisconsin, says the popularity of winter trout fishing has increased so dramatically in recent years that new fishing restrictions may become necessary in Wisconsin.

Whenever possible, Pratt stocks brookies, browns, and rainbows in the same lake because each contributes to the fishery in a different way. Brook trout are easy to catch, so they have immediate impact on angler harvest. Often from 50 to 70 percent of the brook trout stocked in a reclaimed lake are caught the first year. Rainbow trout show a similar exploitation rate, but usually spread over several years.

Many of these fish get big. Brown trout, in particular, are more wary and therefore often attain trophy size. Pratt also confirms that the majority of big browns caught during any year are taken by ice fishermen.

Most designated trout lakes fall within two categories: reclaimed lakes and two-story lakes. Each requires a somewhat different fishing approach.

Reclaimed Lakes

Reclaimed lakes usually are small lakes or ponds that don't support healthy warm-water fisheries. Fisheries departments treat them with chemicals to remove undesirable species. Then they add stream trout to turn once unproductive lakes into wonderfully productive trout fisheries.

Many reclaimed lakes are small, bowl-shape, and seemingly without structure. During summer, trout spend much of their time within a preferred temperature zone in deeper water. During the Cold Water Period, however, they aren't restricted by water temperature.

"Trying to locate roaming fish in a structureless lake covered with ice sounds frustrating, but it's easy," Dave began the discussion with Al and Doug. "The structural blandness of a reclaimed lake is usually offset by its small size and the fact that trout love the littoral zone—the shallow water from shore to the deepest point where light penetrates to the bottom.

"During summer, warmer water temperatures make this area off limits to trout. During colder-water periods, however, trout are most often found in 3 to 10 feet of water as they forage on minnows, crustaceans, and insects. Frequently you see the trout. In fact, ice fishing in a reclaimed lake is often a visual affair."

Al continued the discussion. "The 3- to 10-foot band of water around a reclaimed lake is your 'contact zone'. Sure, trout can suspend throughout the lake, but you aren't likely to find them consistently. Occasionally, a few prominent structural elements like bars or humps also attract trout.

"The best fishing is during a two-week period at first-ice. Fish activity decreases as winter progresses, although trout can be caught all winter.

Presentation

Vertical jigging probably is the most productive fishing technique, although tip-ups are effective too, particularly for brown trout. Small Jigging Rapalas and flash lures like Kastmasters are favorite jigging lures, along with small airplane jigs.

Where legal, tipping a jig with bait such as a minnow, minnow head, or

Winter Trout Location in a Reclaimed Lake or Pond

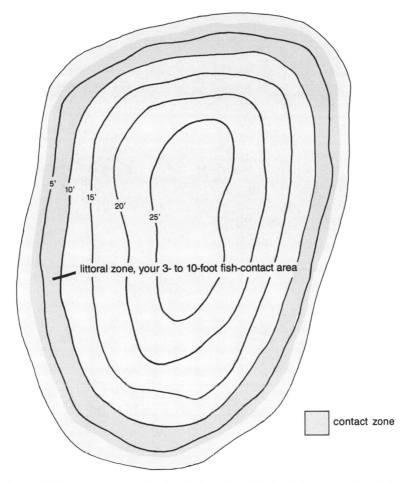

5' 10' 15' 20' 25'

littoral zone, your 3- to 10-foot fish-contact area

contact zone

Reclaimed lakes are notoriously bowl-shaped and lack obvious structural ele-
ments. During the Frozen Water Period, however, trout frequent the littoral
zone (from shore to the deepest water sunlight penetrates).

Concentrate your fishing in the shaded area, and be sure to check a variety of
depths at each location. If you don't catch fish or see them, move. Pay extra
attention to areas with forage-attracting weedgrowth and rocks.

grub often greatly enhances its effectiveness. Where bait isn't legal, try
Berkley Power Baits.

If you jig for other species, you probably own much of the gear needed
for trout fishing. Light-action spinning rod-and-reel combinations rigged
with about 6-pound-test line are standard fare. This, however, is overkill
in many lakes where smaller trout call for lighter "panfish" tackle. Many
fishermen like short rods so they can fish close to the hole while they

Where at least two lines are legal, a combo approach using a tip-up in conjunction with jigging is an efficient approach for stocked trout. Jigging, though, is the most efficient single method.

watch for trout cruising below.

Regardless of how long a rod you use, it should be stout enough to set the hook, but limber enough to absorb the sudden run of a larger trout. We discussed rods at length in the equipment chapter, so you no doubt already have the idea. Colder water deprives fish of some of their pep, but a big 'bow or brown hooked 5 feet below your boots will really run some line.

To find fish, work your way around the shoreline. At each spot, cut several holes at varying depths in the 3- to 10-foot zone. Be quiet. Trout are spooked by noise in shallow water.

"Browns and rainbows move constantly, so you may have to move, too," Dave observed. "Brook trout, on the other hand, are homebodies, often remaining in an area until they're caught.

"Live minnows are a good bait to fish under tip-ups, but seldom legal on inland designated trout water. Other popular baits include insect larvae such as Eurolarvae (maggots), wigglers (the aquatic stage of the Hexagenia mayfly), or any other grub commonly used for panfish. Big trout love tiny grubs, particularly maggots.

"Regardless of what type bait you use," Dave continued, "light line and small hooks are important for presenting baits naturally. Check the

Tip-up Riggings

split shot about 18" above hook

egg hook

light-wire hook

quick-strike rig

Two popular tip-up rigs include single hooks like Mustad or Eagle Claw egg hooks for salmon eggs, spawn sacs or corn, and any light-wire hooks for nymphs and grubs. Hooks should run from #4 to #6 for spawn sacs, #8 to #12 for salmon eggs, and #10 to #14 for grubs.

Quick-strike rigging is popular for bigger trout, especially browns and splake. Use #8 to #14 hooks tied in tandem from 1 inch (3-inch baits) to 2 inches (4- to 6-inch baits).

panfish chapter for details on learning to 'tackle down' to get bit by big fish, including trout."

"But don't ignore traditional trout baits like jarred salmon eggs and cheese baits," Doug said. "Whole kernel corn also is a good bait, although it too is illegal in some lakes because trout can't digest it. Berkley Power Baits have gained a powerful following in many parts of the country. And then, the favorite bait of our friend and winter trout expert Robert Reznak of Ashland, Wisconsin, spawn sacs like those used by steelhead fishermen on the Great Lakes."

Two-Story Lakes

Two-story lakes support both cold-water and warm-water fisheries. The "two-story" designation is appropriate because warm-water species like bass use the upper portion of the lake, while trout use the lower level. At least this generalization applies during summer.

A sort of reversal or mixing of the two groups often occurs during cold-water periods. In winter, warm-water species often are found in deeper water, while trout actively feed right under the ice.

In addition to stream trout, splake are stocked in many two-story lakes. And some states are experimenting with kokanee and Atlantic salmon.

"Two-story lakes offer more structural diversity than reclaimed lakes,"

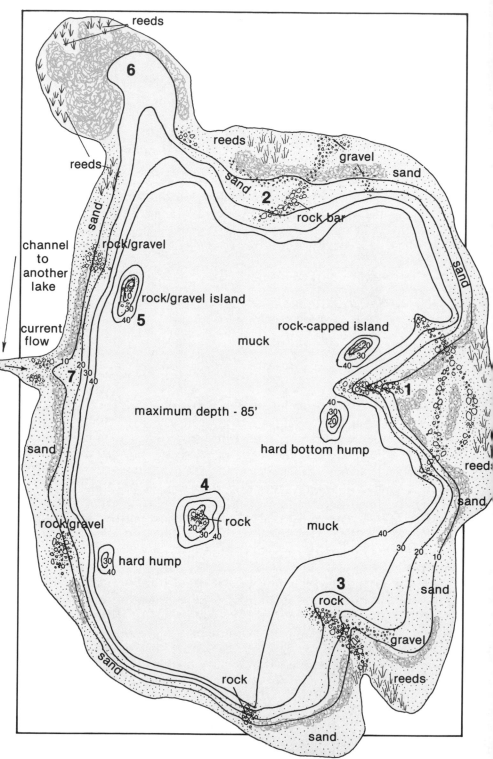

Trout Location in a Two-Story Lake

During the Frozen Water Period, trout can be anywhere. Ice fishermen must be willing to systematically search obvious structural elements to find fish.

Bar 1 *probably is the best winter trout location because the large shallow food shelf contains remaining weeds. But the combination of a quick-breaking point and two humps also make this an excellent deep-water location, especially for brown trout or splake—two stocked trout that relate to deeper water than rainbows or brookies.*

While probably not as productive as Bar 1, Bars 2 *and* 3 *are worth checking. Concentrate your effort near remaining weedgrowth and along rock bars.*

Hump 4 *could be a good deep-water location, particularly when heavy surface activity (noise) spooks fish from shoreline spots.*

Hump 5 *could also be a good producer, being close to a good shoreline spot.*

Surprisingly, Bay 6 *could be a good winter spot. The 10-foot trough leading into the bay is large enough to lure trout back to forage in standing weeds.*

Area 7: *Whenever the combination of current, rocks, and weeds is adjacent to deep water, trout will be there. Only* Bar 1 *is better.*

Doug observed. "Look for bars, points, and humps, especially those with rocks or standing weeds.

Shallow areas with current are trout magnets, too. Look for stream inlets as well as narrow necked-down areas where water flows between lakes.

Check outlets, too. They may be weed-choked during summer; hardly good trout water. But after turnover, trout use them.

Other prime winter trout locations are distinct shoreline structures like bars and points. These too are more productive if they have remaining weedgrowth. Rocky areas, on the other hand, host crayfish and insect larvae, forage that trout love. In short, many of the "classic" structures popular for first-ice walleye fishing also attract trout.

"Trout use deep water, too," Doug continued. "The number of trout using deep water is often increased by a shortage of productive shallow structural elements, noise from fishermen and snowmobiles, a recent cold front, or the presence of deep-water forage like ciscoes. Brown trout and splake particularly tend to use deep water more than rainbows or brookies."

Trout in deeper water tend to school more, and quick-breaking structures keep a school from spreading horizontally. Trout and particularly rainbows, by the way, occasionally school vertically.

Presentation

Use the same tackle you'd use for reclaimed lakes, but it might have to be heavier because you may be fishing deeper.

Even though it sometimes pays to wait for fish to move onto a spot or

Weeds Mean Winter Trout

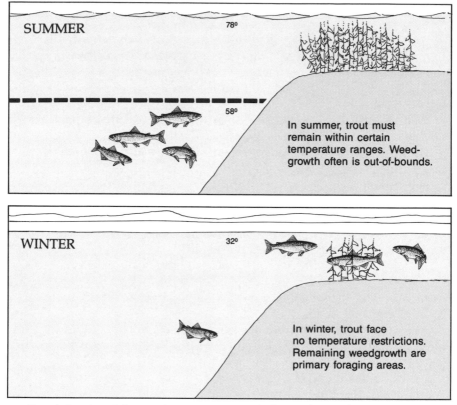

In winter, trout face no temperature restrictions. Areas of remaining weed-growth become primary foraging areas.

Most fishermen associate weeds with bass and pike, but after turnover, trout are attracted to weeds because weeds attract forage—trout feed on—bullheads, bluegills, and invertebrates.

become active there, try moving until you find active fish. Systematically fish major structural elements.

On lakes that get daytime fishing pressure and snowmobile activity, fish shallow structural elements early, moving to deeper locations as human activity increases.

Great Lakes Bays

Ice fishing for Great Lakes trout can be spectacular, for the trout are big and plentiful. Most Great Lakes fishing can be divided into two categories: near-shore shallow fishing and deep fishing. What is shallow and what is deep? Sixty feet is the dividing line.

The shallow-water fishery is for steelhead, brook trout, and splake in bays and harbors. The deep-water fishery is for lake trout.

The brown trout held by Robert Reznak is but one species of stocked trout offering ice fishermen some of the most consistent, exciting, and productive winter fishing anywhere in the world. Head for a stocked pond, lake, or Great Lakes' bay. Trout on!

For the most part, fishing in bays takes place on the Great Lakes in water from 10 to 60 feet deep because Great Lakes forage species—smelt

Trout Location In A Great Lakes Bay

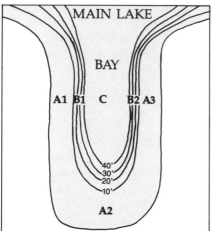

Many Great Lakes' bays have a deep trough entering the bay. The banks that form the sides of a trough are used by trout.

Shallow Flats A1, A2 and A3 are primarily used by warm-water species like walleyes, pike, and perch. Trout using these flats are scattered.

Banks B1 and B2 are hot spots. Although trout can be on the bottom at a variety of depths, they're rarely far from the bank.

Trough C sometimes draws lake trout from the main lake.

and alewives—relate to moderately deep water during winter. Shallow areas rarely attract forage. Also, many potentially productive shallow areas are too far removed from deep water to attract trout.

In late fall, as water temperatures begin to cool from the surface down, most trout species (steelhead being the major exception) congregate near the bottom. Sometimes these schools are huge and the fish are active, cruising around banks and points, searching for food. These schools stay together and remain active for several weeks after freeze-up. Then they become less concentrated and active.

Many bays are characterized by a single deep trough extending into the bay from the main lake. The banks formed on either side of the trough are the focal point for fish activity. Warm-water species like walleyes, pike, and perch frequent the shallow flats. On the other hand, lake trout sometimes filter from the main lake into the deep trough. But browns, brook trout, and splake relate to mid-depth banks. Steelhead are mostly suspended and scattered, and the best place to catch them through the ice is in shallow harbors.

A Great Lakes bay can cover thousands of acres, but location and presentation approaches, which are similar to trout fishing in other environments, remain constant. Your perspective must change, however. A bar on an inland lake can be measured in feet, while banks in the Great Lakes run for miles.

Tip-ups work, too. Where more than one line is legal, tip-ups let you cover more water. Live emerald shiners and smelt are popular baits, although dead smelt are a successful bait too.

Robert Resnak recommends "bank cutting" to find Great Lakes trout. Members of a fishing party stagger their lines down one of the main banks bordering the center trough of the bay. If trout are located at a particular level, everyone switches to that depth. If you aren't catching fish, move farther along the bank.

As always, you're searching for fast action and fun . . . fine eating, too!

C H A P T E R   1 2

LAKE TROUT

Years of experimenting has changed the way we fish for lake trout through the ice. We've discovered a world of action left untouched by traditional lake trout tactics.   Al Lindner

The lake trout fits ice fishing. A fish of cold northern climes, winter is more hospitable to lakers than stagnating summer heat that forces them to retreat to deep water. Al and Doug know this from experience. That's why they get so excited—particularly Al, for clearly the laker's his favorite winter fish.

"One of the ultimate go-have-an-adventure trips in the fishing world," he said through a big smile. "You usually won't have fast fishing, but no other fishing opportunity offers the same chance to really get smacked hard, to really stick a horse!"

The long and glorious past of ice fishing for lake trout has spawned traditions that guide today's laker icers. Sometimes, though, tradition gets in the way of progress. Many traditions aren't the most effective approaches for finding lake trout under ice. Without a doubt, more overlooked winter lake trout locations exist than traditional ones.

Breaking with Tradition

"Lakers like winter," Doug said. "They're forced into deeper, cooler water during summer and can only survive in oligotrophic waters (deep, cold waters with few nutrients). Sure, lakers are found and caught deep in winter. After all, tradition says lakers love deep water. But they also roam shallow flats where few anglers look for them.

"Mostly they like to eat. And most plankton growth is shallow, so most minnow forage is shallow . . . so you know where most lakers are."

Lake trout are almost always active in winter. Moving a lot—cutting a lot of holes and quickly seeing if fish are below them—is one key to con-

One of the ultimate go-have-an-adventure trips left in the fishing world . . . the chance to get smacked hard and stick a horse!

sistent catches. Mobility, however, is important in successful ice fishing for all species.

"Too many lake trout fishermen drill one hole, drop a jig, and sit in the same spot for two days," Al said, shaking his head. "They've been following that pattern for 50 years. They've caught some fish, and that's the way they'll continue fishing until arthritis confines them to watching fishing shows on television."

Traditionalists primarily fish one type of spot—bluff banks. They head for the steep walls of a lake trout lake and look for suspended fish.

"Granted, bluff banks are potentially good spots. But how many years can you take fish off the same spots and expect them to continue producing?" Al asked. "These days, unless you fish virgin territory, bluff banks hold mainly 2- to 3-pound fish, with an occasional 5- or 6-pounder and the odd 30."

"The chief mistake, though, is spending too much time fishing deep water. Experience shows that most of the time, water shallower than 40 feet is much more productive than deeper water. But with lots of water less than 40 feet, where do you start?

"Focus on humps and flats in 35 to 40 feet of water," Doug said. "Winter water temperatures and oxygen levels in lake trout lakes are about equal throughout, except close to the surface and near bottom.

Camp Mobile! In Canadian lakes that don't get much pressure, one secret to catching lots of fish is to move, move, move . . . into an area, cut lots of holes, catch the aggressive fish, and move on. Traveling with a group's always a good idea in remote country.

Lake trout can move freely without environmental restrictions. Again, most preyfish stay shallow."

"And those wintertime feeding machines stay nearby," Al said with a smile.

Fishing shallow water is more efficient. You can fish roughly twice as fast in shallow water as in deep water. You can use lighter baits and get to the bottom faster for checking more spots during a day.

"Like we said," Al observed, "winter trout are active. Drop a lure to them and the odds-call is you'll get bit in the first minute. If you don't get bit within about three minutes, don't expect to clean up in that hole. That's not to say you should move every three minutes. But I'd never sit over a hole for more than 15 minutes without a bite or a fish."

"Come on," Doug said. "I've never seen you stay in the same spot for more than 7 minutes."

According to Doug and Al, even though lakers can use any depth, they tend to hold in water about 20 to 40 feet deep. Large concentrations of their favorite winter baitfish—ciscoes and small whitefish—are often found at this depth, so lakers don't stray far.

"Ciscoes and small whitefish roam open-water areas feeding on plankton and small fish, so lakers have the best feeding opportunities where large structural elements occur at this depth," Al instructed. "Look for points; sunken islands; troughs between islands; and larger hard-bottom sandy flats in 25 to 65 feet of water.

"Doug and I probably catch three-fourths of our lakers through the ice in less than 45 feet of water, and 85 percent to 90 percent in 60 feet or less. Again, it's only partly because lake trout aren't holding very deep; it's because we're more efficient fishing shallower, so that's what we do.

"Scan the map of a typical, lake trout lake or a bay of a larger lake," Al continued, holding up a lake map. "**Area 1** contains a classic structural element typical of a Canadian Shield trout lake—a point with a reef and sunken hump nearby, connected by deeper saddles. This is a gathering area for baitfish and the trout that prey on them.

"Saddles between the shoreline break and the reef and between the shoreline break and the sunken hump are natural funnels. Inside turns along these funnels could be the key spot."

Traditional lake trout wisdom would be to fish off the islands and deeper points. Instead, Al and Doug would concentrate on major flats.

"Start on the big sand flat in the northwest corner in about 18 feet of water and work your way down into the saddle," Al said. "I guarantee that trout will be on those flats all winter—and no one fishes for them."

"The variety of available forage is the key to the attractiveness of shallower flats," Doug observed. "Lakers on flats eat perch, crayfish, ciscoes, or anything else that comes in to feed on plankton or bottom-dwelling organisms. When you clean a trout caught off a flat, you often find all these forage types in them. In trout caught off bluff banks, you find ciscoes and whitefish—and maybe an eelpout. No perch, no crayfish, nothing else.

"Goes back to a concept we've preached forever—all the fish in a body of water aren't doing the same thing at the same time. This is as true of lake trout as of any other fish species. Break with tradition and catch fish that haven't seen a lure since the boys put away their wire line months ago."

"By the way," Al said, still holding his map, "**Area 2 is** a classic point with potential as a trout spot. But because it doesn't have as large a flat or reef as the associated hump and saddles, it probably won't be as consistent a producer as **Area 1**."

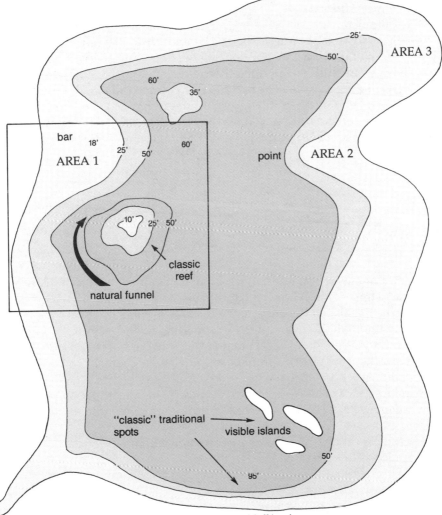

Troughs

Troughs like **Area 3** at the northeast corner of the lake are another little-known lake trout hangout in winter, according to Doug. Troughs aren't easy to find without a contour map. Try checking for them at the mouths of major bays.

"Troughs produce because when fish are roaming, and lake trout roam a lot, they funnel into an area and concentrate," Doug said. "Troughs stockpile big fish like shoppers going up an escalator.

"In **Area 3**, the 25- to 50-foot zone is a flat food shelf, an ideal fishing zone. But lakers may also move into the shallow portion of this bay; so always check the shallower water, too."

Underwater Humps

Al continued, "What we've learned about fishing humps in the last couple years will save you years of trial and error. The best lake trout humps aren't the classic, sharp-breaking 'walleye' humps everyone looks for. Slow-rolling hills outproduce sharp-breaking humps every time.

"That's the good news. The bad news, if you can call it bad, is that you have to fish fast and keep moving. You might have to check the entire hump before contacting fish. Lakers can be in 35 or 40 feet of water, or up on top in water 15 or 18 feet deep. One locational shortcut is seeing clouds

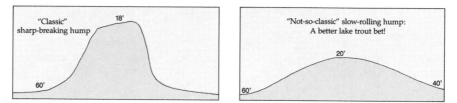

of baitfish on the depthfinder. Where you find baitfish, you'll find lakers.

"Can't stress enough how vital it is to use a depthfinder. I've used one every time I've fished through the ice for many years. I couldn't imagine fishing without it. If I didn't have a properly rigged depthfinder, I don't know if I'd go ice fishing. I feel that strongly about it. That's true especially for lakers, because they can be holding at any depth from bottom to top, and they're so easy to see."

Contour maps of lake trout lakes reveal sections of comparatively shallow water, such as good-size bays and arms with maximum depths of 50 to 60 feet or less. Again, trout will be there, but it's best to avoid those areas and concentrate instead in areas with maximum depths of 70 to 100 feet or more. That's true lake trout country.

"That might sound like a contradiction to our advice about fishing shallower than 40 feet, but it's not," Al said. "Within those deeper sections, look for 25- to 65-foot zones with major structural characteristics. Move beyond other anglers and past tradition, into lake trout spots of the '90s."

Location: Another Look

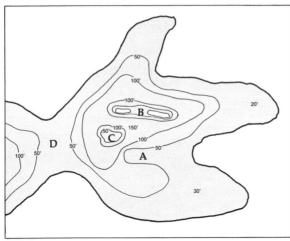

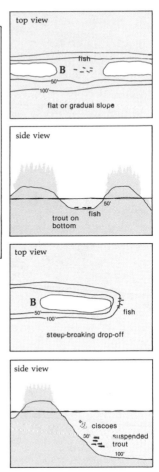

Shallow bays on lake arms aren't trout water. Instead, look for trout in deep main-lake sections.

Relatively shallow water is still important for locating concentrations of trout, however. Not just any shallow water, though, but shallower structural elements in the deep portion of the lake. Points like AREA A, saddle areas between islands like AREA B, humps like AREA C, and saddle areas between points like AREA D are potential trout attractors.

Say you're fishing AREA B. Trout using the 50 foot deep top of AREA B would probably be bottom-oriented. That is, when trout are lying on top of a flat surface or gradual slope, they often feed right on the bottom.

If the fish are along the quick-dropping edge of the area, however, chances are they'll be suspended over deep water. They might be at the same depth (50 feet) as the top of the saddle. Or they might be suspended at the same depth as a school of wandering ciscoes.

Finally, yes, it's possible to find trout over deep, open flats. But they're hard to contact because searching is inefficient in water beyond about 60 feet deep. Trout hold on shallow flats, too, though, and they're much easier to contact there.

Lures

Fishing for lake trout calls for jigging. The 1980s tradition called for a certain staple lure, the airplane jig. We'll discuss the airplane jig in a moment, but first let's look at a new angle on winter lake trout lures—gitzit-type plastic lures of bass-fishing fame.

"After hearing of guys in Colorado smoking big 'greasers' on tube jigs, we took a selection into Canada," Al noted. "Big tubes on a standard jighead were by far the most productive lure on most of our trips."

With modifications, you can get tube jigs ready for lakers. Don't push the jighead completely to the front of the hollow tube. Leave a nose sticking out, so the lure swings to the side when you work it, similar to the action of an airplane jig. Also, pack the inside of the tube with scent, cut bait, or other meat for extra triggering power.

Rigging A Gitzit For Lake Trout

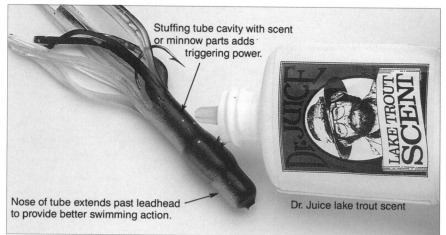

Stuffing tube cavity with scent or minnow parts adds triggering power.

Nose of tube extends past leadhead to provide better swimming action.

Dr. Juice lake trout scent

Rigged this way, gitzit jigs offer the components of a prime lake trout lure. They swim out and return when you jig 'em and never settle back the same way twice. They attract fish from a distance and also provide a lot of triggering power. Lakers hit tubes on a dead rod or when you just barely jig it, because the long tentacles on the tube body quiver even when no action is imparted.

"As for colors?" Al questioned outloud. "We've had success with white and silver, but I think orange would work well, too. And don't overlook phosphorescence—added visibility can be a plus at times.

"I'm not saying we've quit fishing the airplane jig, the bait from the 1980s," Al continued. "Still take 'em on every trip."

The most popular airplanes are from Northland Tackle. The 3/4- to 1-ounce jigs have treble hooks on the wings and a rear stinger treble. Fish are hooked on the stinger almost every time. Because airplane jigs spin, rig them on a ball-bearing snap-swivel to minimize line twist.

"Lots of times you don't have to switch from the airplane jig to anything else, Al said. "It remains the standard against which other winter lake trout lures are measured, because it catches fish.

"Briefly, one way to fish an airplane jig is to: (1) tip it with some kind of meat. (2) Drop the jig into the hole, free-lining it to the bottom under light

Laker Lures

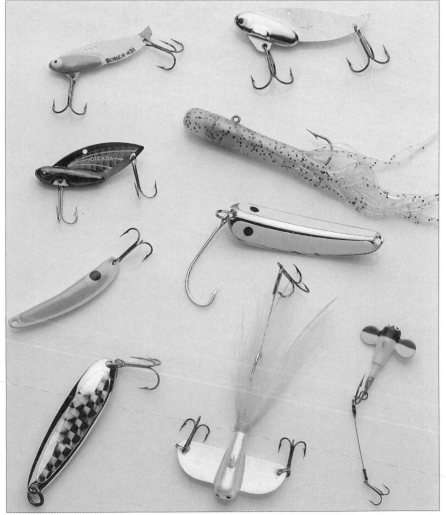

You don't need a big tackle box to be a versatile lake trout jigger. Since you'll be fishing from 20 to 80 feet, lures that sink fast are most efficient. Try blade baits such as the Heddon Sonar, Bullet Bait, and Cicada in the heaviest sizes. Four-inch tube baits like Creme's Super Tube, with a selection of leads from 3/8 to 1 ounce, are a new frontier in laker fishing. And don't hesitate to experiment with other types of plastics. Jigging spoons like Jig-A-Whopper's Knocker Minnow and Hawger Spoon, or Luhr Jensen's Krocodile are effective with meat added. Air-Plane Jigs ranging from 1/4 to 1 ounce complete your selection for lakers.

tension. (Bites occur on the drop, so keep the line slightly taunt on the way down.) The jig will swim in a circle as it drops, like a circling air-plane. (3) Once the jig hits bottom, lift it up and slowly pump it 3 or 4 feet a few times.

"Now reel up about five feet of line and repeat the process. Until you define a depth pattern or until you see fish on your depthfinder, use this method all the way to the surface."

Leadhead jigs tipped with meat, jigging spoons like the Jig-A-Whopper Hawger Spoon, bladebaits like Heddon's Sonar or Reef Runner Cicada, and rattlebaits like Normark's Rattl'n Rap or Jig-A-Whopper's Knocker Minnow work for vertical jigging, too.

Rods and Reels

For jigging for lakers, Doug and Al break from another long-held ice fishing tradition and use relatively long rods. Try rods like the heaviest of the Berkley Northern Lites series or Jig-A-Whopper's rods made by Thorne Brothers, ranging in length from 36 to about 48 inches. These rods, as was mentioned in the chapter on jigging, offer "measured give," not pool-cue stiffness, so you can work lures effectively in deeper water. And they're forgiving tools for fighting a rolling, slashing fighter like the lake trout.

Baitcasting equipment has a slight advantage over spinning tackle when you're constantly changing depths. On a casting reel, just press the button and thumb the spool on the way down; it's easier than opening and closing the bail on a spinning reel. But spinning equipment is most available and works fine.

Try 8- to 10-pound-test mono for most lake trout jigging. But if you're on water that offers a crack at really big fish, or if you want your lure to work slower, try 12- or 14-pound test.

Strategy

Because lake trout are active in winter, a run-and-gun strategy puts the odds in your favor, especially if you want to catch lots of fish. And who doesn't?

For giant lakers, though, it's hard to beat bottom fishing with a big chunk of scrungy meat. Wait them out on a high-percentage spot.

Al and Doug prefer the numbers game. They'll fish circles around guys who sit with their bait on the bottom.

"Couldn't fish like we do without power augers," Al said with a smile. "Stay away from anything designated 'light.' Carry the heaviest, meanest piece of machinery you can handle. We're talking lots of ice and lots of 10-inch holes.

"In your fishing group, designate one person as the hole-driller, at least to begin with. The driller drills holes, shallow and deep, in a zigzag fashion across the area you plan to fish. A partner works with the driller, checking depths with a sonar unit. If you have more companions, they follow, clean out holes, and start fishing. Making 'Swiss Cheese,' as we call this, lets you work quickly from hole to hole.

A longer rod means efficient presentation and a ton of fun.

"The noise of drilling may or may not spook trout," Al continued. "Frankly, I've seen as many situations where I think it attracts trout. Lots of times we catch a trout on the first drop after drilling.

"If you're fishing alone, you have to do everything yourself. That doesn't make multiple holes any less important—just takes a little more time to get fishing."

"When you move to the next area," Doug said, "rotate so the driller becomes a fisherman, the sonar person becomes the driller, and so on. Everyone shares the work, no one sweats too hard, and everyone gets a chance to be first to drop a bait down fresh holes.

"Where it's legal, Al likes to fish two rods. Not me—just too much

Fishing A Swimming Jig

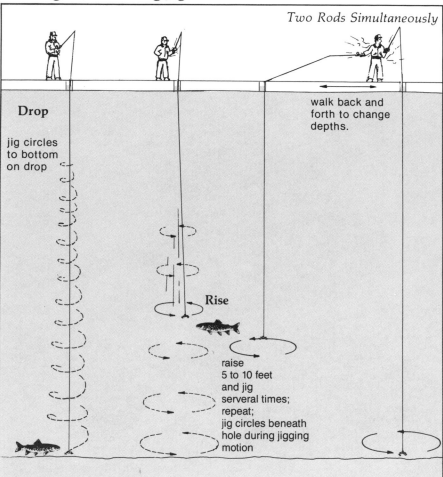

Two Rods Simultaneously

Drop

jig circles
to bottom
on drop

walk back and
forth to change
depths.

Rise

raise
5 to 10 feet
and jig
serveral times;
repeat;
jig circles beneath
hole during jigging
motion

Freeline the tipped jig to the bottom under light tension. Bites occur on the drop, so keep the line fairly taut on the way down. The jig spirals and swims in a semicircle.

Once the jig hits the bottom, lift it off the bottom and slowly pump it up and down a few times. Reel up 5 feet or so and repeat the process. Until a depth pattern develops, fish this method on the way to the surface. Trout can see farther in shallow water, though, so work in 10-foot increments in less than 30 feet of water.

Another method: Cut two holes 20 feet apart at either the same of different depth levels. Take one rod and drop the jig to the bottom. Take another rod and drop the jig halfway down. Walk back and forth between the two holes with a rod in each hand. As you move toward one hole, that jig drops, while the other rises.

Tipping

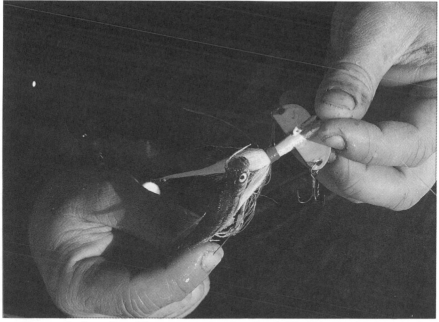

Tip an airplane jig with meat—strip of sucker belly (1 inch wide by 4 inches long) or a sucker or shiner minnow the same length. If you have a choice, use shiner minnows. Compared with the fat, round bodies of sucker minnows, the flat body shape of shiners functions better on an airplane jig. Shiner-tipped jigs tend to swim in a wider circle that's more attractive to trout.

If you can't use fresh bait, keep precut belly meat or minnows by placing them in a plastic bag (no water) and pouring table salt over them. The bait won't freeze, even in cold weather. The salt keeps the minnows or meat semifresh and ready to use. Soaking the bait in water once it's on your jig puffs the bait back almost to its original shape. You can also keep bait fresh by placing it in sawdust liberally doused with anise oil or a scent product with an anise oil base.

work. Al, though, drops an airplane jig down and fishes it to the bottom in 10-foot spurts—drops it down 10 feet and jigs it, drops it down another 10 feet and jigs it. He repeats this all the way down. Then he fishes the bottom for 30 seconds and finally leaves that rod sitting on the snow with the bail open or the button pushed, so a fish can take line if it hits.

"Then he goes to a second hole and works a gitzit down the same way, stair-stepping it to the bottom. It's amazing how often he comes back to the first rod with the bait lying on the bottom and sees the line swimming away.

"He fishes the two rods back and forth until he moves to another area where he starts the whole thing over again. On a good trout lake, he contends you get plenty of extra fish every day that you wouldn't otherwise

Hole Patterns

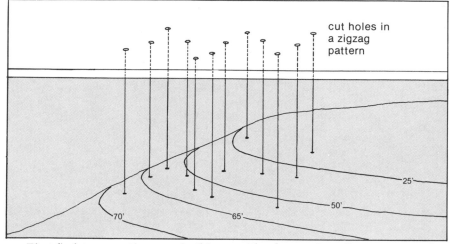

cut holes in a zigzag pattern

First find a prospective area; in this case, it's a large point. One person carries an auger, the other a portable deptfinder.

Find the approximate edge of the structural element, and then cut holes in a zigzag pattern along the length of the area from shallow to deep water.

have had. Perhaps. But the same argument can be made for concentrating on fishing one rod effectively. But why argue. Try both approaches."

How Often Should You Move? "The longest I think you should fish without a bite is 15 minutes, even after you've caught several fish," Al suggests. "If you drill 10 holes and catch 3 fish in 15 minutes (and that's common), it might take you 3 more hours to catch 3 more fish. Better to move to another spot and punch 10 more holes.

"The typical fisherman will drill one hole, drop the jig 35 feet, and sit there for 3 days. It's been done that way for 50 years. No matter the conditions, you have a better chance if you drill a lot of holes. And odds call for a bite in the first few minutes of jigging in each hole."

When you're on an unfamiliar lake trout lake, don't fish where everyone else is fishing. Study a map, cut holes, and start catchin' instead of just fishin'!

"Tradition calls for fishing along bluff banks," Al concluded. "Don't head to bluff walls because that's traditionally where lake trout are fished for in winter. Lakers use bluff banks. But if you're only fishing bluffs, you're missing most of the fish most of the time. And you only have so much time . . . and none of it's worth wasting!"

Tip-ups

A tip-up makes a good second line while you're jigging. Set lines are usually placed on the bottom or suspended just a few feet off bottom. They're usually more effective on top of the flat portion of a point or sunken island where lakers are likely to be on the bottom.

FINAL TIPS

If lake trout rush your lure but won't bite it, drop to 8-pound-test line and a smaller airplane jig or other lure. Next time a fish rushes your lure but doesn't bite, crank it toward the surface as fast as you can for about 10 cranks and stop. Don't drop it back down. Often, they'll come up and strike it.

When your partner hooks a trout, drop your line about 20 feet down a nearby hole and jig it a few times. "You won't do this 10 times without catching a fish," Al guaranteed. "Lakers follow hooked fish because they often regurgitated food."

Time of Day? "Seems like early morning is the key bite most of the time," Doug said. "You need the sun up a bit, but 50 to 60 percent of your fish go during that first 2 to 3 hours on most days. Morning is the key time.

"My guess is that lakers, like pike, don't feed effectively after dark. They're hungry in the morning."

Weather? Al Lindner: "Sunny seems better than overcast. But in winter, that doesn't necessarily mean a classic cold-front day. Ideal conditions? A warming trend and stable weather."

Selective Harvest? Catch all you want, but limit the keeping. It takes a long time to grow a big lake trout. You can damage a lake trout population quickly if you keep too many big fish.

The good news is that lakers through the ice are very releasable, as long as you don't pull them from the hole and bounce them around on the snow and ice. Remove the hook and quickly get the fish back down the hole.

CHAPTER 13

PIKE...
AND MUSKIES

Frozen water means big pike. At least it can. Or let's say it should. Or let's say it will. If you know a few simple tricks to ice a pike.
Doug Stange

"**P**ike so big the slime alone weighed 10 pounds," Toad Smith laughed over the phone. "You hadda see it to believe it."

"Yeah, well, you're right about that. And would you be offering to guide me now, ayee?" Doug asked, practicing his central-Canadian end-of-the-sentence "ayees" in anticipation of a trip to Manitoba, Ontario, or where the heck was Toad fishing?

"Secret."

"Come on," Doug pleaded. "You didn't just call to talk pike. You want to show me. You gotta! I'll show you how to catch them if you take me to them."

"Already can catch 'em."

"But I'll show you how to catch 'em better."

Challenge made and accepted, Doug and Toad headed to Manitoba in search of "iceopiketric" exercise.

There's only one doctor-recommended iceopiketric exercise, and that's pike fishing. Toad Smith gets plenty.

Toad is one of those back-to-the-basics guys with an uncanny knack of finding big pike. The Dakotas, Iowa, Minnesota, Manitoba, Ontario. Territory conquered.

"Been East?" Toad asked Doug once.

"Yep."

"Eastern pike like western pike like northern pike?" he asked, enjoying his play with words.

"Pike's pike. Same fish, same basic tactics."

Toad's particularly good at location. No fooling. He moves around a

WHERE?

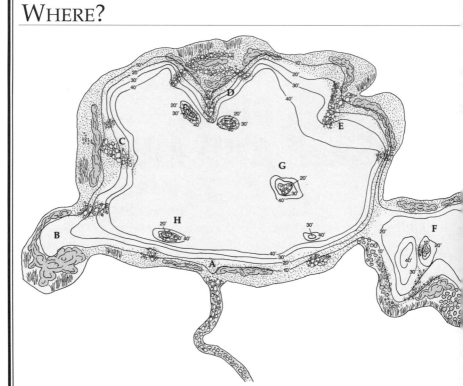

A prominent structural element like a bar with a variety of habitat including points that drop off into deep water are the primary key to pike location during winter. Prominent bars gather baitfish and pike, and combination habitat holds them.

Large bays also gather traveling baitfish and pike. If there's enough deep water and enough combination habitat, pike may use the bay all winter. The biggest pike tend to use bays during early and late season, however, and prefer main-lake habitat during midwinter.

lake with the mystical flair of a well witcher. When he says here, he means here; right here, big pike, maybe not today, but if not today, tomorrow, and if not tomorrow, the next day.

But right here. Here! That's the way Toad is and that's the way big pike are during winter.

"You wanna catch little pike," Toad will say, "spend your time up on shallow flats. You'll get exercise. You wanna catch big pike, figure on waiting."

Toad waits well. He's taken a couple hundred deer, several dozen bear and antelope, plus elk, turkey, buffalo, boar, and who can keep track of

---

FEEDER CREEK A—Current attracts pike at early and late ice. Concentrate on the weed breaks at the mouth of the creek.

BAY B—Good depth leading into this bay. Big pike are likely to use the weededge all winter. Primarily a first- and final-ice spot, however, for during midwinter, larger pike tend to move to main-lake areas.

BAR C—Combinations! Weeds, rock, and sand on a bar that protrudes into the lake. Plus rocky points that drop into deep water. Structural combinations plus the combinations of BAY B near BAR C make this area potentially one of the most consistent pike producers in the lake.

BAR D—This bar will hold pike all season. Plenty of weededges, rock edges, rock drop-offs, plus two rocky sunken islands pike use at midwinter. You can spend the entire season fishing the options on this bar.

BAR E—Another good one, but without the total combinations of BAY B and BAR C, or BAR D. Worth fishing only if better areas are pressured by other fishermen.

BAY F—Because of its size and depth, consider this bay a separate lake. During early season, fish the inside corner near the outlet and the weed point. Switch to the saddle area between the weed point and the sunken island, and fish the sunken island during midwinter. Pressure? Try the weededge in the not-so-prominent inside turn on the north shore.

ISLAND G—Too small and isolated to hold many pike, but worth checking during midwinter when prominent lake areas get lots of fishing pressure. The key is fishing it before anyone else catches the few, but likely large pike holding there.

ISLAND H—Same comments as ISLAND G; however ISLAND H is a more traveled area. Pike holding near CREEK A or in BAY B, for example, could move to ISLAND H as winter progresses.

whatever else, with a bow from various stands around the country. Toad has spent half his life waiting. He's deadly patient. Shwack! Another whitetail. Thump! Another pike. Toad. Ultimate predator.

"Sleek, mean, and lean. Float like a butterfly, sting like a bee. That's me," he says. "Like a cheetah, maybe, or a panther, or a muskie."

"Like a barrel-chested, grizzled, whiskered shovelhead cat," Doug says.

Doug doesn't wait well, so Toad and Doug make an interesting fishing pair.

"No more coffee," Toad'll say as Doug begins to pour. "Relax! It'll happen. It always happens."

"I know. But I want it to happen now," Doug will say.

"Relax!"

"Think I'll take another round with the ice ladle and clean the tip-up holes."

"Relax."

Waiting's hard work. To make it pay, make sure you're waiting on one of Toad's "right heres." Nothing mystical about a good spot, though, for pike location under ice is like this.

Structural Prominence

"Pike like to eat," Doug offered. "Therefore they spend most of their time on major food-gathering areas, which for the most part means a major structural element like a bar—shoal. So you don't misunderstand, sunken islands are bars, too; and points may be portions of bars.

"In a reservoir with large creek arms, key on bars in a creek arm. In flowing rivers, pike hold on or near bars within river lakes, backwaters, or side channels. And in lakes or reservoirs without major creek arms, the best spots tend to be combination areas—bars with points near bays or small creek arms."

The larger and more prominent the structural element, or better yet, combination of structural elements, the more likely they are to consistently attract forage that consistently attract pike.

"For example," Doug said, "the primary structural element I fished on my first winter pike trip to Manitoba. Al Lindner and I plus Winnipeg, Manitoba, friend and hunting and fishing guide Ted Jowett fished a mile-or-so-long finger (bay), almost a creek arm I suppose, off a portion of the Winnipeg River, which flows from Lake of the Woods generally northwest to Lake Winnipeg. Halfway down the finger, a one-acre sunken island rises from 45 feet of water to 10. A 25-foot-deep saddle connects the island to shore. Lots of rocks and a few weeds are atop the island. The weeds aren't vitally important to this structure.

"What is important is the combination of the saddle and hump that protrudes halfway across the finger. Like a long arm, it gathers wandering baitfish and pike. The 8 bigger pike we caught there on our first trip

Bar D

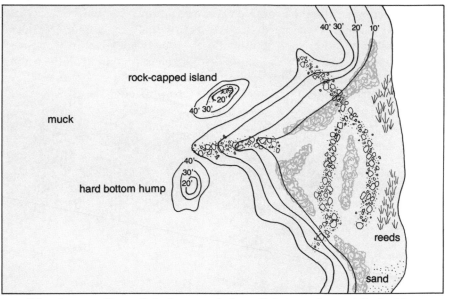

Pike chase small preyfish along weededges. Points, and especially inside turns in weeds, tend to concentrate both prey and predators. Another important location, especially for larger pike, includes spots like the tip of the bar and the sunken humps near it. Large pike use deeper water for most of the year, so they're often in deeper areas at first-ice.

ranged from 18 to 23 pounds. They were using the drop-off breakline on the saddle side of the island, or the saddle itself."

Al entered the discussion. "I've never seen a distinctive saddle portion of any major structural element that didn't attract pike, even when the outside or sharp-dropping portion of the island looked good, too. Saddles are that important. If the saddle hadn't been present, the deep edge of the bar would have been the most important area."

The point though is that prominent structural elements gather pike. But we know some of you don't like a Canadian example because you'll say, "Sure, go where the fishing's easy and the fish are big; what does that prove when I fish a lake outside Chicago?"

Try fishing West Okoboji in northwest Iowa sometime. It's a big, clear, deep body of water out of place in the Iowa landscape. It's one of North America's most intensely used bodies of water.

Iowa. The number and average size of the pike change, but the structural story's the same: Major structural elements attract pike. In this case, choose from many major structural elements, but two key elements are bars that block the entrance of two major bays, Smith's Bay and Emerson's Bay. The pike move along weededges, rock edges, and drop-off edges on the inside and outside of the bars.

Structural Variety

"After considering the prominence of a structural element, consider its structural variety," Al suggested. "Weedgrowth attracts forage. So does rock-rubble and other rock combinations. Weeds and rock in combination with sand transitions in shallow water mean pike in shallow water during portions of the winter season. But when pike go deep, as they often do during midwinter, rock-rubble drop-off edges and especially

Toad Smith wrestling a good one that hit a deadbait suspended 8 feet down in 12 feet of water near the edge of major main-lake bar.

deep rock humps near shallow cover are usually where they hold.

"Suspended pike? Sure, in some lakes. But most pike suspend relative to prominent structural elements. No use worrying about those that don't, because there's no consistent way to find them."

What is worth worrying about is basic seasonal pike movement based on the portion of the winter season. Think shallow, deep, and deep and shallow during early-, mid-, and late-ice, respectively.

Seasonal Movement

"*Early-ice.* Think shallow. Think great fishing," Doug said. "Some pike will always be deep because some forage is always deep. But by early-ice, most pike, many of them large, have settled into a routine centered around prominent shallow foraging areas.

"Shallow at early-ice means plankton, which means zooplankton, which means small fish, which means larger fish. Food! As the season progresses and the ice thickens, light penetration decreases along with water temperature. Shallow is no longer so inviting or advantageous.

"The second reason pike tend to be shallow early is because for months they haven't been bothered much by fishermen or boat traffic."

Doug continued, "Pike and other fish populations tend to drift deeper as the season progresses. Deeper water means stability to carry fish through midwinter. But lack of fishing pressure and activity on the ice lengthens the time pike stay shallow. Pressure hastens their retreat to deeper water. By midseason, only on seldom-fished lakes are many large pike holding shallow.

"Early, concentrate on shallow edges on or along prominent bars. Remember again that bars include sunken islands. The outside or deep side of the weededge usually is the key. Increase your odds of contacting pike by fishing pockets (inside turns) and points in the edge. Weedless pockets in weedgrowth on top of bars, sometimes well away from a drop-off edge or the outside edges of a weedline, also attract pike, however. Experiment. We know little about everything, almost nothing about some things, and when it comes to pike, well, they're always where you find them."

"Think combination," Al observed. "Points or turns in bars or weed-lines that coincide with rock bottom and drop-offs attract more pike. Toad likes points that drop off in stair-step fashion as opposed to points that crash immediately into deep water. Agreed. I would add, too, that the best weededges don't grow to the edge of a sharp drop-off. The best weededges have a clear holding-ramp kind of area before the drop-off.

"Find a combination structural area, place your trap (bait) properly, and if a big pike's around, you'll get him. Timber, by the way, may replace weeds as a primary source of attractive shallow cover. And don't forget current areas early, although they poop out quickly and don't get hot again until late-ice."

Midwinter Concentrates Bigger Pike

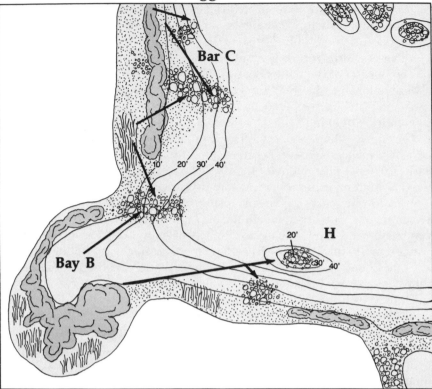

Pike activity usually slows during midwinter, but it can still mean some of the season's finest fishing. Bigger pike often concentrate in specific areas that are rarely heavily fished because they're rocky and deep. Too many pike fishermen think pike only relate to shallow weeds.

Probable scenario in this lake area? Bigger pike in BAY B will gradually move from the bay and concentrate on the deep-dropping rock point at the mouth of the bay. Some pike may also wander from the other side of the bay and hold on rocky sunken ISLAND H or the small adjacent rocky shoreline point. The pike from the shallow flat on BAR C will tend to hold in deeper water near the rocky slide at the face of the bar. Set a trap and wait.

Midseason. Think deep, according to Doug and Al. Many pike fishermen could turn poor midseason fishing into good fishing by not spending all their time working weededges. Look for rocky drop-offs or rock humps near shallow holding areas. Isolated midlake humps may be worth fishing if obvious areas are being pressured.

Pike fishermen who don't want to fish deeper rocky structural elements should be resigned to catching smaller pike. Great eating!

"Another option is a trip to a remote lake where pike haven't been

Seasonal Trends

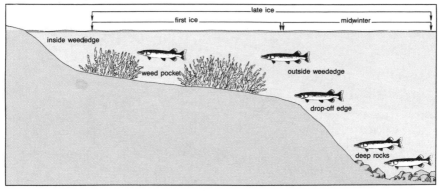

Pike location revolves around shallow flats, drop-off edges (which may coincide with the outside weededge), and deeper rocky areas including drop-offs or points, or portions of sunken islands.

During early season, bigger pike are evenly distributed deep and shallow. Some big pike will be using shallow flats, especially weed pockets on the flats and the outside edge of the weedgrowth near deeper water. Distinct inside weededges may also be used. The pike are shallow because their food's shallow and they-haven't been bothered by fishermen for several months.

By midseason, most bigger pike retreat to deeper water. That means the outside edge of weedgrowth or the drop-off edge, but also deeper rocky areas including portions of rock drop-offs and sunken islands.

At late-ice, big pike are again evenly distributed from shallow to deep water.

bothered," Al said. "It's the reason we travel to Manitoba at least once a winter. You still find big pike shallow in remote lakes, but even there, be willing to fish deeper rocks during midseason or you'll miss big fellas."

Doug noted, "I've jigged pike from 55 feet (fishing for walleyes), by the way, and caught them on tip-ups set 50 feet deep (fishing for pike). Agreed, however, that in most lakes, most bigger pike come from 15 to 35 feet of water during midwinter. Granted, too, depth is relative. Twelve feet is relatively deep in a body of water where weedgrowth ends at 6 feet and the maximum depth is 25 feet."

Late season. Doug and Al agree, think shallow and deep. In lakes where the pike season runs until ice-out, look for bigger pike to gradually abandon deep water and roam shallow again as ice-out approaches. Deeper weededges on sections of bars adjacent to shallow spawning bays are good spots. Check weedgrowth near current, too. Late season is one of the best times of year to catch a huge pike.

Presentation

Tradition holds that during winter, pike fishermen sit in one place . . . and wait for a fish to bite, or their minnow to die of old age, or their five-

Depth Set Zones for Tip-ups

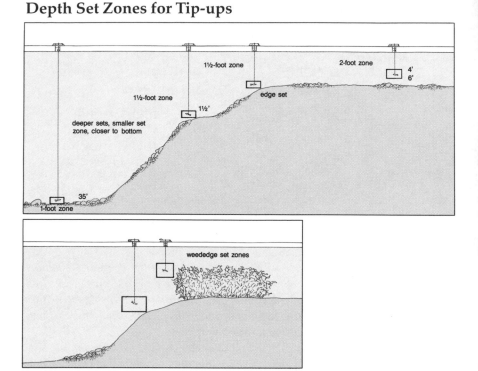

gallon bucket to screw a hole in the ice so they can fall through and get it over with. As Toad says, sometimes waiting patiently can be a good idea—if you're waiting in the right spot.

Waiting, to many folks, means fishing a tip-up. Winter pike and tip-ups are another long-standing combo. Tip-ups. Properly set traps. Is there another way, a better way to consistently ice big pike?

"A few years back I would have said no," Doug said, "for in 25 years of ice fishing, I'd caught more pike with tip-ups than anything else. What could be better? You set the trap and wait. Set the trap in the right spot, and it'll happen. And with the addition of quick-strike rigging, a tandem-hook arrangement that lets you strike immediately after a pike hits, when pike hit you almost always have them.

"But several years of serious experimentation with jigging techniques has convinced me that in most bodies of water, jigging will outfish stationary tip-ups 10 to 1. Go one step farther, though, and use jigging in conjunction with a tip-up system to ensure success.

"I would never say that jigging a pike on a rod and reel is more fun than catching a pike on a tip-up. Playing a big pike on a hand-held line, feeling the instant surge and power of each move, feeling the icy line stripping through your fingers is an ice-fishing tradition. I hope it remains so.

"But a 15-pound pike on a medium-action rod-and-reel combo is a thrill or two, too. Ready for a tackle-testing run when you set the hook? Drag work? Better not make a mistake at the hole!"

Jigging Versus Tip-ups

"Although most of the ice-fishing world still doesn't agree," Al explained, "in most instances, jigging is the most efficient way to catch fish through the ice. It's a matter of percentages, a matter of covering

Jigging offers the potential to outproduce tip-up sets by 10 to 1. And jigging triggers pike, large and small.

Ready to jig.

more water searching for fish, rather than sitting soaking a bait, waiting for fish to come to you. In short, it's a matter of efficiency."

OK, you might be saying. That might be true for panfish or walleyes. But there aren't many big pike. Jigging won't get much action. I'm better off waiting if I'm in a good spot.

"Comparatively speaking," Doug offered, "jigging still is more efficient and therefore usually more effective than stationary sets. Jigging is more work, but you'll catch more pike in the long run. And again, if you have confidence in tip-ups—we do!—use a jigging approach coupled with a stationary set. In most states, at least two lines are legal through the ice."

Not only is jigging a more efficient way to find fish, it's usually a more efficient way to trigger them. Think of each presentation choice in terms of attracting and triggering. Each presentation move has an attracting phase and a triggering phase.

Jig a flash lure like the Rocker Minnow for walleyes, for example, and the immediate lift-fall portion of the maneuver is the attracting phase, the phase that catches a fish's eye and draws it to the bait. The settle-back-below-the-hole action, plus the time when the jig sits still below the hole, make up the triggering phase—what makes the fish hit after it's attracted to the bait.

With a tip-up, you depend on the inherent qualities of your bait to attract and trigger pike. These qualities can be enhanced by the liveliness of the bait or by using a flap-armed tip-up (wind tip-up) that moves the bait.

"That may or may not be enough to do the job," Doug continued. "At times, more attraction or triggering means more fish. Jigging allows perfect control of the relative amount of attraction and triggering portions of the presentation. It's more difficult with a tip-up.

"Say you're fishing a dead bait like smelt below a tip-up. Smelt are a fine, oily, attractive pike bait; but the typical 6-inch smelt is too small to consistently attract big pike. An 8-inch sucker is a better bet and smells

Aggression Spectrum For Pike

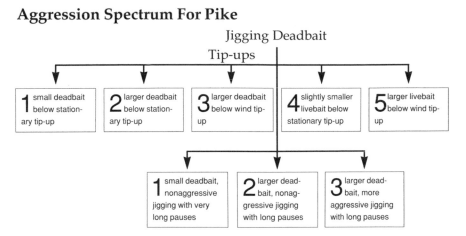

just as good. More importantly, this bigger bait can be seen better—more attracting power."

When you're fishing, even when you're using a stationary approach like a tip-up, make a judgement about the activity level of pike. Tailor your presentation package to match it. You're looking for a proper balance of attraction and triggering.

A dead bait is a good choice for inactive pike. But an inactive pike can't eat what it can't see. Active pike, on the other hand, eat almost anything they see. In both cases, seeing is the vital first step in the triggering process.

With a tip-up, adding more attraction to a dead bait presentation may be as subtle as using a bigger bait (*Step 1* in the "aggression spectrum"). Coupling a bigger bait with a wind tip-up presentation that adds movement to the bait is more aggressive (*Step 2*). Replacing the big dead bait with a slightly smaller live bait is still more aggressive (*Step 3*). Finally, for maximum aggressiveness, add a big, lively bait (*Step 4*).

"In each instance, visual qualities are added to the bait (your presentation)," Doug explained. "Pike must see the bait before they can eat it. But the presentation must not be so aggressive that a fish in a certain feeding mood is intimidated once it gets to the bait. A proper measure of attraction followed by a proper measure of triggering means success with a tip-up or a rod and reel.

"But jigging lets you control the relative measures of attraction and triggering in your presentation better than a tip-up. A jigging approach also lets you move easily, and keep moving."

Move

To compare a jigging approach to a tip-up approach for winter pike, Doug and Al suggest you imagine you're fishing a main-lake bar adjacent to a large bay. Both the bay and the bar attract forage and pike. Say, how-

Move!

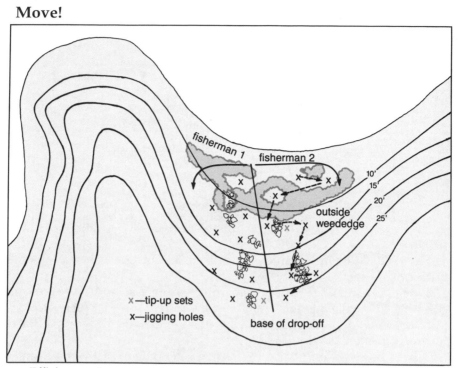

fisherman 1

fisherman 2

10'
15'
20'
25'

outside
weededge

x —tip-up sets
x —jigging holes

base of drop-off

Efficiency. In most states, two fishermen can each fish two or more lines. Four tip-ups set in good spots should get pike action. Let's set one tip-up on the flat, two along the outside weededge, and one deep at the base of the drop-off. That's good coverage, but not the most efficient coverage you could get with a combination jigging and tip-up approach.

Cut lots of holes in key spots. Divide the bar in half perhaps. One fisherman can set a tip-up shallow and the other fisherman a deep one. Begin jigging quietly, moving from one hole to the next after 5 minutes. You'll get much more efficient coverage for the time you spend.

ever, it's midwinter and most of the pike are relating to the main-lake bar, a bar with a large flat containing some remaining weedgrowth that ends at 12 feet. The drop-off edge of the bar has scattered rock that slides into 25 feet of water.

Pike will roam the flat. Other pike will relate to the edge of the weeds or the edge of the bar. Pike will also hold in deep water at the base of the drop-off.

It'll take at least 3 guys fishing 2 tip-ups each to cover the bar. You'll want several tip-ups on the flat, several along the drop-off edge, and several at the base of the rock slide.

"A fine approach for bigger pike," Doug said, "would be to each place one tip-up along the drop-off edge and another at the base of the rock slide. But a lot of water's not covered, even by 3 fishermen."

One fisherman, using a combination jigging and tip-up approach, can cover the bar better than 3 guys using only tip-ups. Drill plenty of holes, enough to cover the top, the edge, and the base of the bar. Let things quiet down while you set out a tip-up, probably over the base of the drop-off.

Begin jigging. Move from hole to hole to hole. Never stay at any hole longer than 5 minutes, unless you're convinced pike are right there, right now (such as seeing them on a depthfinder or getting strikes). If pike are there and you're jigging right, you'll have them soon if they're going to bite.

Al concluded, "Tip-ups may do a better job with very inactive pike, the ones that may take an hour to decide to strike. But jigging will get everything else in short order. Efficiency! Walk quietly, though. Pike can be spooky in shallow water under ice."

Rigging

We won't get into detail about what makes a good jigging rod for heavier baits, because we did that in the equipment chapter. You'll want to know more, though . . .

Line—If 100-pound pike existed, you could handle them on 12-pound-test line. Twelve-pound line is right for handling lures, baits . . . and pike. Try Stren; clear Berkley XL; Bagley Black Label Silver Thread; or the newer entry, Berkley Cold Weather line. "You don't need a super-tough line to fish through ice," Doug offered. "I've never seen high-quality monofilament fray on the ice. I think the fraying so many writers refer to is a hallucination caused by spending winters in Florida writing about ice fishing."

Leaders—Wire is absolutely necessary. "Don't talk to me about heavy monofilament," Doug said. "Use it and you'll lose fish and get fewer strikes. Stranded wire is thinner and less visible than monofilament of the same test."

You can get stranded wire from several sources mentioned in the equipment chapter. (Get some 8 pound, too, for walleyes!) Order break strengths from 12 to 27 pounds. You'll need forceps, #6 or #8 trebles, and #10 swivels to tie your own leaders. Pretied quick-strike rigs are available from H.T. Enterprises or Bait Rigs Tackle Company.

Baits

Airplane jigs, modified flash lures, and several other lure options trigger pike. The best bet, however, is to jig a dead bait on a quick-strike rig.

"I prefer 8-inch baits like suckers, ciscoes, or very large smelt, for reasons mentioned earlier," said Doug. "Big chubs also work, when you can get them, and I'm sure other local baits will work, too.

"Suckers work well because they have a big, heavy head that sinks slowly without having to add shot. Big ciscoes tend to roll and spin and sink horizontally, which most fishermen assume is perfect.

At the Hole

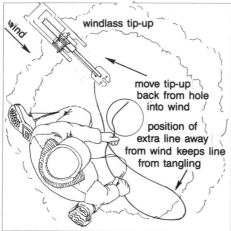

windlass tip-up

move tip-up back from hole into wind

position of extra line away from wind keeps line from tangling

You've properly positioned your wind tip-up upwind from the hole. Handle a strike by gently lifting the tip-up and moving it another foot away from the hole. You should be kneeling at a right angle to the wind so your line blows away from the hole. This keeps your line from tangling as you give and take line. The procedure is the same for a stationary tip-up. Always shovel snow from around the hole so your line doesn't snag on it as you fight a pike.

- Don't strike hard with light tackle. A "lift" or straight pull will do it.
- Take your time. You almost can't lose.
- Gaffs are only for fish you keep.
- Gently but firmly lead the fish's head into the hole. Once his head starts coming, the rest follows.
- Head out? Grab the fish below the head with gloved hands.

"Important point: Use the term 'jigging' and most anglers instantly think of open-water jigging, where a bait is moved forward. When you tip a live bait on a jig for open-water fishing, it makes perfect sense to place the head of the live bait so it looks natural moving forward.

"But you want just the opposite effect while fishing vertically through the ice. When you jig, bring the tail of the bait up first so it flutters and sinks head first on the fall, and holds head-down while it sits still.

"It's wrong," Doug continued, "to believe that baits must hang horizontally to be attractive to pike. Baits that sink head first tend to be grabbed head first, right where your lead hook us. If a bait doesn't sink head first, add a 3/0 shot to one tine on the treble hook nearest to the head of a bait."

Two reasons for quick-strike rigging: First, you'll hook more pike; second, you'll hook them in the mouth. If you fish often, you'll catch enough pike to release the bigger fellows. Takes a long time to grow a 16-pound pike. Keep a few smaller guys for pike patties.

Insert the hook farthest up your leader into the bait just behind the dorsal fin. The end hook should be just behind the bait's head. If pike are taking the bait too aggressively—too deeply—move the tandem rigging toward the bait's tail. If you're jigging right, pike almost always grab the bait head first.

Jigging Technique

"Say you're fishing the edge of a bar 14 feet deep," Al said. "Your bait is hanging head-down just above the hole; your rod tip is about 2 feet above the hole. Proceed in one of two ways.

"Open your bail and place your index finger on the spool to control the amount of line spilling from the spool. Let out enough line to slowly drop the bait about 5 feet. Hold there momentarily to give a pike a shot at the bait. When you're in less than 15 feet of water, pike may be riding anywhere in the water column, and it isn't unusual for one to snap the bait on the first drop. In deeper water beyond the drop-off, they almost always hold within 3 feet of bottom.

"After a moment, lift your rod tip about 2 feet to jig the bait and send it

Cover the Column

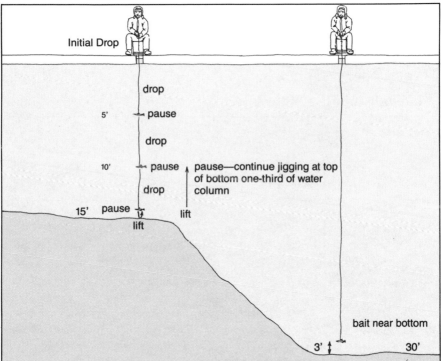

Doug Stange suggests these rules for covering a column of water effectively:

When fishing water less than about 15 feet deep, consider the entire water column pike territory. On your first drop, let your bait fall to 5 feet, pause; let it fall to 10 feet, pause; and let it fall to the bottom before pausing it a foot above the bottom. Then spend the majority of your time with the bait suspended at the top of the bottom one-third of the water column. In other words, at 15 feet, raise the bait to about 10 feet. This gives pike at each depth a chance to see the bait.

In deep water, keep your bait near the bottom. If you're using a depthfinder, raise your bait only when fish come through at other levels.

careening to the side and fluttering down. At the top of the lift, let another 3 to 5 feet of line spill from the spool. Follow the line down with your rod tip after you place your finger back on the spool to keep more line from spilling out. Again, let the bait settle and wait a moment.

"By now your bait is about 10 feet down in 14 feet of water—prime territory. Jig again, however, and let the bait drop to the bottom before lifting it up a foot off bottom and holding it there. Then bring the bait up to the 10-foot level to continue jigging."

(Yes, use your depthfinder to alert you when a pike swims below. But it's still necessary to "cover the column" in this fashion, because pike can be holding out of sonar cone coverage and yet be attracted by your jigging.)

"When you tiptoe to a new hole," Doug continued for Al, "the first series of drops is the highest percentage series. If a pike doesn't take on the first drop series, place your bait in the top of the bottom third of the water column; in other words, in 14 feet of water, fish at about 9 or 10 feet. At this level, pike hugging bottom can see your jigged bait and so can fish hovering high."

An Angle on Pike

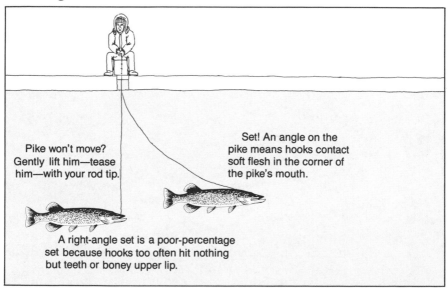

Pike won't move? Gently lift him—tease him—with your rod tip.

Set! An angle on the pike means hooks contact soft flesh in the corner of the pike's mouth.

A right-angle set is a poor-percentage set because hooks too often hit nothing but teeth or boney upper lip.

Some pike will grab a bait and run; others will grab and move off slowly; and still others will grab and stay put. The softest flesh is in the corner of a pike's mouth. It's difficult to hook the corner of the mouth when you set with the pike directly below you.

If a pike absolutely won't move off even as you patiently wait for a minute, take a chance and set. Sometimes you can make a pike move by teasing him—lift him gently with your rod tip. You'll rarely miss pike that are at an angle away from you when you set.

"Continue jigging by slowly raising your entire rod, not just the rod tip, about 2 to 3 feet and then letting the bait fall back to the intended depth as you follow the line and bait back with the rod.

"Always keep your rod tip several feet above the hole. Pike may charge, grab, and keep moving. If your rod tip is inches above the hole, you can't react other than with a scream."

Doug and Al suggest reacting to a take by steadily giving line. Just let it flow easily under the finger that's pinning line on an open spool. You're in control and can feel exactly where the pike is going.

When you're ready, grab the line with your index finger and set. Pull steadily is a better description. Don't set too hard. Put a solid bend in the rod and keep it there. When the pike runs, control line release with your finger until you close the bail and let the drag do the work. This system of reel, line, and rod handling takes practice, but works best in our estimation.

An alternative procedure is to fish with your drag set so loosely that a pike can always take line without much resistance. To drop your bait, strip line with your free hand. Set the hook either by tightening the drag or by holding the spool with your free hand.

Notes

If a pike grabs your bait below the hole, give him a moment to move before you set. A right-angle straight up-and-down set is a low-percentage move. "I can't remember a fish I missed that I let move off just a bit before setting the hook," Doug added.

Always keep your rod tip several feet above the ice during battle with a pike. This gives you time to react when the fish makes a quick run. Keep your drag loose and control runs by putting pressure on the spool with your free finger. Pump the fish up with your finger on the spool.

"Now don't hurry a fish at the hole," Doug emphasized. "Chances are it's well hooked, and the only way you'll lose him is with too much pressure at the hole.

"If you absolutely want to keep the fish, use a gaff. H.T. Enterprises makes a gaff that works as well for walleyes and other large predators in open or frozen water as it does for pike.

"If you want to release the fish, keep firm pressure on it at the hole. Wait for an opportune moment when its head is at the hole. Then lift. Once the fish's head is coming, the rest will follow. And once the entire pike is in the hole, he can't swim backwards; so with a bit of gentle but firm pressure, he'll swim up to you. Grab him with gloved hands and put him on ice.

Releasing small fish: Grab a small fish behind the head, keeping it in the hole. Use a Baker Hook-Out to remove the hook. Lift the fish out, turn it and slide it down. If the weather's cold, return pike immediately or the surface of their eyes freeze. We don't know if this is fatal, but it's reason-

Capture the moment with a photo . . . then release big fish.

able to assume it could be.

Releasing big fish: Same technique as for small fish. If the fish is badly hooked and the weather's cold, wrap the fish in a wet towel or sack, being sure to cover the eyes. Turn the fish on its back, sit straddling the fish, and use one hand to open its jaw while you man the Hook-Out with the other hand. Watch out for teeth.

Keep moving. That's the advantage to jigging. While your tip-up is constantly working for you, keep fishing actively, covering 10 times more territory. In many cases, that can mean 10 times the pike and 10 times the winter fun.

MUSKIES

Berkley and Company

Almost 40 pounds of muskie. The Iowa state record—through the ice.

Muskies. Perhaps the ultimate challenge in freshwater fishing, any-time, anywhere. Including through ice?

Doug: "I don't know why people don't fish for muskies through the ice. In some cases, of course, the season is closed in winter. But in a lot of others, it's closed only in the minds of fishermen. Maybe they're too used to the pounding (as in 12- to 14-hour days of casting) it takes to fish the buggers in open water."

"Right," Al said. "They get used to that level of challenge so they don't find any compelling reason to try to catch a big fish through the ice. Cold weather finally snaps reason into their heads, and they wander off to fish other species until the ice leaves."

Yet of all seasons of the year, muskies may be as concentrated at early-ice as they ever get.

"Basically," Doug said, "muskies are active enough to be caught during the first month of ice cover. They can potentially be caught throughout winter, but there's a huge decrease in activity at midwinter. It's almost the opposite of what we see in big pike, which are cold-water creatures. Pike may slow down in winter, but they still feed actively. Most people would be hard-pressed to catch a muskie on demand in January. But it's not so difficult to catch a muskie at first-ice on a good muskie lake."

First-Ice Advantages

A muskie hunter has impressive advantages at early-ice. First, the fish haven't been bothered much by fishermen in the weeks prior to ice-up. Few fishermen are grizzled enough to launch their boats into the teeth of icy winds.

We know where the high-percentage spots are, from fishing experience just before ice forms. Precise placement of bait in a known muskie area equals success; once the trap is set in the form of a tip-up or two, as Doug says, "it's bound to happen."

Locating Muskies at Early-Ice

Early-ice. Think deep water and hard bottom. When the waters of muskieville get cold, major changes take place. Most of the lunker-class fish aren't where they were during much of the open-water period. Deep water usually is the key.

No doubt this idea's foreign to many anglers, because muskies so often hold shallow during summer. But anglers who venture out just before ice-over, and the even smaller group who fish muskies through the ice, find success with approaches for deep water.

Initially, the thought of fishing deep water intimidates many muskie hunters. Yet the deep-water haunts of big muskies are easy to locate once you know what to look for. In addition, the areas usually are limited in size, making precise, pinpoint location possible. At any other time of year, muskies often are scattered over flats and slower-tapering bottoms, holding in shallower cover, or suspended. But not in late fall and during early-ice.

Look at a map of your favorite muskie water and imagine a giant siphon sucking the water off the flats, leaving only the deep basin hole.

Muskies Where?

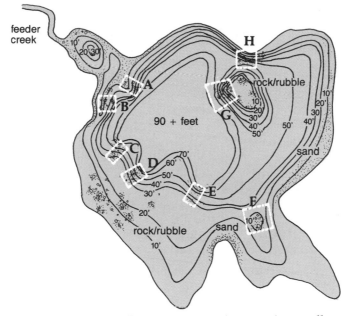

Muskies roam where walleyes roam. Find areas where walleyes roam deep basin areas and you'll also find muskies.

Areas A *through* H *appear to be potential spots.* Rule out Area F, *though, because it's too isolated from the deep area of the lake, and the flat on top is too small.* Area H *could hold some fish, but has low potential because it's not adjacent to the largest area of deep water.* Area E *has the wrong bottom content.*

That leaves Areas A, B, C, D, *and* G. *All of these could have muskies, but let's eliminate* Areas C *and* D; *instead of plunging directly into deep water, these areas break in a sloping stair-step fashion. There are better areas to fish.*

Areas A, B, *and* G *are good shots. They all plunge from the first drop-off all the way to deep water. They also have hard, rocky bottoms. Of course, you'll have to fish the areas to see if they produce.*

Now that the lake is "drained down," what key areas are left underwater that have (1) cover, (2) hard bottom, and (3) quickly break into the deepest water? Only a few areas usually are evident. These are prime early-ice lunker muskie hangouts.

The deepest rim of hard bottom surrounding the main lake basin forms a breakline. As muskies intercept cover and irregular features along this perimeter, they may stop and hold there. "Key contact areas," Doug said. Muskies holding in these areas at early-ice are catchable. But you have to effectively present a bait.

"To summarize," Doug said, "at first ice most muskies have pulled off shallow structural elements into deeper water surrounding those elements.

"Say a major point or bar has other points and inside turns on it. While occasionally muskies would roam over the top of the 10 to 15 foot point, they would probably spend most of their time pulled off the side in water 25 to 45 feet deep.

"In part, location depends on the forage in the lake. In most muskie lakes, the forage base is perch, walleyes, and ciscoes or whitefish. As winter rolls in, most muskies don't seem active enough to roam open water around points and sunken islands. They hold near bottom, off or adjacent to obvious structural elements. Therefore, the ciscoe connection becomes less important in a lot of cases. Preyfish holding in these same areas, such as perch and walleyes, become much more important.

"So the majority of muskies caught through the ice are accidentally caught by walleye fishermen. The reason more muskies aren't caught is that walleye anglers aren't comfortable fishing in deep water. Lots of muskies hold from 25 feet down to 60 feet and deeper.

"Tell you a little story from my days fishing on Lake Okoboji in Iowa.," Doug reminised. "Back in the 1970s, at a time when the muskie population wasn't as good as it is today, a small core of good ice fishermen spent a lot of time fishing deep water for walleyes. They would set tip-ups in the 35- to 55-foot zone. And despite a small population of muskies at the time, it was common to catch some."

Late-Ice Muskie Location

Throughout midwinter—suggested by scientific study—most muskies move very little. They sit, almost in a stupor, and almost never feed.

But at late-ice—the last month before ice-out—muskies become more active. They're often seen and occasionally caught by panfishermen on shallow bars where weedgrowth still exists. Smaller, more aggressive male muskies often roam the same shallow bays where they'll eventually spawn a month or so after the ice goes out.

"At last-ice," Doug observed, "panfishermen typically are over bars or shallow organic-bottomed bays. That's why they sometimes make muskie contact, although they're undermatched tacklewise and rarely actually land the muskie they hook."

Even at this time, don't ignore the most abrupt, shelf-like spot on a point or sunken island, these same "contact points" that were the key to muskies at early-ice. Muskies will still be there, as they move from deep to shallower water.

"Fish shallow late," Doug said, "but I think your best chance of finding a concentration of fish is near deep spots. The muskies are probably not any more active there, but the odds of putting your bait in front of one are better on these concentration points.

"Presentation? Nothing new to say. Read about tackling pike," Doug said. "The same rigging, especially tip-ups, that score pike will ring up muskies. Jigging works, too. Experiment with something that's due to get hot in pike circles—jigging dead baits.

"Don't get us wrong. Finding and catching muskies isn't easy any season. On any given day, it might seem like nothing's there, because the fish just aren't active. It takes time to catch a fish or two."

That's the challenge. Do it, though, and you'll join a small group of fishermen who have.

MANUFACTURERS OF ICE FISHING EQUIPMENT

Acme Tackle Co., 69 Bucklin St., Providence, RI 02907, 401/331-6437 (Ch. 2,4,7,8,9,10,11).

Acton Angling Center, Attention: Jim Meles, 187 Old Oak Road, East Acton W3 7HH, England (Ch. 2).

Altus Technology Corp., 11569 Encore Circle, Minnetonka, MN 55343, 612/935-6595 (Ch. 2).

Angostura Ice Rig, P.O. Box 460, Hot Springs, SD 57757 (Ch. 2).

Arctic Fisherman, 500 E. Burnett St., Beaver Dam, WI 53916, 414/885-3118 (Ch. 2).

Bagley Silver Thread, P.O. Box 110, Winter Haven, FL 33880, 813/297-8090 (Ch. 2,5,12,13).

Bait Rigs Tackle Co., P.O. Box 4153, Madison, WI 53711, 800/236-RIG1, 608/256-3232 (Ch. 2,4,5,12,13).

Baker Manufacturing Co., P.O. Box 28, 131 Locust St., Columbia, PA 17512, 717/684-2816 (Ch. 12,13).

Bay de Noc Lure Co., P.O. Box 71, Gladstone, MI 49837, 906/428-1133 (Ch. 4,8,9,10).

Berkley Inc., One Berkley Dr., Spirit Lake, IA 51360, 800/237-5539, 712/336-1520 (Ch. 2,3,4,5,8,10,11,12,13).

Blue Fox Tackle Co., 645 N. Emerson, Cambridge, MN 55008, 612/689-3402 (Ch. 8,10).

Brainerd Outdoor Sports, 5049 Hwy. 371 S., Brainerd, MN 56401, 218/828-4728 (Ch. 2).

Bruins Boxmeer, Steenstraat 111-113, 5831 JD Boxmeer, Holland, 011-31-8855-71192 (Ch. 2).

Bullet Bait Co., Inc., P.O. Box 770, Blountville, TN 37617, 615/538-4493 (Ch. 12).

Cabela's, 812 13th Ave., Sidney, NE 69160, 800/237-4444, 308/254-5505 (Ch. 2,3,4,5,7).

Class Tackle Products, P.O. Box 837, Minden, LA 71058, 318/371-2151 (Ch. 2,4,5,6,7).

Coleman Co., Inc., 250 N. St. Francis St., Wichita, KS 67202, 316/261-3211 (Ch. 2).

Comet Tackle, 2794 Midway St., Uniontown, OH 44685, 216/499-3366 (Ch. 2,5,7).

Creme Lure Company, P.O. Box 6162, Tyler, TX 75711, 214/561-0522 (Ch. 12).

Custom Jigs & Spins, Inc., P.O. Box 27, Glenview, IL 60025, 708/729-9050 (Ch. 4,6,7,8,9,10).

Daiwa Corp., 7421 Chapman Ave., Garden Grove, CA 92641-2193, 714/895-6645 (Ch. 2).

Du Pont Co., 1007 Market St., Wilmington, DE 19898, 302/774-4040 (Ch. 2,12,13).

Eagle Claw Fishing Tackle, Wright & McGill, 4245 E. 46th Ave., Denver, CO 80216-0011, 303/321-1481 (Ch. 11).

Express Bait, 15941 Tippecanoe St., Ham Lake, MN 55304, 800/451-2576, 612/434-0550 (Ch. 7).

Fanatics, P.O. Box 10880, Golden, CO 80401, 303/232-7027 (Ch. 2).

Feldmann Engineering & Mfg. Co., Inc., P.O. Box 908, 520 Forest Ave., Sheboygan Falls, WI 53085-0908, 800/344-0712, 414/467-6167 (Ch. 2,4).

Fishing Specialties, 315 Short St., Auburn, MI 48611, 517/662-6347 (Ch. 2).

Flambeau Products Corp., P.O. Box 97, Middlefield, OH 44062, 216/632-1631 (Ch. 2).

FOF Inc., 1505 Racine St., P.O. Box E, Delavan, WI 53115, 414/728-2686 (Ch. 2).

Frabill, Inc., P.O. Box 499, Allenton, WI 53002, 414/629-5506 (Ch. 2,3).

Frontier Industries, 19285 Highway 7, Excelsior, MN 55331, 612/474-0641 (Ch. 2)

Genesee Fishing Specialties, P.O. Box 284, Genesee Depot, WI 53127 (Ch. 3).

Gerhardt's, Steve Sports Center, 3008 E. Washington Ave., Madison, WI 53704, 608/244-2300 (Ch. 1).

Glacier Glove, 4890 Aircenter Circle, Suite 206, Reno, NV 89502, 702/825-8225 (Ch. 2).

Gore-Tex, W. L. Gore & Associates, Inc., 100 Airport Rd., Building 2, Elkton, MD 21921-0729, 301/392-3500 (Ch. 3).

Gudebrod, Inc., Griffith Towers, P.O. Box 357, Pottstown, PA 19464, 215/327-4588 (Ch. 2,5).

Handishop Industries, Inc., 1411 N. Superior Ave., Tomah, WI 54660, 608/372-3289 (Ch. 2,5).

Harmony Enterprises, 704 Main Ave. N., Harmony, MN 55939, 507/886-6666 (Ch. 2).

Heat-Pack, P.O. Box 7366, St. Cloud, MN 56302, 800/228-HEAT, 612/253-5020 (Ch. 2).

Heddon, PRADCO, 3601 Jenny Lind, Fort Smith, AR 72901, 501/782-8971 (Ch. 12).

Hengelsporthuis, Bruins Boxmeer, Steenstraat 111-113, 5831 JD Boxmeer, Holland (Ch. 2).

Heron Manufacturing, 1620 Central Ave. N.E., Minneapolis, MN 55413, 800/426-7804, 612/781-3860 (Ch. 4,5,8,10).

Hodgman, Inc., 1750 Orchard Rd., Montgomery, IL 60538, 312/897-7555 (Ch. 2).

Hondex Marine Electronics, 13161 56th Court, Suite 203, Clearwater, FL 34620, 813/573-1870 (Ch. 2,3,8).

HT Enterprises, Inc., P.O. Box 909, 139 E. Sheboygan St., Campbellsport, WI 53010, 414/533-5080 (Ch. 2,3,4,5,8,10,12,13).

Hypark Specialty Co., P.O. Box 1413, Minnetonka, MN 55343, 612/931-9022 (Ch. 2).

Ice-N-Easy, P.O. Box 191, Gothenberg, NE 69138, 308/537-7503 (Ch. 2).

IKH Industries, 4013 S. Shady Lane Dr., Eveleth, MN 55734, 218/744-5496 (Ch. 2).

Ins-Tent, 402 Arch St., P.O. Box 650, Cloquet, MN 55720, 218/879-9712 (Ch. 2,3).

Jig-A-Whopper, UMM Holdings, Inc., P.O. Box 411, Hwy. 56 S., Dodge Center, MN 55927, 507/374-2480 (Ch. 2,3,4,5,6,7,8,9,10,12,13).

J-Moe Mfg. Co., 7854 Vernon Rd. S., Clay, NY 13041, 800/776-5663, 315/452-0002 (Ch. 2).

K & E Tackle, 2530 Barber Rd., Hastings, MI 49058, 616/945-4496 (Ch. 7).

L.L. Bean, 32 Birch St., Freeport, ME 04033, 800/548-4305 (Ch. 2).

La Crosse Footwear, Inc., P.O. Box 1328, La Crosse, WI 54602, 608/782-3020 (Ch. 3).

Lake Country Products, P.O. Box 367, Isle, MN 56342, 612/676-3440 (Ch. 2).

Lindy-Little Joe, Inc., P.O. Box C, 1110 Wright St., Brainerd, MN 56401, 218/829-1714 (Ch. 3,4,10).

Lowrance Electronics, Inc., 12000 E. Skelly Dr., Tulsa, OK 74128, 918/437-6881 (Ch. 3).

Luhr Jensen, 400 Portway, Hood River, OR 97031, 800/535-1711, 503/386-3811 (Ch. 12).

Mankato Tent & Awning, 1021 Range St., N. Mankato, MN 56001, 507/625-5115 (Ch. 2).

Micronar, Hondex Marine Electronics, 13161 56th Court, Suite 203, Clearwater, FL 34620, 813/573-1870 (Ch. 8).

Mitchell Sports USA, Inc., Johnson Fishing, Inc., 1531 Madison Ave., Mankato, MN 56001, 800/227-6433, 507/345-4623 (Ch. 2,4).

Mustad, O. & Son, Inc., 247-253 Grant Ave., Auburn, NY 13021, 315/253-2793 (Ch. 11).

Normark Corp. (Rapala, Pilkies), 1710 E. 78th St., Minneapolis, MN 55423, 612/869-3291 (Ch. 1,2,3,4,8,9,10,11,12).

Northern Lite Mfg., 412 S. 6th St., P.O. Box 77, Brainerd, MN 56401, 218/829-8584 (Ch. 2).

Northland Fishing Tackle, 3209 Mill St. N.E., Bemidji, MN 56601, 218/751-6723 (Ch. 2,4,6,7,8,9,10,12).

Osceola Power Equipment Corp., 411 Washington Ave. N., Minneapolis, MN 55401, 612/338-4021 (Ch. 2).

Plano Molding Co., P.O. Box 189, Plano, IL 60545, 708/552-3111 (Ch. 2).

Reef Runner Tackle Co., Box 939, Port Clinton, OH 43452, 419/798-9125 (Ch. 8,9,12).

RefrigiWear, Inc., 71 Inlp Dr., Inwood, NY 11696, 516/239-7022 (Ch. 3).

RT Copfer Co., P.O. Box 1381, Erie, PA 16502 (Ch. 2).

Schooley & Sons, 13700 14 Miles Rd., Greenville, MI 48838, 616/754-3266 (Ch. 2).

Sevenstrand Tackle Corp., 5401 McFadden Ave., Huntington Beach, CA 92649, 714/891-2431 (Ch. 2,5,12).

Shakespeare, Fishing Tackle Division, 3801 Westmore Dr., Columbia, SC 29223-4700, 803/754-7000 (Ch. 2,5,8).

Shaw, Joe, Tower, MN 55790, 218/753-3322 (Ch. 2).

Shimano American Corp., P.O. Box 19615, One Shimano Dr., Irvine, CA 92713-9615, 714/951-5003 (Ch. 2).

Shurkatch, 507 Alden St., Fall River, MA 02722, 800/272-4223, 508/678-7556 (Ch. 2).

Slater's Jigs, P.O. Drawer 688, Indiannola, MS 38751, 601/887-3548 (Ch. 2).

St. Croix, P.O. Box 279, Park Falls, WI 54552, 800/826-7042, 715/762-3226 (Ch. 2,4).

Stinger Tackle Co., 6087 Hwy. 51 S., Hazelhurst, WI 54531-9744, 715/356-4633 (Ch. 5).

Strike Master, Inc., 411 Washington Ave. N., Minneapolis, MN 55401, 612/338-4021 (Ch. 2).

Tackle Marketing, Inc., 3801 W. Superior St., Duluth, MN 55807, 218/628-0206 (Ch. 5,12).

Tackle Tamer Products, Inc., P.O. Box 715, Keewatin, MN 55753, 218/778-6249 (Ch. 2,3).

Talon Tackle Mfg. Corp., 10121 W. Sharon La., P.O. Box 25340, Milwaukee, WI 53225, 414/464-1537 (Ch. 5).

Thill Tackle, 706 W. Bradley, Urbana, IL 61801, 217/384-5240 (Ch. 4,5).

Thorne Brothers, 7500 University Ave. N.E., Minneapolis, MN 55432, 612/572-3782 (Ch. 2,4,5,10,12).

Trade Management Services, 7400 Metro Blvd., Suite 126, Edina, MN 55435, 612/835-1702 (Ch. 2).

Tru-Turn, Inc., P.O. Drawer 767, Wetumpka, AL 36092, 205/567-2011 (Ch. 5).

U.S. Line Co., P.O. Box 531, Westfield, MA 01085, 413/562-3629 (Ch. 2).

Uncle Josh Bait Co., P.O. Box 130, Fort Atkinson, WI 53538, 414/563-2491 (Ch. 8).

Vexilar, Inc., 9252 Grand Ave. S., Minneapolis, MN 55420, 612/884-5291 (Ch. 2,8).

Wazp Brand Products, P.O. Box 837, Minden, LA 71058, 318/371-

2151 (Ch. 4,5,7).

Whitefish Manufacturing Co., 215 N. 3rd Ave. W., Duluth, MN 55802, 218/727-8675 (Ch. 2).

Winter Fishing Systems (Genz), 859 Manor Dr., Minneapolis, MN 55432, 612/786-7648 (Ch. 1,2,3,5).

Wisconsin Tackle, P.O. Box 285, Hartland, WI 53029, 414/367-1104 (Ch. 2,4,6,7,8,9,10).

Witchcraft Tape Products, P.O. Box 937, Coloma, MI 49038, 616/468-3399 (Ch. 8,10).

Worden's Lures, Yakima Bait, P.O. Box 310, Granger, WA 98932, 800/527-2711, 509/854-1311 (Ch. 8).

(The) Worth Co., P.O. Box 88, Stevens Point, WI 54481, 715/344-6081 (Ch. 2).

Zebco/MotorGuide, 6101 E. Apache, Tulsa, OK 74115, 918/836-5581 (Ch. 2,8).

IN-FISHERMAN MASTERPIECE SERIES

- **WALLEYE WISDOM:** A Handbook of Strategies
- **PIKE:** A Handbook of Strategies
- **SMALLMOUTH BASS:** A Handbook of Strategies
- **CRAPPIE WISDOM:** A Handbook of Strategies
- **CHANNEL CATFISH FEVER:** A Handbook of Strategies
- **LARGEMOUTH BASS IN THE 90's:** A Handbook of Strategies
- **BIG BASS MAGIC**
- **FISHING FUNDAMENTALS**
- **ICE FISHING SECRETS**

Each masterpiece book represents the collaborative effort of fishing experts. The books don't represent a regional perspective or the opinions of one good angler. Each masterpiece book teems with information applicable to all areas of the country and to any fishing situation.

In-Fisherman Inc., Two In-Fisherman Drive, Brainerd, MN 56401, 218/829-1648